Leadership
and Group Dynamics
in Recreation Services

Leadership
and Group Dynamics
in Recreation Services

H. DOUGLAS SESSOMS
University of North Carolina

JACK L. STEVENSON
Clemson University

ALLYN AND BACON, INC.
Boston   London   Sydney   Toronto

Library of Congress Cataloging in Publication Data

Sessoms, Hanson Douglas.
    Leadership and group dynamics in recreation services.

    Bibliography: p.
    Includes index.
    1. Recreation leadership. 2. Social groups.
3. Social group work. I. Stevenson, Jack L.,
1928–   joint author. II. Title.
GV181.4.S47   790   80-26874
ISBN 0-205-07282-8

Printed in the United States of America.

Printing number and year (last digits):
10 9 8 7 6 5 4 3 2 1   86 85 84 83 82 81

CONTENTS

PREFACE

This book is a text and training manual for students wishing to apply group dynamics techniques to recreation service environments. It consists of ten chapters: Introduction, The Nature and Art of Leadership, The Nature and Function of Groups, Forces Affecting the Functioning of Groups, Small Group Techniques, Large Group Techniques, Group Problems, Leadership Development, Supervision and Consultation, and Evaluation. This work is unique in its attempt to integrate group dynamics principles and techniques, strategies, leadership functioning, and leadership development, and the nature of supervision and consultation to the recreation and leisure service delivery system. Furthermore, it provides, uniquely, the opportunity for laboratory learning as a teaching technique.

The materials are a blending of theoretical and research findings developed by small group theorists and contemporary students of recreation programming and administrative functioning. Each chapter contains suggested exercises and illustrative materials. By using the exercises, the recreation student and instructor can immerse themselves in the group process. Both experiential (laboratory) and conventional learning are afforded through this process. Without these exercises and illustrations, the work stands as a conventional text; by application of these suggested learning techniques it becomes, in addition, a manual or handbook of group practices as they apply to recreation services.

Our specific objectives are:

1. To describe the elements involved in group dynamics so that students can become more sensitive to their presence and effects.
2. To provide a theoretical basis for, and understanding of, the application of these principles and techniques to specific situations.
3. To have students develop a sensitivity and awareness of themselves in various group settings so that their participation becomes a constructive rather than a destructive group force.
4. To describe various leadership techniques and methods and to offer practical suggestions for, and illustrations of, their application.

5. To heighten students' sensitivity to the importance of communication and feedback and to offer techniques for evaluating group process and leadership functioning.

6. To provide the reader with illustrations, case studies, and training exercises.

It may be useful for the student and the instructor to skim the entire book, including the exercises, before beginning the course. Some of the exercises, such as those in Chapter Eight that pertain to leadership development, can serve as a philosophy and guide for the use of the book. The suggestion for a personal journal is one the instructor and student might find very useful.

A certain body of knowledge and exercises common to group work is used by nearly all who practice that art. Within it are scores of exercises and drills. Probably the best collection of these can be found in Pfeiffer and Jones's series of annual booklets titled *A Handbook of Structured Experiences for Human Relations Training*. We recommend them for supplemental exercises, since many can be easily adapted to the leisure service profession.

We have enjoyed developing and writing this text. We hope you will find the application of group dynamics principles as exciting and fulfilling as we do in our everyday work and living.

Leadership
and Group Dynamics
in Recreation Services

Chapter One

INTRODUCTION

For the United States the twentieth century has been an era of expansion. The first fifty years of the century were given to materialistic growth with an abiding optimism for increased productivity. Investments in technical know-how and breakthroughs in such industries as steel, chemicals, and electronics characterized the industrial order. During the first half of this century, the majority of American workers were employed in the blue-collar fields; the nation fought two major wars and laid the groundwork for a standard of living unsurpassed by any previous society. Organizational management and the applied sciences were the foundation of the country's expansion; increases in consumable goods and leisure were the by-products of their effort.

With these rising levels of industrial productivity and personal consumption came some interesting consequences. Industries clustered in selected communities; metropolitan districts were created. Improved technology reduced a need for long work hours; more free time with shorter work weeks and longer vacation periods resulted. Advances in chemistry and physics affected medical care and increased life expectancy; a larger retired and older population resulted. To get the goods and services to markets, bureaucracies and conglomerates were formed. Understanding and shaping behavior became important; service professions were created with psychology, sociology, and the social sciences serving as their cornerstones.

By 1955, the white-collar service industries had replaced the blue-collar worker industries as the major employer of Americans. Services, essential to the quality of life, as well as products were promoted and consumed. Both have a direct bearing on the activities of the leisure services profession.

To accommodate our free-time interests, a variety of services and products developed. Many were commercially feasible; others were seen as the responsibility of governmental concerns. Some, like the manufacture of sports equipment and recreation vehicles or the operation of resorts and entertainment centers, became a part of the traditional industrial order. Others, like adult educational programs, recreation and parks services, youth and group work activity, became elements of a publicly supported human service system.

RELATIONSHIP OF ADULT EDUCATION, GROUP WORK, AND RECREATION

Adult education, recreation, and social group work all have a common heritage. Each is a product of the social welfare reforms that occurred in our cities and industries at the turn of the nineteenth century. Their founders shared a similar belief—they were concerned with the quality of life and believed that through the "proper" use of leisure, it could be achieved. In fact, all three cite Eduard Lindeman, a central figure in the federal government's programs and services during the years 1932–39, as a major contributor to their early thinking and literature. Lindeman said all should be concerned with informal educational activities, not with operating facilities or providing entertainment. Others could do the latter.[1]

As is often the case, general concerns become specific. In time, adult education, recreation services, and social work became distinct professions, with specific concerns and well-defined areas of activity. Informal learning activities were seen as education, the responsibility of the public school system. Consequently, adult education specialists were developed and employed by schools and departments of education, even though the motivation of many of the students was recreational. They were there to learn new skills, new ways to enjoy their leisure. The adult educator was there to teach them.

A similar crystallizing of function and identity occurred among group workers. They were viewed as social workers, concerned with delinquency prevention and the activities of youth; they developed their own methods, processes by which individual behaviors were shaped and influenced through group structures and peer activities. Increasingly, group workers were employed by social work agencies; consequently their professional preparation occurred in schools and departments of social work. Although much of their concern was recreational, they did not see themselves as recreation specialists since they used activities as techniques for involving and shaping behavior, not as ends in themselves. To their clients, the activities were free-time expressions, but to the group worker they were therapeutic programs.

With both adult education and social work establishing their turf, recreation services did the same. Although some recreation specialists were concerned with the therapeutic or socially rehabilitative activities or with teaching and developing leisure skills and attitudes, the recreation profession set as its primary concerns the management of recreational environments and the offering of free-time activities. Outdoor recreation and sports programs became its program focus. Recreation professionals were employed by governmental units, such as park commissions and recreation and park departments, though their programs of professional preparation were largely administered by schools of natural resources and divisions of recreational leadership in departments of health, physical education, and recreation.

Although adult education, social work, and recreation services are now separate professions, they continue to have a common concern and rely upon a similar methodology. Their similarities are much greater than their differences. In fact, they are cousins to all the professions that comprise the human service system. Social planners, human relations experts, personnel managers, counselors, and the like all rely on the same concepts of human behavior and techniques of "working with people" as adult educators, recreators, and social group workers. One common denominator and concern is group dynamics.

DEFINITION OF GROUP DYNAMICS

Group dynamics is a study of human interactions in specific group settings. It is also the application of specific techniques and principles to accomplish specific group goals, a process of achieving collective action. Malcolm and Hulda Knowles state that the term *group dynamics* is used in four different ways: (1) to describe "what's happening" in groups at all times, whether the members are aware of those forces or not; (2) to describe that branch of social science concerned with "why groups behave as they do"; (3) to identify the body of knowledge about group behavior that has been developed through research and study; and (4) to identify and classify those practices and methods that affect group interaction and improve group performance.* Although the first use of the term is of some special interest to recreation and park professionals for training purposes, the last one interests them most. To recreators, group dynamics involves being aware of the many forces that affect the way individuals act in group settings, and, once aware of them, using those dynamics in a manner that enhances the quality of the group experience and moves the group toward achieving its goals.

For the most part, recreation and park professionals are not students of the group process. Nevertheless, they practice it. After all, many of our recreation experiences occur in a group setting; most political and policy decisions are effected through group efforts; and most working environments require the staff to interact with participants and other profes-

* From *Introduction to Group Dynamics* by Malcolm S. Knowles and Hulda F. Knowles, Copyright 1972. Used by permission of Follett Publishing Company, a division of Follett Corporation.

sionals. To some extent, the quality of our service is directly related to our understanding and use of the principles of group dynamics.

There are many misconceptions about group dynamics. Some think of it as group therapy or sensitivity training. To them, group dynamics is a means of manipulating behavior and therefore should be used only by those highly trained in the group process. Others see group dynamics as a form of personnel and leadership development. They assume it can be used only in a training situation or in a controlled learning environment. Both perceptions are partially correct. The concepts and principles of group dynamics are used by therapists who intend to modify behavior. This is most often accomplished through therapy and encounter groups. It is a form of experience-based learning in which the individual or group with the problem is "led" to an understanding and solution by a therapist. Some national organizations such as the National Training Laboratories use group dynamics to train leaders and improve interpersonal relationships of key management and organizational personnel.[2] The assumption is that as individuals come to know themselves and the way others view them, they become more effective managers and administrators. These training laboratories and training programs are directed by specialists in the group process.

It is not the intention of this text, or of most recreation and park professionals, that recreators become group therapists or laboratory training specialists. The recreation professional is concerned with providing meaningful leisure experiences, not group therapy. Recognizing, however, that individuals do grow through group experiences and that the recreator can provide an optimum environment for self-realization, we become students of the group process. By being aware of the factors that affect the quality of the recreation experience, the recreator can maximize those that enhance it, while minimizing those that detract from it. In a sense, group dynamics is the science of group functioning; leadership is its art.

Interest in group dynamics has grown rapidly during the past two decades. It has become a fertile field of research for the psychologist and sociologist. Departments of adult education, social group work, and speech have contributed to the academic development of its methods and practices. Organizational theorists and practitioners promote it as an effective means of leadership development. Politicians advocate it as a basis for participatory democracy. This interest has developed for several reasons. Among them are the growth of urbanism, the emergence of the "social sciences," the expansion of the human service systems, and the growth of the civil rights movement. Common to all of these is our desire to humanize our bureaucracies, living environments, and concerns.

It seems inevitable that as we become more dependent on each other, our need for appropriate group functioning and understanding increases. Laws, guidelines, and other forms of social control are necessary but impersonal. Opportunities for individual expression have been reduced in our living and working environments, yet the need for identity and recognition remains. These needs can be partially met through recreation behaviors, especially when those behaviors are supported through the application of the principles of group dynamics. Possibly that is why the advocates of participatory democracy and civil liberties are so enthusiastic about its use.

Central to group functioning is an understanding of leadership and leadership techniques. To some extent, the study of group dynamics evolved from the study of leadership. Why are some people better able to lead than others? Can leaders be developed by improving their understanding of group functioning, or is leadership a gift, a power given only to a few? These kinds of questions provoked the thinking of the earlier students of the group process.

DEFINITION OF LEADERSHIP

Leadership has been defined in many ways. It is seen as the act of commanding and directing, the actions of leaders, the process by which groups achieve their goals, the antithesis of followership. All of these views are valid. Leadership is the act of moving people toward goal achievement. It is the process by which we find collective satisfaction. To achieve such a goal, there must be followers, group goals, and leaders. Leadership, then, is an interaction of the three. (See Fig. 1–1.)

When people are asked to define leadership, they often respond by giving the name of a national leader. When pushed further for a definition, they frequently cite the head of their company or organization or give the name of people in positions of authority. The more authority one assumes or is given, the more he or she is believed to be a leader. Leaders command and those with authority are in a position to command. That is one concept of leadership.

A second concept of leadership holds that leadership is a process, one in which many people share roles and responsibilities. Those who subscribe to this view say that leadership is always present in any group situa-

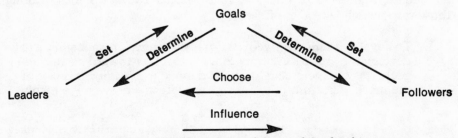

FIG. 1–1. Leadership: Moving People toward Goal Achievement

tion; it is a set of tasks that, if completed, results in the group achieving its goal. This concept of leadership does not stress leaders but the process by which groups achieve satisfaction. It holds leadership to be a group phenomenon. The various concepts of leadership are discussed more fully in Chapter Two.

Both types of leadership are appropriate to recreators and the leisure service delivery system. There is a direct relationship between authority and leadership. By their very nature, positions of responsibility and power confer upon their holders the means of command. If leaders execute, followers obey, and goals are achieved, then leadership has occurred. Likewise, if individuals share responsibility and accomplish their goal collectively, then leadership has occurred but without heavy influence of a designated authority or head. The process holds in both illustrations. Through leaders/leadership, goals are achieved.

There are many types of leaders. They may be appointed or elected, or serve because of the position or status they hold in the organization. Some emerge from the process of the group or function as leaders on an informal basis. In all instances, the end result is the same—the goals of the group are achieved. If not, then the "leaders" were ineffective and, in the final sense, not leaders at all. Leadership is an absolute condition. It requires followers and goal attainment. When there are no followers, there is no leadership. Likewise, when the goals of the group are not met, leadership has not occurred. Leadership is a dynamic process.

Headship must not be confused with leadership. When individuals are appointed to a position of responsibility, they become "heads." Whether they become leaders depends on their ability to assess their followers' needs and to develop techniques for meeting those needs. Since individual needs vary and group needs change, so must the techniques and processes of leadership. Because one is successful in reading the dynamics at work in one situation does not necessarily mean he or she will be successful in another. However, being *aware* of those dynamics may assist in successfully executing leader responsibilities.

Certain responsibilities are inherent in leadership. In their book on new understandings of leadership, Ross and Hendry devote a chapter to "What the Leader Must Do." Their materials, based on research, hold that all leaders, regardless of position, share similar responsibilities. Among those responsibilities are the following*:

1. To develop a sense of "we-ness." It is the leader's responsibility to develop the group's capacity to work together toward a common goal. This characteristic has been defined as *viscidity*. It is one of the more important criteria of group effectiveness and is highly

* From *New Understandings of Leadership* by Murray G. Ross and Charles E. Hendry, Copyright 1957. Used by permission of Follett Publishing Company, a division of Follett Corporation.

correlated with leadership adequacy. The more effective the leader is in developing the group's tendency to "pull together," the more productive the group will be.

2. To develop the *hedonic* tone. It is the responsibility of the leader to develop a pleasant group climate or to see that one is established. Group members who like each other and the group tend to work together more productively. There is a strong relationship between a group's hedonic tone and its degree of viscidity. Both relate to the group's feeling about itself as a group, rather than to the leaders' skills which are necessary to achieve its goals.

3. To identify *goals*. The key to successful group functioning is the group's ability to identify its goals and objectives. It is a leader's responsibility to facilitate that process. The ability to analyze both the situation and the group's capacity to deal with the situation is needed.

4. To organize for *goal achievement*. Goal achievement is closely related to goal identification. Groups want leaders who can help them achieve their goals; in fact, goal achievement is the ultimate test of leadership. To accomplish the group's objectives requires a sensitivity to organization. Organizing the group for action implies a sense of priorities, the recognition and utilization of individual group member's skills, and the ability to motivate the group to act.

5. To initiate *action*. Leaders initiate action. Having initiative is fundamental to group goal achievement. We tend to follow those people who act first on our behalf and whose actions seem to suggest success. Possibly that is why aggressive people seem to be more likely to achieve leadership positions. However, hyperaggressiveness can be a negative characteristic, one that may turn people off and inhibit action toward goals.

6. To develop a *pattern of communication*. Good leaders are effective in facilitating communication. A group cannot function for any period of time as a unit unless there is sufficient and meaningful communication within it. The leader is the key in the communication pattern and provides the model for other members on matters of communication—what is communicated and in what form.

7. To facilitate *group structures*. Every group needs some structure. One of a leader's major responsibilities is to establish and maintain the group's structure. The group's plan of action reflects its structure, much as the group's tone reflects its personality. Leaders must work in both areas of functioning—group feelings and group productivity.

8. To develop and implement *group philosophy*. The implementation of a philosophy helps the group obtain its objectives. When group members are constantly reminded of their objective

and the importance of goal attainment, they tend to have a greater sense of purpose. Groups reflect the philosophy of the leader, but they also respond to the leader's public statement of their purpose and underlying principle.

When leaders do the above—develop group tone and tendency to pull together, identify and obtain goals, initiate action, develop communication patterns and organizational structures, implement a philosophy—they help groups establish their own personalities. Each group does have its uniqueness, and its leadership contributes to that quality.

FOLLOWERSHIP

There are many explanations about why people follow leaders. Most of them center around the notions of *efficiency* (it's easier to let someone else do it for you), *satisfaction* (when you are content with the way things are, you tend to follow it), and *experience* (if you are used to having someone else lead, then you are probably conditioned to follow). People cease to be followers when they are bored, discontented, or dissatisfied with their lot and feel something can be done about it. This is true in any setting, especially in the recreation environment where we have great freedom of choice and, therefore, great latitude for change. Professional recreation and park personnel are *formal* leaders with participants as followers. If, however, these professionals fail to provide the programs and services that meet the needs of the participants, the participants are not required to continue to depend on the recreation system for their recreation experiences. They seek them elsewhere. When this occurs, recreation and park professionals fail to be leaders although they may remain agency or program heads.

GROUP DYNAMICS AND THE RECREATION SYSTEM

Recreation services and recreation leadership are the concerns of this text. We are interested in developing more effective recreation and park professionals—individuals who, through their leadership and use of group dynamics, will provide more opportunity for meaningful leisure expression.

Much has been written about the organized recreation and park system and its needs for leaders. The late Harold D. Meyer always referred to leadership as the key in the development and operation of a recreation system. Many of the earlier programs for preparing professional recreation specialists were called recreation leadership curricula. Their mission seemed to be to develop program and activity leaders. Later, they became known as departments of park and recreation administration or departments of recreation resource management, name changes which reflected the profession's growing concern with the administrative aspects of leadership.

The relationship between leisure and recreation has long been recognized. Recreation is an active phase of leisure; it is composed of those free-time activities and experiences that give pleasure and satisfaction. Recreation experiences are highly individualistic. Regardless of what form they take, when or in what setting they occur, only the participant knows if they are recreational. The participant, not the professional recreator, determines if an activity is recreation.

Since it is difficult to determine the motivations of participants or to activate such an individualistic concept as recreation, society has tended to define recreation in terms of activities—more specifically, those activities in which individuals participate when they are not at work and for which they do not receive payment. They tend to be diversionary and "for fun." Both the public and the recreation professionals have come to accept this description. When people are asked what they do for recreation (in their free time), they normally cite one or more activities from this set. In other words, there is a generally held cultural image of the recreation experience.

Recreation theorists, however, argue that the recreation experience is not limited to a single set of activities. They say it may occur spontaneously and in any setting or context. Likewise, they hold that leisure is not a time set but an attitude about existence. It simply is a matter of who defines the experience. From the personal view, the theorists are correct; from an operational view, the public and recreation practitioners are correct. In reality the recreation and park professionals never really provide recreation, only opportunities and activities with recreation potential.

To maximize the resources for providing these experiences, communities have established park and recreation systems. (See Fig. 1–2.) Industries have found it profitable to produce the desired and needed equipment and clothing for the so-called recreation experiences. Businesses have developed in response to the public's tastes for amusement inappropriate for governmental sponsorship. Clubs and private associations have been formed to meet the specific recreational interests of their members. Collectively, these four elements—government, industries, commercial enterprises, and private associations—compose the organized recreation system.[3] The last three are primarily concerned with organizational structures and the activities and opportunities they provide; the first (government) is both a manager of physical resources and a provider of activities. Consequently, when park and recreation professionals refer

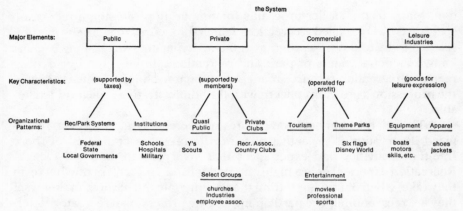

FIG. 1–2. The Organized Recreation-Park System

to organized recreation services, they are speaking of those programs and facilities provided by a formal organization for the purpose of recreation. Although the term implies leadership, not all recreation experiences are under the direct supervision of a recreation leader. However, the activity would not have been provided were it not for the organization.

The elements of the system are constantly interacting. For example, industries provide the equipment, such as boats and motors, which can be used at the owner's discretion. The participants determine when they have the time (their leisure) to engage in recreation (boating or fishing). The organized recreation system provides and/or manages the resource (lake, river, boating area) for the experience. Although it is highly unlikely that the participant would consider boating or fishing an activity organized by the system, were it not for the system, the experience might never have occurred. The requirement for leadership in this context of recreation is quite different from that in which a participant actively seeks out a recreation expert, such as a tennis or crafts instructor or program supervisor, for instruction and direction.

An illustration of recreation leadership involvement, in the activity sense, occurs on playgrounds and athletic fields where recreation specialists provide instruction or supervise play. When the recreator schedules the time for the Little League baseball game, obtains the officials to supervise it, and has the participants adhere to the rules and policies of the recreation service, his leadership is present even though less obvious than when he is teaching a class in ceramics or telling a story on the playground. In all instances—providing physical resources, scheduling activities, or instructing an event—the recreator provides the opportunity for recreation; the participant determines if the experience was recreational.

APPROACHES TO THE RECREATION SERVICE

Just as there are formal and informal leaders and organizational and individual elements of the organized recreation system, so there are formal and informal organizational approaches to provide recreational opportunities. Some elements of the organized recreation system have established formalized procedures and instructions for providing and monitoring their activities and resources. Others approach the task on a more *ad hoc* basis. Differing philosophies form these approaches. The former relies primarily on the concept and notions of bureaucracy, with centralized decision making, well-defined lines of authority, and a chain of command. It is a more static structure. The latter approach emphasizes decentralized authority; it is dynamic and temporal in its form. Though it relies on a different leadership style, as does the more bureaucratic form, it has a well-defined structure or approach to its process.

These two approaches to the provision of recreation and park services can best be illustrated in the following manner. The National Park Service is a highly structured bureaucracy. Its personnel have defined roles and responsibilities. Formalized procedures and policies must be adhered to throughout the system. Campgrounds are opened on a certain date and operated according to a specific schedule of hours and policies. Yet, within this structure, individual campers are not encumbered by the policies of the bureaucracy and may be totally oblivious to them. To the participants, the park service provides a recreation experience; they, the campers, are in charge of that experience.

The college student union provides a good illustration of the second approach to services. The union encourages various student groups to organize and develop their own programs. It may offer technical assistance and advisors to the students, but the content and structure of the program are left largely to the individual groups. The union operates from a general framework of resource management, but the programs vary tremendously from semester to semester depending on the inclinations and interests of the students and the kinds of groups they form.

As a leader, the recreation/park professional has two constituents: the agency or community that employs him and the participants in his program. Each requires a different set of understandings and expectations; both are grounded in the same principles of leadership practices and techniques. The talented recreation specialist is able to discern which technique best fits the situation and the group served.

Briefly, let's look at each of these two major expectations. As a member of the official leadership body of the community (town government), the recreation and parks specialist is expected to assume the role of expert. After all, he or she is trained to be the specialist in leisure services and to know more about recreation and park administration, program design, facility operation, etc., than any other person in the community. The director of the park and recreation service is the titular head of the agency and thereby the designated leader of the recreation and park department; through his staff, community recreation leadership is provided. It is really a team effort since, ideally, no one recreation specialist is expected to know "the most" about every facet of recreation programming, service, and operation.

As leaders in the program/participant setting, the recreation and park specialists might be expected to assume one of several roles. They might find themselves functioning as technical experts on equipment or the rules and regulations. They might be facilitators, allowing the participants to create their own situations and experiences, the latter occurring because the leaders made available the optimum resources for those experiences. They might be coordinators, the focal point in the communication link between various participants and agencies. Their leadership techniques may be subtle or overt, depending on the types of groups served, the situation, and the expressed needs of those served. The principles of group dynamics apply to all situations.

Leadership, as we see it, may occur at any level of organization or functioning, whether it is administrative, supervisory, or "face-to-face." Actually, all professionals, regardless of their position in the organization, assume all three roles or functions. When working directly with the participants, or indirectly through managing and supervising staff, the recreator influences group behavior and therefore provides leadership. Fundamental to the recreator's influence is the ability to monitor and structure the setting and situation of the recreation or the staff experience; in other words, to provide administration and supervision. In the final analysis, the recreator is a manager of leisure opportunities and resources.

THE RECREATOR AND GROUP DYNAMICS

To achieve these various roles successfully and provide leadership, the recreator must become a student of group dynamics and group processes. Central to the satisfaction of both the participants and the recreation staff is the involvement of those affected by the decisions made. Granted that in some situations, such as instructional classes in which the participant is merely interested in getting information or developing an activity skill, the importance of group decision making is minimal; the creation of a proper environment for the execution of the task is the primary concern. However, in those settings in which responsibilities and pleasures are jointly agreed upon and shared, such as a teen club activity, personal satisfaction is heightened when the participants "choose" their goals and means of participation.

There are at least four major recreation situations that suggest the application of group dynamic principles. Two have been mentioned previously. They are "working with participants" and "working with the recreation staff." The other two are working with volunteers and policy formulation groups and working with other community or agency groups to effect social change or promote better interagency relationships. Recreation and park services are not mandatory but exist at the pleasure of those served. Recreation leadership, therefore, is the art of *influence* rather than of command. Group dynamics is fundamental to the development and application of that art.

Briefly, let us look at these four situations, the need for group understanding and action, and the role of the recreator in each.

Participant Situations

Recreation and park units exist to serve the leisure interests of the public. Participant satisfaction is enhanced when the participants feel free and unencumbered with rules and regulations. Their involvement in recreation situations is voluntary; they are there to be served. It is axiomatic that satisfaction is directly related to involvement. The more participants feel a part of the planning and decision making, the more commitment and benefit they have. Program settings that allow participants to decide the activities they wish to pursue and set the tone for their involvement are the ones that provide the most benefit. This is true whether it be at a campground in a national park, playing bridge in a community building, or participating in a leisure counseling encounter group. Even when participants must abide by the rules, such as when playing in a softball league or receiving instructions in a ceramics class, if they feel they had some input in creating the activity—its objectives, the time and place of its occurrence—their participation will be more intense. It is in this context that the recreation department ceases to provide entertainment and offers opportunities for fulfillment. *The recreator becomes an enabler, a facilitator.*

Staff Relations

Although there are differing levels of responsibility within any organization and a necessary bureaucracy, each professional within the organization is a peer with all other professionals. The effective administrator understands this and involves his or her personnel as equals in planning and organizing the agency's work. Developing personnel policies and procedures, formulating and enforcing rules and regulations, and establishing and maintaining a system of recognition and awards are critical to staff morale and staff functioning. Despite differences in decision making and the carrying out of responsibility, the former can and should involve group planning and group dynamics; the latter becomes a responsibility of the individual who has been delegated to perform specific tasks. If junior staff members or lower echelon professionals feel left out of decision making, they may become hostile, apathetic, or passive towards the agency's responsibilities and functioning. The result may be a deterioration of their ability to lead and effectively create meaningful leisure experiences for the participants. On the other hand, when they are involved in shaping the agency's goals and procedures, they "stretch" themselves, grow professionally, and add to the life quality of both the agency and community. Good staff functioning and staff morale are essential to effective programming and public relations. *The recreator is the administrator, the manager.*

Volunteers and Policy Groups

There is a limit to what professionals in an organization with a limited budget can do to promote their service and effectively meet the public's demand. The use of volunteers and part-time staff extends the leadership resources of the agency and may partially compensate for budgetary deficiencies. The reliance on an advisory policy board to assist in developing and interpreting agency policies and program priorities aids in legitimating the recreation service and improves the chances for budgetary increases. Those members serving in an advisory capacity to the department, as well as those who offer their program and administrative skills freely, are volunteers. Their rewards come from the satisfaction they derive from serving others. Their satisfactions are enhanced when they feel a part of the team, not outsiders invited to serve when the staff is unable to do its job. Since these volunteers are members of the community, their commitment to the department through their activities extends back to their community groups in the form of support for the recreation agencies' goals and policies. They are a critical element in the link with public relations. Commitment rather than authority binds them to the agency's goals and the tasks they must execute. They do not have to follow the department's leaders and leadership; they do it because they are committed and influenced by the agency's leadership and aspirations. *The recreator becomes the supervisor, the counselor.*

Interagency Relations

Recreation departments and agencies should not operate in a vacuum. They are a part of the human service system and both influence that system and are influenced by its functioning. The success of recreation bond elections, program development efforts, and community support are directly related to the perceptions other professionals have of the importance and functioning of the recreation service. If the medical officials believe recreation is important to the community's health, if school officials are positive towards the services and program objectives of the recreation department, if public administrators respect the operations of the recreation agency, then the recreation department will play a stronger and more instrumental role in influencing community life. If its efforts are only tolerated by these other professionals, then its scope of service will be limited and negatively affected. Recreation and parks will have little voice outside the activities of its own department. Effective public relations efforts and sound programming are fundamental in establishing and maintaining good interagency cooperation. The involvement of key personnel and volunteers from those agencies in the general thinking and planning of the recreation service is essential if their commitment to recreation is to be maintained. The application of good group process principles nurture that support. *The recreator must be an interpreter, a consultant.*

A SYNOPSIS OF WHAT IS TO FOLLOW

It is the intent of this book to provide the student and the practitioner of recreation and parks with a working knowledge of group dynamics and of the application of group process principles to the recreation services environment.

It is an effort to extract from the literature and experiences of group dynamics those principles and understandings that have immediate application to the everyday functioning of recreation and park professionals. It should be useful in the in-service training of both staff and volunteer workers, contribute to the improved functioning of board advisory committees, and heighten the reader's sensitivity to the environment in which he or she lives. We begin this study with a discussion of the nature and art of leadership (Chapter Two). There we look at the various concepts and theories of leadership, the responsibilities of leadership, and the problems leaders face. Since leadership is a group phenomenon, Chapter Three discusses the nature and significance of groups and the types of groups that constitute the recreation/park environment. This discussion is followed (Chapter Four) with the identification and discussion of those forces that affect the functioning of groups. Attention is given to both the internal and external dynamics that shape group behavior and that, to some degree, may be controlled by the leader.

Having developed some of the theoretical aspects of group functioning, Chapters Five and Six are devoted to a description of various techniques leaders may use when working with groups. Chapter Five, written by Cynthia J. Hampton, concentrates on small group techniques, while Chapter Six is a discussion of those things leaders can do or use to affect large group functioning. Illustrations, case studies, and practical suggestions are included in each.

Since all groups experience conflict and have occasional problems, leaders need to know how to cope with these disruptions. Chapter Seven deals with these problems, why they exist, and the means by which they may be resolved. Specific attention is focused on the nature of interpersonal relationships and the application of a problem-solving methodology to group functioning.

The final three chapters relate to specialized leadership roles (supervision and consultation), leadership development strategies, and evaluation techniques. This grouping of information begins with the discussion of leadership development or training techniques (Chapter Eight). Suggestions on the organizing and conducting of in-service training programs, workshops and conferences are offered. The nature of supervision and consultation and the functioning of supervisors and consultants are considered in Chapter Nine. Suggestions for implementing social change within a community or agency are included in this discussion. The final chapter (Chapter Ten) emphasizes the importance of evaluation and the various techniques and efforts that can be applied to assess the effectiveness of leaders, the quality of the group's experience, and the factors which influence both.

Through the integrating of theory, illustrations, and discussions of interlying dynamics and group techniques that may be applied to various group situations, we hope to strengthen the leadership of park and recreation professionals and to add measurably to their understanding of the significance of group dynamics in their professional lives.

EXERCISES AND STUDY SUGGESTIONS

The following exercises and study suggestions, and those following each chapter, are designed to enable both instructors and students to experience the concepts discussed in the chapters. "Processing" or discussing the experiences reinforces the identification of specific learnings from the experiences as well as the reading in the chapter and other suggested readings. The authors strongly urge the considered use of these exercises and study suggestions to develop the most efficient overall learning experience.

To get the group process going, it is suggested the class or group try some warm-up activities. Among those which are available are:

I. *First Names, First Impressions*

Objective:	To get acquainted and to study the nature of first impressions.
Time Needed:	45–60 minutes
Setting:	Group members should be in a circle, facing each other.
Process:	Have each person give his first name only, or what he wishes the group to call him, and two significant facts about himself.

Once all have done this, each person turns away from the group and writes down as many names as he can remember.

After three minutes, have the group turn their chairs back so all are again facing the group to see whose names they forgot. They can now ask for more information to attach to the names they may have forgotten.

Then, discuss reasons for remembering or forgetting names.

Once this phase is completed, have each person note his or her first impression of each person in the group. Share them with the group. Seek consensus of impression—were they similar? Discuss the value and problems associated with first impressions.

II. *Fantasy Land*

Objective: To free up the group and assist in getting acquainted.

Time Needed: 30 minutes

Setting: Circle arrangement.

Process: One at a time, have each person tell the group: (1) what he wishes the group to call him; (2) what he would like to do if he had all the skills or resources necessary to do it (his life fantasy); (3) where he would go and what he would do if he could take his ideal vacation.

While performing this exercise, it is critical that the leader interact with each person as he or she expresses his or her fantasy. When all have spoken, discuss the exercise and the importance of having "dreams," then have one of the group members name all the other members in the group.

III. *Goal Setting and Agenda Building*

Objective: To state publicly your goals for yourself in this group and your goals for the group; seek to build an agenda (set of expectations) for the group.

Time Needed: 1 hour

Setting: A room with a chalkboard.

Process: Have each person write one personal objective for himself and one group objective; collect them and write each on the chalkboard under the appropriate heading—*Personal Goals; Group Goals.*

Once all have had time to read this list, have the group discuss the order in which they want to work on group goals. Also, ask them to discuss the possible problems they may encounter in meeting these goals and how these difficulties may be overcome.

Finally, have the group discuss the value of setting personal and group goals; also, have them determine if these goals are realistic within the time constraints and resources of the group.

In addition to the above and similar warm-up exercises, you may want the group to discuss the following topics:

1. Are leaders made or are they born?
2. What is leadership?
3. What differentiates leaders from followers? What must a leader do?
4. The application of group dynamics processes and techniques to recreation services.

Other suggestions to get started with the study of groups are:

1. Have various members interview professionals in social work, adult education, and recreation services and report their findings to the group. Have the group discuss the similarities and differences in these professions and their use of group techniques.
2. Begin sensitizing the group members to their role as observers of the group process by using such instruments as the *Process Observation Form* and *Consultation Guide* when group members are asked to observe other classmates. Those who observe should share their observations with those who were functioning as discussants.
3. Try to alter the size of the discussion groups to see the effects of size on participation. Begin with two-person groups, then four- and finally eight-. Have the groups talk about the dynamics of group size as it affected their participation.

PROCESS OBSERVATION FORM

Make notes in the blank spaces provided. Record *who* did *what*.

Organization: How did the group get started?

How did members begin sharing their resources?

What procedures did they develop to solve the problem?

Data Flow: How did the group get out all the information?

What data were accepted? Rejected?

How was the information collated or compiled?

Data Processing: How did the group stay on track?

What rules emerged to guide decision making?

What visual aids were employed?

How was consensus achieved and tested?

CONSULTATION GUIDE

These forms are for the purpose of assisting each member of the group to record his or her perceptions and to compare and discuss them with the other members. After any group discussion, rate your performance.

HOW YOU WOULD RATE YOURSELF NOW:

Thinking back over your performance in the discussion group sessions, place a check at the appropriate point on each scale.

I. Response to most of the other group members:

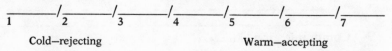

Cold—rejecting   Warm—accepting

II. Response to group needs:

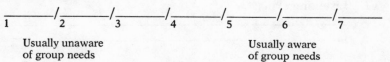

Usually unaware   Usually aware
of group needs   of group needs

III.   Level of participation:

———————————/ ————————————/ ————————————

Tendency to over   Realistic amount   Tendency to under-
participate   of participation   participate

IV.   Degree of Problem-Centeredness:

———/———/———/———/———/———/———
1   2   3   4   5   6   7

Rarely stayed with   Usually stayed with
the issues; unattentive   the issues; attentive

V.   Communication Skills:

———/———/———/———/———/———/———
1   2   3   4   5   6   7

Communicated in   Communicated thoughts
vague manner   clearly

VI.   Listening Skills:

———/———/———/———/———/———/———
1   2   3   4   5   6   7

Frequently did not   "Hears" objectively
"listen" to others

Use this guide to indicate briefly the ways in which you intend to change
your performance in group sessions.

I.   Response to most of the other group members:

_____

_____

II.   Response to group needs:

_____

_____

III.   General participation:

_____

_____

IV.   Degree of problem-centeredness:

_____

_____

V.   Communication skills:

_____

_____

VI.   Listening skills:

_____

_____

ENDNOTES

1. Eduard C. Lindeman, *Leisure—A National Issue* (New York: Association Press, 1939), 61 pp.
2. Leland P. Bradford and others, eds. *T-Group Theory and Laboratory Method* (New York: John Wiley & Sons, Inc., 1964), 498 pp.
3. H. Douglas Sessoms, Harold D. Meyer, and Charles K. Brightbill, *Leisure Services* (Englewood Cliffs: Prentice-Hall, 1975), 362 pp.

SUGGESTED READINGS

Beal, George M.; Bohlen, Joe M.; and Roudabaugh, J. Neil. *Leadership and Dynamic Group Action.* Ames, Iowa: Iowa State University Press, 1962.

Johnson, David W., and Johnson, Frank P. *Joining Together.* Englewood Cliffs, N.J.: Prentice-Hall, 1975.

Knowles, Malcolm and Hulda. *Introduction to Group Dynamics.* Revised ed. New York: Association Press, 1972.

Pfeiffer, J. William, and Jones, John E., eds. *A Handbook of Structured Experiences for Human Relations Training.* La Jolla, Calif.: University Associates, 1979. All volumes, especially those on getting acquainted and sensory awareness.

Chapter Two

THE NATURE AND ART
OF LEADERSHIP

It is desirable for the recreation or park professional to have a solid grasp of the concept and the importance of leadership. People in the United States are parts of groups in many settings including social, educational, work, and religious activities, as well as at play and recreation. In nearly every group some form of "leadership" either is present or emerges from the group. An understanding of the nature and the art of leadership can enable the recreation professional to be more efficient in the performance of his or her job.

The efforts of behavioral scientists to isolate and analyze the phenomenon of leadership have been only partially successful. We are certain leadership exists; we see it in action and note its results. There is, however, considerable diversity and limited agreement concerning a definition of leadership.

The Latin and Greek words for "leadership" shed much light on our study and on our efforts to define the word. "Leadership" is derived basically from the verb meaning *to act*. Arendt shows that two Greek verbs *archein* ("to begin," "to lead" and finally "to rule") and *prattein* ("to achieve," "to pass through," "to finish") have corresponding verbs in Latin, *agere* ("to set in motion," "to lead") and *gerere* (which originally meant "to bear").* Each leadership action can be said to be logically divided into two parts: the beginning, made by a single person; and the achievement, which is performed by others who see the activity to completion by "bearing" and "finishing" it.[1]

Furthermore, the two verbs designating the verb *to act* in both Latin and Greek are closely related. The leader begins an action and depends on his or her followers for help in taking the action to completion. The followers, likewise, need the "beginner" to develop or initiate their cause for

* Adapted from *The Human Condition* by Hannah Arendt by permission of The University of Chicago Press. Copyright 1958 by The University of Chicago.

action. Eventually, the original interdependence for action between leader and follower became divided into two functions. To the leader went the function of giving commands; to the followers went the duty of following or carrying out the commands. The very act of initiating or beginning—of leading—tends to isolate a person from others who might have joined him and assisted in completing what he began.

It becomes clear that leadership, when traced to the original Greek and Latin, did not mean necessarily that followers were completely dependent upon leaders. In fact, the interdependence of leader and follower was obvious then as it is now. Both leader and followers need each other. *Leadership, then, is that activity of ideas or behavior of one or more persons in a group that affects the ideas or behavior of one or more persons in the group; a leader is any person who exerts leadership on other persons.*

THEORIES OF LEADERSHIP

As results of the study of leadership have accumulated over the years, many theories of leadership have emerged. In this section we will examine some of these theories which can prove useful especially to the recreation professional. These theories tend to emphasize either the nature of leadership, that is, characteristics and traits of leaders, or the influencing factors and situations which condition the emergence and practice of leadership.

"Great Man" Theories

One interesting approach to leadership, as suggested by Eugene E. Jennings, is called "The Great Man Theory." Building from his premise that a conspicuous personality is required of a truly great leader, Jennings says that our society is basically without "great man leaders" because we are part of a highly organized society. Organizations of this nature inhibit the historic and practical function of great leadership.[2] Jennings' theory provides other perspectives on leadership. The following several pages (up to the section "Superior Person Leadership") draw largely from Jennings' writing.[3]

Princes.   Some great men are motivated by a desire for power over others. These can be called "Princes." Examples from history include Julius Caesar, Fredrick the Great, Mussolini, Henry Ford, and Franklin Roosevelt. The classic model was provided by Machiavelli in *The Prince and the Discourses*.[4] A true Prince must both want power and be able to use it. He needs the skills of a fox (to recognize traps) and the fearlessness of a lion (to frighten away wolves). His leadership style uses both power and cunning and is self-serving in developing a power base and power program.

The Prince type of leader has a personality characteristic that Machiavelli called *virtu*, which we translate as drive, spirit, or ambition. According to Machiavelli, a leader controls himself and others, often enduring extreme difficulty and persisting through personal danger. Coupled with the Prince leader's drive is the tendency to be fraudulent or deceptive. Cunning and deceit often serve this type of leader better than force. In fact, the less confidence and integrity this leader type has as permanent traits of personality, and the greater his capacity to instill fear without causing hatred, the more likely he is to succeed as a Great Man (Prince) leader. While this state of leadership is sometimes lumped under the heading *autocratic*, in its pure form, it is far more manipulative and potentially destructive than what we often think of as autocratic leadership.

Heroes.   Thomas Carlyle was another who chronicled much of the Great Man Theory. He believed that "among the undistinguished ant-like masses are men of light and leading, mortals superior in power, courage, and understanding." [5] The history of mankind describes the lives of many of these great men. They possess superior intuitive insight and great sincerity and are followed, admired, and obeyed almost to a point of worship. From Carlyle, we derive an image of a Great Man leader as one possessing extraordinary insight with a "seeing eye," the ability to see through to the pattern of facts and future events. To these men others bow in duty and service or follow in hero worship.

Today, we think of this kind of leader as a kind of "charismatic, benevolent, autocrat" with superior insight and concern for betterment of the community or society. Carlyle called these leaders "heroes." He believed they possessed a sort of religious or mystical awareness of a better life beyond mere surface appearance, viewing events with more a "moving heart" than simply a clear, rational head. Carlyle believed that the selfless dignity of man would result from unity in fighting for a purpose, a community generating wonderful power under the leadership of a hero who would elicit a commitment and morality of the strongest human emotions: love for one another, for duty, and for truth. Many recreation and park professionals aspire to be this type of leader; not "heroes" in the ego sense, but in the mode of Carlyle—one dedicated to service.

Democratic Hero.   Another view of the Great Man Theory comes from John Stuart Mill. He believed that the democratic process would allow the selection of a Great Man as leader of a large group such as a state or a nation. In this way, people of superior intelligence would be selected by the masses to lead them, and these leaders would peacefully discharge leadership without consolidating personal power. Through the democratic process, this superior leader would emerge by the choice of people who rationally discussed the merits of potential leaders and selected the one best suited to rule or lead them. The persuasive power of discussion was a major emphasis of Mill in the decision process.[6]

Great Average Man.   Ralph Waldo Emerson adapted Carlyle, and transferred much of the focus on analysis of leadership to the American continent.[7] Emerson believed heroes are needed in both aristocracy and democracy, but that those in democracy were of a different breed. He saw the hero as a "Great Average Man," a mystic who thinks in realms higher than those of most of his followers. A high level of energy and participation are two major characteristics Emerson saw belonging to the hero leader. A third characteristic was that of the leaders developing their leadership to such a level that successors would be spurred to even greater heights in their leadership roles.

Receptive Man.   William James took the democratic ideas of Emerson and Mill a major step further. He saw a dynamic relationship between the situation and the leader, including those who accept and follow his leadership. His concept was called "receptivity of the moment." By this he meant the time is right, the situation is appropriate, and the inherent forces present in the situation seem to draw the leader into the position of leadership. Many believe that it is the *situation*, not the person, which makes leadership happen. Or, in other words, events create leaders. His famous essay *The Will to Believe* shows James' commitment to success depending on energy of action, and this energy is derived from the will. The will of a person gives the belief that one will succeed.[8]

Eventful Man.   Sidney Hook brings the "hero theory" closer to the present in his contrast between the eventful man and the event-making man. He defines the eventful man in history as one whose behavior influenced events along a course different from what would have been if his actions had not been taken. In contrast, the event-making man is an eventful man whose outstanding character and intelligence cause his actions to be what they are. He is a hero, according to Hook, more by virtue of who he is than of what he does. For Hook, a democracy would do best if it realized that heroes can be developed by fitting social opportunities to talents of specific individuals. A democracy should be regulated by the ideal slogan, "every man a hero." [9] Here we have an historical basis for leadership development programs.

Jennings is careful to conclude his pages dealing with heroes (Great Man Leaders) by encouraging us to see the difference between a hero-type who will crush other people in his effort to make his mark in life, and the leader who works well within the bounds of representative government. He finally draws upon Carlyle, Mill, Emerson, James, and Hook to develop his definition of a hero. The hero leader today is one who is a starter, an initiator, one whose efforts are both conditioned by and also have a molding effect upon the environment. The leader is not determined by the situation, but is definitely relevant to the situation. He "sees purpose and possibility and places his faith upon initiative. In general, he inspires and motivates in ways to which men are not generally predisposed but which immeasurably improve their welfare." [10]

It is important to understand that a hero leader, in Jennings' view, is more than merely the person at the top of a formal organization. Anyone in this position has, at least in theory, the same amount of power inherent in the organization. Nor is a leader recognized solely for his or her executive ability. The personal resources the individual person brings to the situation in which he functions as a leader identify him as such.

Nietzsche's Superman.   Another approach to "The Great Man" theory of leadership is the *poetic* picture of the Superman, based on the writings of Friedrich Nietzsche.[11] Nietzsche felt that the combination of democracy and Christianity had overbalanced emphasis on personal and moral values that reduced the capacity for individual strength. He believed that people had lost their own sense of human worth and dignity, and were no longer self-directed. They had lost much of their capacity for true freedom, creativity, and originality in thinking and behavior. Nietzsche believed life to be a struggle not for existence but for power. His was not a will to live but a will to power. For him, humanity needed to reevaluate its social values and make weakness the ultimate disgrace and power the ultimate virtue.

To understand Nietzsche it is necessary to clarify his meaning of "power." Apparently he meant the power of self-overcoming. That is, he meant that a person should develop to the highest he or she was capable of becoming. This would be in contrast to conforming to what others had in mind. Nietzsche felt that one's conscience was introjected by society, and that this inhibited one's natural passions, which lie in turmoil beneath the surface. Thus, conformity was weakness, the easy way out.

Nietzsche wanted people to work through these passions, throw off that conformity, and develop their fullest, most true selves. This was real freedom, the end to which most people grope but which few attain. The one who does is the self-directed, fully free individual. This ideal person for Friedrich Neitzsche was a Superman.

Psychological and Sociological Theories

In the foregoing paragraphs we have looked at leadership through the eyes of authors who have observed historical leaders in action. Their writings describe the operating style of these leaders. In the following section we will examine leadership as social psychologists have looked at the interactions between leaders and the human elements in their environment.

One of the earliest psychologists to write about leadership was Alfred Adler. He believed people developed a resistance to domination and an eagerness to dominate, and that each person has areas of inferiority, real or imagined.[12] These feelings of social, physical, or mental inferiority stimulate goals of superiority by means of compensation. The will to power drives one to compensate for feelings of inferiority. Demosthenes, the stammerer who overcame his personal problem to become one of history's greatest orators, is a good example. For Adler, individuals establish a compensatory life pattern that enables them to learn to respond to all of life's situations with the refusal to be dominated, the will to personal power and success.

Modern child psychologists have also noted that the onset of self-assertive behavior comes at an earlier stage of development than feelings of inferiority. This may mean, as Nietzsche suspected, that there is in the early life of the individual an innate impulse to dominance. According to Otto Rank, the general population can be divided into three primary groups or types of persons.[13] The first type surrender their will to whatever group they are with. They conform and, as a result, have fewer conflicts. They have less power and are less creative. To the second group of personality types belong the neurotics who cannot conform to group will, but also cannot express their own will. They are not happy either alone or with other groups making up their social environment.

The third type of individuals extend their ego into reality. These are "creative man," the personalities whose ideals are not taken from the group—as are those of average people—or from the battle between self and others, but rather from their own interdependence with the social groups with which they interact. In a real sense, these persons create themselves through interaction with the other selves in their environment, both giving to them and taking from them. It is well to note that Rank's creative man does not place himself in adversary or conflict relationships with the group as does Nietzsche's Superman, even though each fully affirms and accepts himself as a person.

A further example of ideal man is drawn from Erich Fromm.[14] People who are "marketing man" sense themselves as commodities to be bought and sold, and thus mold themselves to fit whatever qualities they perceive to be in demand. As chameleons, they vary with the situation, and people see them as unstable and unfixed in character. Without tangible character, they often feel empty and alone. In contrast to marketing man is "productive man," who uses his strengths to realize his inherent potentialities. He has wishes other than popularity or marketability; he desires to become independent and feel full of self-respect. Such people enjoy living and live confidently. Their leadership reflects it.

One final contribution to the theories of leadership which is relevant to our understanding is that of David Riesman.[15] In his book *The Lonely Crowd* he describes a change in American independence. Before World War I most Americans were "inner-directed" (Rank's third personality type); their behavior was motivated from inner values and goals emphasizing self-reliance and conquest over new or challenging situations. Their introjected inner gyroscopes gave them stability in difficult times.

Riesman says that typical Americans of the post-World War II period have become "other-directed" (Rank's first type). They seek more to "fit in" than to be independent. They seem to compute the cues others continuously send them and respond to these cues in terms of what they think others expect of them. They have lost their internal emotional centers of motivation. Thus, they often seem characterized by passive and apathetic attitudes. Another way to describe them is that they have a low "will to power." They seem almost incapable of charting their own courses and then following the charts with willed determination. What Riesman describes in the other-directed person is the social individual who never becomes fully independent. (See Fig. 2–1.)

"Superior Person" Leadership.   For the field of recreation services we suggest the Jennings leadership model of the "superior person."[16] This model is a composite and an ideal formulation of people who have the essence of self-directedness—self-respect. Their goal is to become the best they are capable of becoming, and they do this by willing it. They will their successful becoming. They are not adversely affected by approval or disapproval or personal hurt. They have considerable positive pride but are not vain. They see themselves as leaders and are willing to accept the pain of loneliness of leadership. They realize the job with power over others does not come without the discipline and even the anguish of power. They will suffer and struggle as part of the process of inner strength and freedom.

They are free of the control of the radar that picks up and computes the cues from others and that controls much of the other-directed person's behavior. They may or may not have the internal gyroscope of the inner-directed person placed there by the authorities of their youth. Rather, "superior people" have worked through the introjections of authorities of their youths and have worked out for themselves their own values, goals, and norms, which are specific to them as mature and unique individuals.

In contrast to Princes and Heroes of today, Jennings' "Superior Man" stands out. Such people may or may not dominate others. In either case, it results from self-control and using inner resources effectively. They do not manipulate or maneuver or compromise as may strong-willed princes in their drive for power. Neither will superior people allow themselves to become tools for the organization or the group, as might weak-willed princes. Although this ideal leader is mythical, over-idealized, and seldom found in one person, we can learn much from the perfection Jennings so purely describes.

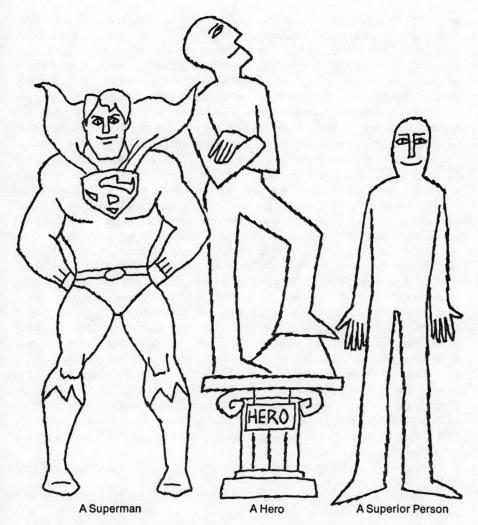

| A Superman | A Hero | A Superior Person |

FIG. 2–1.   Superman, Hero, Superior Person. Which Do You Choose to Be?

Trait Theories

Another theory for examining leadership is to consider the *traits of persons* who are leaders or are possibly soon-to-be leaders. For some fifty years Americans have tended to evaluate leaders in terms of their characteristics or traits. From about 1930 to 1955 leaders were frequently judged or evaluated by the traits they possessed or brought to the job. Emory Bogardus (1934) and Ordway Tead (1935) wrote in these areas.

Tead summarized fifteen or more traits as physical and nervous energy, a sense of purpose and direction, enthusiasm, friendliness and affection, integrity, technical mastery of the job or information, decisiveness, intelligence (of which evidence is imagination and sense of human teaching skill), and faith or deeper resources.[17] Bogardus presents a similar list of traits that originate in personality. He adds other sources of leadership in heredity and in "social stimuli" or environmental forces.[18]

Ralph Stogdill examined over 150 studies on leadership traits as described by researchers from 1904 to 1947.[19] He summarized the conclusion of fifteen or more of these traits, and his findings show that the average person in a leadership position exceeds the average of his or her followers in intelligence, scholarship, dependability in exercising responsibilities, socioeconomic status, and activity and social participation. Ten of the studies reported that the average leader exceeds the average follower in sociability, initiative, persistence, knowing how to get things done, self-confidence, alertness to and insight into situations, popularity, adaptability, cooperativeness, and verbal facility. Moreover, as seems obvious, certain situations cause other traits to be highly valued, such as athletic ability by an athletic team, and physical strength and nerve by boys' gangs. Other highly valued traits with the highest overall correlation in relation to leadership were popularity, originality, aggressiveness, judgment, desire to excel, humor, cooperativeness, and liveliness. A low correlation to leadership was demonstrated by such variables as chronological age, weight, height, physique, appearance, energy, dominance, and mood control.

Stogdill noted that the research findings on leaders' traits during the first half of the twentieth century suggest that leadership is not truly a passive status, or even a combination of traits. It is, rather, a working relationship between members of a particular group wherein the leader achieves this status by actively participating with the group, and by carrying tasks to completion.

The traits could be classified according to the six functions in Table 2–1.

To check on his earlier work of leadership studies from 1904 to 1947, Stogdill surveyed 168 leadership studies conducted between 1948 and 1970.[20] From the earlier to the later study, value was apparently reduced in each of the following traits: age, appearance or grooming, education, judgment or decisiveness, adaptability, alertness, dominance, extroversion, persistence against obstacles, responsibility in pursuit of objectives, ability to enlist cooperation, cooperativeness, popularity or prestige, social participation, and tact or diplomacy.

In contrast, the following traits were found to have maintained value or increased in value from the earlier study of 1904–1947 to the later 1948–1970 study.* (Those items marked with an asterisk [*] show a strong

* List reprinted with permission of Macmillan Publishing Co., Inc. from *Handbook of Leadership* by Ralph M. Stogdill. Copyright © 1974 by The Free Press, a Division of Macmillan Publishing Co., Inc.

TABLE 2–1.   Leaders' Traits Classified According to Six Functions

Functions	Traits
1. Capacity	intelligence alertness verbal facility originality judgment
2. Achievement	scholarship knowledge athletic accomplishments
3. Responsibility	dependability initiative persistence aggressiveness self-confidence desire to excel
4. Participation	activity sociability cooperation adaptability humor
5. Status	socioeconomic position popularity
6. Situation	mental level status skills needs and interests of followers objectives to be achieved

Reprinted with permission of Macmillan Publishing Co., Inc. from *Handbook of Leadership* by Ralph M. Stogdill. Copyright © 1974 by The Free Press, a Division of Macmillan Publishing Co., Inc.

positive correlation increase in the 1948–1970 study. Two asterisks [**] indicate items that appear in the 1948–1970 study and not in the 1904–1947 study.)

activity and energy*
social status
mobility
intelligence
knowledge
fluency of speech
adjustment or normality**
aggressiveness or assertiveness**
ascendance or dominance*
emotional balance and control

enthusiasm**
independence and nonconformity**
objectivity**
tough-mindedness**
originality and creativity*
personal integrity and ethical conduct
resourcefulness**
self-confidence*
tolerance of stress**
desire to excel or achieve*
drive for responsibility
enterprise or initiative**
task-orientation*
administrative ability**
attractiveness**
nurturance**
sociability and interpersonal skills*

While persisting values are clear, new values in traits from 1948–1970 reflect the social changes of the times.

A leader is generally thought to have a strong drive for responsibility and completing tasks, persistence and vigor in pursuing goals, is venturesome and original in solving problems, has self-confidence and a sense of personal identity, is willing to accept consequences of decision and of action, possesses a drive to initiate social situations, is willing to absorb interpersonal stress, tolerates frustration and delay, and possesses the capacity to influence the behavior of others and the ability to order systems of social interaction to deal with the task or purpose.

Although the trait theory approach has appeal, a word of caution is advised. It seems clear that describing the traits others have isolated as being present in leaders has merit, but to subscribe to the trait approach to leadership is patently atomistic. We would by preference be eclectic and holistic in our approach to leadership, to see it as a more complex set of interactions between people rather than simply being the result of innate, individual traits.

We can be equally certain that the situationist approach to leadership, wherein leadership evolves to meet the situation, has merit but is also not fully acceptable as the *only* clear way to understand leadership. For example, an examination of over 100 studies of leadership traits suggested that if there are traits that can be characteristic of leaders, patterns of these traits are likely to vary with the requirements for leadership in various situations. Groups tend to accept as leaders, it can be said, those persons who demonstrate characteristics and skills that will better enable the group to accomplish the task it perceives as its own. As far back as 1918, Bogardus proposed a theory along this line.[21] One logical conclusion of this manner of thinking is that leadership resides in a situation rather than in a person. It seems an appropriate conclusion that leadership in fact resides somewhere between the trait approach and the situationist approach and involves important features of both approaches.

Personal-Situational Theories

The trait theory adds to our understanding of leaders and leadership but is not sufficient in itself to describe leadership itself or its emergence. Those who theorize that leadership develops in the environmental situation also contribute much to our understanding of leadership. Sufficient reason exists, however, to conclude that these theories represent two extremes, perhaps the two ends of a continuum, and that the truth lies somewhere between or in some combination of the two. The effects must be considered an interaction between the individual's own traits and the situation's own forces. Thus, the "Personal-Situational Theories" of leadership.

As early as 1933 C. M. Case suggested that leadership is produced by the interaction between (1) the leader's personality traits, (2) the nature of the group and the members of the group, and (3) the charge, task, or problem confronting the group.[22] Although there have been refinements by further research and by depth of examination of components of these three areas since Case wrote, they do themselves largely describe the area covered by the personal-situational theorists. *Leadership can be said, in this view, to develop in a dynamic interaction between the traits and skills of the leader, the nature of the group itself, and the situation or work to which the group addresses itself.*

Every professional in recreation, parks, or leisure services should be familiar with the theories and terms developed by Frederick Herzberg, which fit naturally in the area of personal-situational theories of leadership. His original research on job attitudes was followed by research on motivation to work. From these and other research he developed his *Work and the Nature of Man* in which he describes his basic theory on "motivation-hygiene." [23]

Herzberg suggests that the absence of pain is not necessarily the presence of pleasure. He states that "business" is the dominant institution of modern times, and business is harming itself and its employees by not recognizing the bimodal nature of people. Effective leaders need to recognize that a person is composed of equal parts of Adam (possessing physical needs) and Abraham (possessing psychological needs). Herzberg and his followers have asked thousands of persons what gives them feelings of job satisfaction or dissatisfaction, and whether feelings of job satisfaction affect one's job performance, personal well-being, and personal relationships. Results of this research led to the Motivation-Hygiene Theory.

Basically this theory says that five factors, called *Motivators*, determine job satisfaction. These factors are achievement, recognition, the work itself, responsibility, and advancement. A number of other factors, called *Hygienes*, lead to job dissatisfaction. These tend to relate to the work environment. Examples of Hygiene factors include salary, interpersonal relations, company or agency policy, administration, supervision, and working conditions. Good Hygiene factors do not make people happy; they only prevent unhappiness as, in Herzberg's analogy, garbage collection does not make people healthy, but it helps keep them from being unhealthy.

Job satisfiers are motivators to high level of superior job performance. Motivation is primarily an internal stimulus. Leaders need to enrich the job content with opportunity for achievement, recognition, responsibility, and individual growth.

Other Theories

Many have applied theories of leadership in the past three decades to the theories of organizations. The "third force" psychologists have more recently been subsumed under the term *humanistic* psychologists. In this view people are motivated organisms by nature. The development of effective and cohesive organization is a major human goal. Therefore, it is the function of leadership to impact and thus to change the structure and the controlled nature of organizations and thus modify the organization in ways that will allow the individual to meet personal needs while simultaneously contributing to the accomplishment of the organization's goals. The application of humanistic theories of leadership to organizations for these purposes is called "Organization Development."

Douglas McGregor wrote of this in terms popularly called "Theory X and Theory Y." [24] The former leadership style (Theory X) attempts to direct and motivate people to fit the needs of the organization, believing that people are passive, disinterested in work, and resistant to being led. Based on the belief that people possess motivation and desire for responsibility, "Theory Y" leaders work to arrange conditions within an organization so that persons see and work for the fulfillment of their own needs while at the same time working to achieve objectives of the organization. Chris Argyris, Peter Drucker, Abraham Maslow, Warren Bennis, and many other modern organization psychologists have also written in this area of organizational functioning. [25]

Robert Blake and Jane S. Mouton have provided a most useful model upon which to conceptualize leadership (see Figure 2–2). Called "The New Managerial Grid®," the vertical axis represents a concern for people on a scale of 1–9. The horizontal axis, with a similar 1–9 scale, represents concern for production. [26] Throughout the Managerial Grid Seminar, participants are given feedback about their Grid style orientation. People who rank high on *both* axes have a high concern for people and a high concern for production. They develop followers whose sense of interdependence

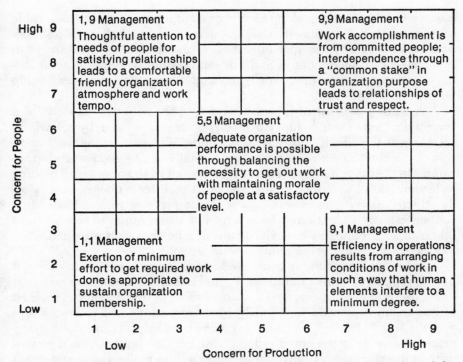

FIGURE 2–2. The New Managerial Grid (From *The New Managerial Grid*, by Robert R. Blake and Jane Srygley Mouton. Houston: Gulf Publishing Company, Copyright © 1978, page 11. Reproduced by permission.)

and commitment to work or production tend to accomplish organizational goals in an atmosphere of respect and trust.

THE LEADERSHIP FOUNTAINHEAD

How does leadership come to exist in a group of persons? How does one get to be a leader—whether in a laboratory or "test-tube" group, a class, an agency, or an organization? "Through any of a variety of ways" is a valid answer. Although no more than one of these is generally operative at a given time, it is quite possible for more than one to be actively visible to the careful observer.

Note that leadership can be either formal or informal. In formal leadership, the leader is so named or titled. He or she is the chairperson, president, manager, professor, coordinator, coach, director, principal, head, supervisor, or any of many other designated titles. The formal leader is in a formally designated position and usually exists so in any organizational description that is set up along formal or traditional lines, such as a Table of Organization. They are "heads." The person who is the formal or designated leader usually has specific duties or responsibilities. With the position goes a certain amount of authority and power. In addition, some status or prestige or esteem is usually associated with the formal leadership position.[27]

A certain amount of power frequently goes with the authority of a formal position of leadership. However, power is often seen by behavioral scientists as the effective exercise of authority. Power is, therefore, a *function* of the authority which goes with a formally designated leadership *position*. On the other hand, *esteem* must be earned by the person functioning as leader. Unlike authority, status, and prestige, esteem does not necessarily adhere to any person who moves into a place of formal leadership. Rather, esteem is what one who is a formal leader hopes to receive from others in the group. This is received only after he or she has provided effective leadership moving the group toward its goals.

Informal leadership is contrasted to the formal. It exists in many, if not all, groups. Persons exhibiting informal leadership often have no designated title and are not charted in a formal table of organization. This kind of leadership is provided informally by those persons who follow or support the formal leaders. An example can be seen in a secretary with many years experience in the organization giving her new boss, who is the manager or director, suggestions that might help him make a wise statement (or refrain from an unwise one) at the next meeting of the board or commission. Again, a group member, picking up on the comment of a formal leader, may add to or clarify that comment so that the group moves effectively toward its goal.

In each case the secretary and the group member provide informal leadership. This does not in any way invalidate or reduce the merit or the impact from these informal leaders. As a matter of fact, the informal leader in a group or agency is at times the only one who effectively leads that group of persons. Still, the leadership is provided from an informal or "untitled" position and is noted here merely to contrast it to formal leadership.

The previous paragraphs in this section describe the basics of informal and formal leadership designations. The person who functions as leader seldom passively falls into that role by default. Usually the formal leader role is filled by designation, election, appointment, competition or run-off, or other means of selection. The power of decision may rest with the group that determines its own leaders. In other cases the power of decision may rest with some higher authority such as an executive, an administrative committee, a search committee, or an elected ruler such as city manager or mayor, governor, or president.

People who are designated to fill formal leadership positions are selected for a variety of reasons. Those who become leaders may possess the skills and/or the traits desired in the position. They might own most of the stock in the company; they might have waged the most effective campaign for the position. Several of the ways one moves into a position of leadership are described below.

Charisma. A charismatic leader is seen as one having unique and special qualities. In a sense the person is blessed—an apt term considering the derivation of the word. "Charisma" is a Greek term used to describe one on whom the gift or favor of God has fallen so that the recipient has some special power with respect to humanity—for example, the ability to heal or perform other miracles. Max Weber introduced this term to the United States' social science literature in 1947.[28] He believed the charismatic leaders have personalities of such nature that their esteem authority projects a kind of spiritual or inspired leadership through strong emotional appeal. When this personality style is combined with an ideology attractive to the dissatisfied, such results as Martin Luther, Mohammed, or Adolf Hitler may be anticipated. While charismatic leaders of yesterday were likely to be religious, those of today are more likely to be political or organizational. Today's charismatic political leaders may inspire in their followers an enthusiasm beyond mere politics. Eric Hoffer has called the followers of charismatic leaders "true believers." He indicates their zeal is based on a sense of their own worthlessness and inadequacy. By identifying with a movement or a superleader, Hoffer says, they gain a sense of personal adequacy and selfhood.[29]

Most leaders on the political scene succeed in part because their followers identify with them. Perceived similarity is a basis for identification. Those in the recreation profession should be aware of the effect of charisma. There are many who seek or obtain professional positions after a career of outstanding local, regional, or national athletic success. Their training may or may not fit them for the recreation position they seek. The professional should know how to confront or to capitalize on the charisma of a famous person in furthering the professional program.

Inheritance. Formal leaders often receive their positions of leadership by inheriting them. The son succeeds his father as president of the family business. An assistant director moves into the position of director when the former director moves out or retires. The Vice-President succeeds to the Presidency, or the vice-chairperson to the position of chairperson. Both valuable and destructive consequences can happen to the agency or organization as a result.

Transference or "Halo Effect." One who is a recognized leader in his or her community—well-known for either prestige of title, social or economic reputation, for business success or educational level (or who for another cause is "looked-up-to" by persons in the group)—is often automatically accorded a position of leadership in another group. The group assumes that persons like this are leaders and will provide leadership in any group of which they are members. Examples would be a physician, clergyman, professor, or someone successful in business becoming chairperson of a church committee, a P.T.A. group, or a community volunteer commission such as a Recreation Advisory Council. His or her "halo" from one position causes the acceptance, election, or appointment to leadership in another group. Success in one kind of group, however, does not guarantee successful leadership in another. The halo effect can cause the transfer of leadership position but not necessarily the transfer of effectiveness. Even so, one who has the drive for success in one situation may well exert the energy or have the self-starting push to bring about success in another situation, therefore reinforcing the "halo" stereotype.

Election.   When a new group is formed, or when formal leadership changes within a group, the members of the group often elect their own leader. Nominations are made, the "floor is closed," voting is done usually on a majority basis, and the new leader or leaders are elected to fill the positions of leadership. At times transference or halo-effect has a strong determining effect on the outcome of the election.

Self-Constituted.   Tead indicates that some persons push themselves for positions of leadership.[30] Historically, this person has often been thought of as the "born leader." In more contemporary times, this person may be recognized as ambitious, aggressive, confident, and either self-serving or group-serving—likely some combination of the last two. An example would be anyone who offers for or campaigns for an office in anything from a recreation club to the United States Senate.

Default.   On occasion a group or organization will find no apparent or willing leader in its midst. In fact, some persons present may have some desire for the prestige or the office, but not feel comfortable making this known. In other situations none may want the job. In these cases someone is usually pushed or coerced into taking a position of leadership. The leadership position is then filled by default.

Emergence.   Successful leaders often come out of the context of the group, the situation, and the personal abilities of the person. Internal and external forces combine to put together a situation in which the leader emerges from among the membership. Many of these occasions lend themselves to a successful leadership experience, for the forces usually prejudge the situation and the persons involved. Pitfalls are present, however, and an automatic policy of "promoting from within," as practiced by many governmental agencies, is suspect.

STYLES OF LEADERSHIP

Through the history of the study of leadership, especially in business and industry, behavioral scientists have examined styles of leadership. Kurt Lewin and his co-workers and followers, especially Ronald Lippitt and Ralph White, have popularized three categories of leadership types: autocratic, democratic, and laissez-faire.[31] (See Table 2–2.) We will examine each of these in some detail. With the examination of each, we shall consider the emotional climate and effective response of those persons who participate in a group with each kind of leadership.

Autocratic

The autocratic leadership style has been associated with a number of words. Some of these would be hard-boiled, authoritarian, dictatorial, leader-centered, production-centered, restrictive, high-pressure, close supervision, tough. Today, we think of this as "Theory X leadership" in McGregor's terms, of leadership moving toward the *9,1* style on the Blake and Mouton Managerial Grid.

The autocratic leader either may be appointed by superior authority, as in the military, or else inherits the position (and perhaps copies the style) from a relative. This person expects obedience from the group and determines group policy, makes decisions (usually alone), and in short runs a one-person operation. This leader is production-results oriented, and manipulates people to obtain the results and production *he* wants.

Members of autocratically led groups tend to "rubber stamp" the ideas of the leader and are frequently squelched when they do not. They ask few questions, for communication is usually one-way—leader to followers. While the group may go through the motions of democratic behavior—voting on issues, for example—the will of the autocrat prevails. Some persons in this group may tend to be either quarrelsome, aggressive,

TABLE 2–2.   Leadership Climates and Effects

Type of Leader	Climate	Motivation	Goals	Effects on Followers
Autocratic	formal	respect fear	leader's	dependent on leader
Laissez-faire	chaotic	self	personal	apathy and anarchy
Democratic	informal	respect love	group's	interdependent

or counter-dependent on each other and on the leader. At other times, the behavior of other persons led by this style may be apathetic, passive, dependent, and without initiative; they act out of fear or conditioning rather than out of desire or respect. When the leader is not present in such a group, purposeful activity tends to drop off or stop. In the group work proceeds at only a fair pace.

Not all autocratic leadership is negative, nor are all followers displeased with it. In some situations, such as the military, it is the preferred type. Some autocratic leaders have great empathy and are "loved" by their followers. They are fair, treat all equally, and work toward ends that are in the group's interests. The key is that the decisions are the leaders', not the groups'.

Democratic

The democratic leadership style is often called "shared" or "participant" leadership. Words naturally associated with the democratic leadership style include equalitarian, facilitative, group-centered, worker-centered, permissive, low-pressure, general supervision, gentle (as opposed to tough). We think of McGregor's "Theory Y," and of Blake and Mouton's style leaning toward a 7,7 to a 9,9 style of management.

Fundamental to American democracy is belief in the dignity of each person. In the light of this belief, democratic leaders treat each person as having dignity and inherent personal worth. They ask opinions of their groups, set goals with them, help each person feel a part of the team as they facilitate their groups' movement toward the goals they have jointly selected. They listen carefully to ideas expressed by group members, try to model the optimum kind of behavior among members of their groups, and hope the groups will copy that model. Their style is designed to help each person *feel* accomplishment, personal worth, and belongingness to the group effort. They have no power beyond that given them by the group, for power remains with the group.

In the democratic group, research has shown that the members of the group have a fairly high level of satisfaction, friendliness, and openness with each other and with the leader. Freedom of action and originality prevail, conflict is minimal but when present is expressed and dealt with openly and directly. An important result is that hostility, tension, and resentfulness are reduced.[32] A sense of interdependence tends to develop among group members, group energy is high, spontaneity and levity are a part of the work effort, work or production is accomplished progressively and smoothly, and continues even when the leader is absent since leadership is shared and the decisions and power of action reside in the group, not in the leader.

Laissez-Faire

In this style of leadership (if indeed it can be called "leadership") some of these words might be applied: no supervision, pressureless, totally permissive, goalless, and disorganized. Neither the X or Y Theory directly applies here, but Blake and Mouton would say this leadership style tends toward *1,1* on the grid.

In the laissez-faire led group, there is a fair amount of haphazard activity, especially in the group's early stages. There can be as much aggression and frustration as under the autocratic style, but there is less sense of accomplishment, less group unity, and less clarity of cognitive structure. Group members are more disorganized and less satisfied than in either the autocratic or democratic groups. Work or production progresses slowly and randomly. This is often because group members spend considerable time on procedural disagreements or arguments among group members on a purely personal basis.[33]

Continued studies through years have shown that the laissez-faire style of leadership is the least desirable of the three, in terms of both production results and participant satisfaction. Neither democratic nor autocratic leadership can be declared better for production results alone; production can be high in either kind of group, depending on many variables. Individual member satisfaction is generally higher under the democratic style of leadership in school or work groups. The satisfaction tends to be highest in smaller, interaction-oriented groups. In larger, task-oriented groups, members often tend to be more satisfied with the autocratic leadership style.[34]

At times people have not clearly understood or differentiated in theoretical or abstract fashion between the democratic and the laissez-faire style of leadership. The two are *not* to be confused. The descriptive words used for each should show some specific differences. The best way to differentiate between the two is to watch groups led by these styles, or better still, work for or be a member of a group led by each style of leadership described in this section. "Experience is the best teacher" is a truism that most definitely applies here. Democratic groups are very structured and highly responsible; laissez-faire ones are rather anarchic and irresponsible. They generally deteriorate or evolve into either an autocratic or democratic group.

CHOOSING A LEADERSHIP STYLE

So much of the potential success of a staff, class, work group, or team of any kind depends on the leadership style chosen by the leader. When one begins with a new group, such as a class at the start of a semester or an agency where a new director assumes office, leadership style can make significant difference in the future relationship between professor or director (leader) and students or staff (followers). It is also important when a new director or supervisor moves into a job or into an agency. "Getting off on the right foot" or "getting a good start" are phrases that apply.

It is logical to ask, should the leader function in autocratic or in democratic style, or something in between? In their classic study, Tannenbaum and Schmidt[35] offer an acceptable answer to this question. In it they develop an authority continuum with seven designated points between "Boss Centered Leadership" and "Subordinate Centered Leadership." (See Fig. 2–3.)

In the earlier alternatives the emphasis is on the manager—on how he or she sees things, what she's interested in and her feelings about things. The latter options emphasize more the interests, views, and feelings of the subordinates. One senses at once a move from a Theory X toward a Theory Y philosophy of leadership as one moves down the list of alternatives.

After considering the possible types of leadership in a situation, one

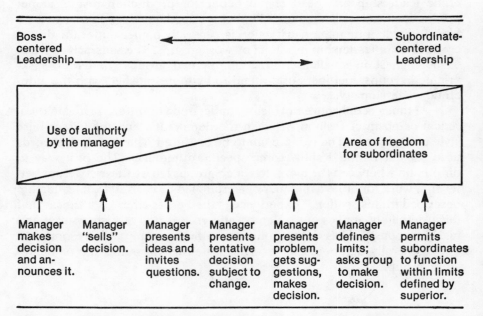

FIG. 2–3. The Tannenbaum-Schmidt Continuum of Leadership Behavior (Reprinted by permission of the *Harvard Business Review*. Exhibit from "How to choose a leadership pattern" by Robert Tannenbaum and Warren H. Schmidt [March–April 1958]. Copyright © 1958 by the President and Fellows of Harvard College; all rights reserved.)

can examine what is desirable and practical. What factors or forces should a manager or leader consider as he or she moves to select an option from among the types of leadership?

Tannenbaum and Schmidt have suggested three broad areas. First, what forces operate personally within the leader? That is, what are his leadership inclinations, his value system, his confidence in his staff of subordinates, and his own sense of security in an uncertain situation? As the leader becomes aware of these personal variables he brings to each situation, he can increasingly understand what needs motivate him to act in certain ways. Thus, he can make himself more effective.

Again, the manager will want to consider forces that affect subordinates' behavior. Each one is, as is the leader, influenced by a number of highly personal variables. Expectations of how the boss should act towards them is another force in staff members. Generally, more freedom can be given subordinate staff in decision making if they have relatively high needs for independence, have a readiness to assume responsibility, have a tolerance for ambiguity, are interested in the goals of the organization and understand the problem in relation to these goals, and expect to share in the decision making process.

In the third place, the effective leader should be aware of forces that operate in the situation. Some of these are the type of organization, the pressure of time, the effectiveness of the group, and the problem itself. The effective leader will be aware of her personal goals for herself, for her employees, and for her organization. Coupled with these, and with her awareness of the forces operating in the situation, in her subordinates, and in herself, she will be better able to choose the style of leadership she will adopt in a given situation. Effective leaders are flexible and maintain a high degree of success in choosing the correct behavior and style for each situation.

In another significant article about choice of style for leadership, Warren G. Bennis has suggested a style he calls "The Agricultural Model." He describes leadership as "an active method for producing conditions where people and ideas and resources can be seeded, activated, and integrated to optimum effectiveness and growth." [36] He describes this kind of leadership as a process. Words like open, developmental, shared ideas and goals, good communication, dynamic, participative, and adaptive come to mind for effective leadership style.

To choose the style most likely to prove successful in a given situation, the leader should have several skills. Included are (1) knowledge of complex human systems; (2) practical theories of intervening in guiding these systems with the leadership style noted by Bennis; (3) "interpersonal competence, particularly the sensitivity to understand the effects of one's own behavior on others and how one's own personality shapes his particular leadership style and value system"; and (4) awareness of one's own values and skills so as to choose when to support and to encourage one's own staff and when to confront them, or if necessary, to enter conflict with them.[37]

Desirable Leadership Skills

Although no one person can encompass all the desirable skills of a leader, there is value in developing as many of them as possible. Among those most desirable are the skills of listening and observing. The recreation professional should be skilled at taking the emotional pulse of a group and reading the emotional tone so that he or she accurately computes the verbal and nonverbal cues sent by the group and its individual members. Recreation professionals should have a high degree of respect for, and expectancy of, each member. Believing in the worth, value, and uniqueness of each member, they expect that the person's potential growth will be affected and his or her assigned responsibilities will be carried out well.

Again, they believe in trust, openness, and honesty among members of their staff or team. They know how their behavior can increase these qualities and conduct themselves to accomplish this increase. They believe in making more leaders and work to enable the leadership capacity of each one in the group to be recognized and developed. They become democratic leaders, and as such take their lead from someone or something greater than themselves. While they may or may not be religious in the sense of being actively identified with a church, they nevertheless have a "spiritual nature," recognizing the worth of others. When this is part of their nature, it is communicated both visually and nonvisually, and the atmosphere of the group shows it.

Democratic leaders must support and believe in their groups and each member. It is sometimes necessary for leaders, as administrators, to maintain some social or personal distance between themselves and their groups. However, in recreation this aloofness can end in limited or broken relationships that reduce or prohibit the effective progress and worth of the recreation program. Therefore, leaders should be able to develop healthy and productive relationships with each individual member of the group. They should be able to enjoy each group for its uniqueness. For example, when working with children, leaders should be able to delight in their games and natural spirit, speak and understand their language, share with them, and be an ideal for them.

The more successful leaders use a positive approach. They must be able to recognize and satisfy the personal interests and needs of each group member. Their approach to leadership should be democratic and positive, appealing to and respecting each individual member's own sense of personal worth, reinforcing and stabilizing confidence, and working toward the independence of self-direction, initiative, and self-actualization.

EXERCISES AND STUDY SUGGESTIONS

Here are a couple of exercises that can start you thinking about leadership, its origin, and effect.

I. *Air Crash**

Objective: To analyze the leadership process and provide a basis for discussing our preconceptions of leadership.

Time Needed: 45 minutes

Setting: Divide the group into subgroups of six discussants and one observer.

Process: Have the group discuss the following problem and offer its solutions; after the discussion, have the observer report on the group's process and the roles played by various group members. Everyone then discusses the exercise and his or her reactions to it.

Situation: A chartered foreign commercial airline has been forced to make an emergency landing in a wilderness mountain area in Northern California. It is in the dead of winter. Fortunately, only the co-pilot was injured when the plane landed. Because of a power shortage immediately before the plane crash-landed, the plane was not sure of its location and was unable to send a distress signal. It is assumed it is within 100 miles of civilization and has only enough food and water to last for three days. There are a limited number of blankets on board, but all artificial means of creating heat are ineffective since the power failure negated the crew's ability to use any of the electrical equipment on board. It is ten degrees Fahrenheit with a chill factor of -35 degrees Fahrenheit. Among the passengers are the following:

Mr. Smith, a prominent sports figure and playboy.

* From Johnson/Johnson, *Joining Together: Group Theory and Group Skills*, © 1975, pp. 34–35. Adapted by permission of Prentice-Hall, Inc., Englewood Cliffs, New Jersey.

Ms. Jones, a stewardess with 15 years of airline experience who spent her childhood in this region of California.

The pilot, a Japanese with no command of the English language. None of the passengers can speak Japanese. The co-pilot can speak both Japanese and English but suffered a concussion when the plane crashed and currently is in a state of amnesia.

Mr. Williams, a self-made businessman who owns several companies.

Mrs. Williams, Mr. Williams' wife, an elected public figure—an alderperson in their home community.

Mr. Thomas, a labor union organizer who has been successful in organizing airline ground crew personnel as unionists.

Father John, a priest.

The immediate emergency is over; the weather is calm; the problem is one of rescue. Which one of these seven people will emerge as leader and how would he/she achieve that position? Why?

II. *Leadership Style**

Objective: To determine one's leadership style—that is, which managerial philosophy to which one subscribes.

Time Needed: 30–45 minutes

Setting: Classroom—each person will be asked to respond to ten questions.

Process: Have each person respond to the following questions; then score their responses and discuss results. After each person has had a chance to review his or her score, ask the group to discuss the merits of each style: McGregor's Theory X and McGregor's Theory Y.

Leadership Attitude Survey—place a check mark in the columns that best describe your feelings.

* From Johnson/Johnson, *Joining Together: Group Theory and Group Skills,* © 1975, pp. 43–44. Adapted by permission of Prentice-Hall, Inc., Englewood Cliffs, New Jersey.

Statement: If I were a leader, I would:

	Make a great effort to avoid this	Tend to avoid doing this	Tend to do this	Make a great effort to do this
1. Closely supervise my group members in order to get better work from them.	____	____	____	____
2. Encourage my group members to set their own goals, objectives, and performance standards.	____	____	____	____
3. Set up controls to make sure that my group members are getting the job done.	____	____	____	____
4. Help each group member accept responsibility for his own personal effectiveness, thereby taking the first step in realizing his potential as a person.	____	____	____	____
5. Make sure that the group members' work is planned out for them.	____	____	____	____
6. Allow group members to make important decisions.	____	____	____	____
7. Set the goals and objectives for my group members and sell them on the merits of my plans.	____	____	____	____
8. Delegate authority to group members on all matters directly affecting their work.	____	____	____	____
9. Push my group members to meet schedules if necessary.	____	____	____	____

	Make a great effort to avoid this	Tend to avoid doing this	Tend to do this	Make a great effort to do this
10. Judge group members' performances on the basis of their success in meeting the goals they have set for themselves.	____	____	____	____

Now score your test to determine your style. Statements 1, 3, 5, 7, and 9 all reflect Theory X. Give yourself 4 points for the most positive (make a great effort to do this), 3 points for second most positive (tend to do this), etc. A perfect Theory X person is 20. Statements 2, 4, 6, 8, and 10 all reflect Theory Y. Give yourself 4 points for the most positive (make a great effort to do this) and so on with 1 point for "make a great effort to avoid this." A perfect Theory Y score is 20. Subtract your Y score from your X score to see which direction you tend (suppose you had 10 on X and 15 on Y, your tendency would be to be a Y person). Discuss your findings.

Theory X holds that people dislike work and will avoid it if they can; therefore they must be controlled, directed or threatened to get them to work.

Theory Y holds that people need to express themselves and that work should allow the worker to feel at least partially in control or a part of the decision making process; therefore, they need to be given a sense of responsibility and authority, not driven to work.

Topics for Discussion

When discussing the following topics have one or more group members serve as observers (using one of the observational guides—see Exercises, Chapter One). After each discussion have them report to the group what they saw—the process by which the group functioned and the leadership pattern which evolved. Have group members discuss their observations.

Topic: Of what consequence is theory—how would a professional recreator act if he/she subscribed to Machiavelli's or Nietzsche's theory?

Topic: Which leadership traits are the most important, the ones which must be present in all leaders? (Justify your view.)

Topic: Who are the power figures in your community? organization? group? How did they achieve that position, and how do you know they have power?

Topic: What would happen in each of the following if the leader did not appear? Democratic Group; Laissez-faire; Autocratic.

Topic: Are Americans becoming more "other directed"? What are the implications of this trend for today's leaders?

Topic: Identify specific situations in which you would use each of the following styles: Tell, Sell, Test, Consult, Join.

When discussing these topics, have the group divide into different sized groups to see what effects size plays on leadership patterns. In some instances, have several small groups (three- or four-person groups) discuss the same topic. Then come together as a larger group to share observations and comments. Have the group discuss the effects of group size and topic on their discussion.

Here are a couple of abstracts that might be of interest. They involve *Power* and *Feedback;* they are abstracted from some materials originally developed by the National Training Laboratory Institute for Applied Behavioral Science.

POWER AND ITS USES IN THE COMMUNITY

Ways of Looking at Power:

1. *Authority*—the legitimate right to influence the behavior of others inherent in a position.

2. *Influence*—the actual or potential capacity to affect the behavior of others through control of allocation and use of resources, rewards, and punishment; may be constructive or coercive.

   Influentials may be of two types: (1) the top influentials are persons from whom particular members are drawn into various systems of power relations according to the issue at stake. Second-line managers, etc. (2) *key* influentials are the leaders among the top influentials, i.e., those who appear in relation to several issues—or decisions.

3. *Capacity to Influence Decision Making* is viewed as the essence of power in the community—as contrasted with social prominence, reputation, or position, which may be "decision facilitating" influences, or help legitimize decisions.

POWER must be viewed as a function of *the person* and as a function of a *social system.*

POWER must be channeled through organization or part of a sub-system. Power is expressed in concrete acts: to work on committees or not; to accept leadership or not; to support or oppose propositions or not; to contribute or withhold funds.

POWER is exercised continuously in the community to maintain arrangements, to prevent the rise of issues, to resist change. It is sharply focused when the established relationships are challenged, when position or allocation of resources must be defined.

One definition: "Power is the chance of a man or a number of men to realize their own will in a communal action against the restraint of others participating in the action." [38]

Types of Power:

Reward—ability to reward
Coercive—ability to punish, coerce
Expertness—knowledge, skill, etc.
Referent—people refer to—defer to
Legitimate—right to influence—authority

The Structure of Power:

1. As a *single* pyramid system
   DECISION MAKERS
   DECISION FACILITATORS
   (Help to legitimize decisions)

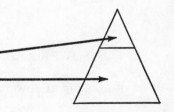

2. As a *multi*-pyramid system
   Separate pyramids in a multi-pyramid system tend to be content or issue-oriented. Sociometric analysis may show a decision maker in more than one of the pyramids, and a "facilitator," too—but not sufficiently concentrated as to form a single pyramid.

Decision facilitators may contribute to the decision by supplying data, by creating "climate" and conditions for decision making, and by helping to legitimize the decision. This distinction between the roles of decision makers and facilitators in many respects is similar to the division of labor between boards and policy making committees in voluntary organizations and the staffs of the organization. Staffs tend to be decision facilitators, and directors and committee members tend to be decision makers. Also, within staffs a role distinction places some closer to the decision making process (boards, etc.), while the others remain almost exclusively in a decision facilitating role.

Analysis of Power:

Some of the methods by which power can be examined are:

- Panels of knowledgeable people to help identify
- Organizational membership lists
- Interviews with those thought to have influence—whom they work with and their ideas about persons with power
- Analysis of specific community decisions on issues to see who made them or influenced them
- Organizational decisions to see who was involved
- Observation
- Sociometric analysis of contracts and interactions
- Study of pyramids of power and their relations with one another.

Access to Power Structure—Decision Makers:

Persons who appear in the power structure may be classified in such terms as these:

1. *Public Sector*—formal authorities elected or appointed to offices in government. Tend to be the upwardly mobile from ethnic, lower socioeconomic groups, and long-time residents.
2. *Private Sector*—the technical or managerial specialists, such as engineers, physicians, attorneys, and the top managers of middle-sized firms, or *just below the top* managers in large firms. Tend to be highly mobile and short-term residents.
3. *Public and Private Sectors*—the top managers of the largest firms and old-line aristocrats.

Some Generalizations About Power and Its Use:

1. The exercise of power is a necessary function in organizations and communities.
2. Power (and leadership) functions within the limitations of the organization or community.
3. Power is a relatively constant factor, and policies and programs are influenced by the exercise of power.
4. Shifts in power among organizations and groups within the community affect the total community.

5. The power of an individual must be channeled through some group or organization to be of maximal effectiveness. If it is so channeled an individual may have more power than he thinks he has. It is always difficult for him to know how much power he has.
   a. The community is a small unit of organized power relationships in which individuals can operate.
   b. The democratic pattern offers the maximum assurance of the individual having a voice in policy and program development and implementation.

FEEDBACK AND THE HELPING RELATIONSHIP

I. General Observations
   1. Different names are used to designate the helping process such as counseling, teaching, guiding, training, educating, etc.
   2. They have in common that the helping person is trying to influence (and therefore change) the individual who is being helped.
   3. The expectation is furthermore that the direction of the change in the receivers of help will be constructive and useful to them (i.e., clarify their perceptions of the problem, bolster their self-confidence, modify their behavior or develop new skills, etc.).

II. The Helping Situation
   1. The helping situation is dynamic, i.e., characterized by an interaction that is both verbal and nonverbal.
   2. The helping person has needs (biological and psychological), feelings, and a set of values.
   3. The receiver of help has needs (biological and psychological), feelings, and a set of values.
   4. Both the helper and the receiver of help are trying to satisfy needs in the situation.
   5. The helper has perceptions of her/himself, of the receiver of help, of the problem, and of the entire situation (expectancies, roles, standards, etc.).
   6. The receiver of help has perceptions of her/himself, of the helper, of the problems, and of the entire situation (expectancies, roles, standards, etc.).
   7. The interaction takes place in relation to some need or problem which may be external to the two individuals, interwoven with the relationship of the two individuals, or rooted in the relationship between the two individuals.

Wherever the beginning point and the focus of emphasis is, the relationship between the two individuals becomes an important element in the helping situation as soon as interaction begins.

Needs		Perception	Perception		Needs
Values	Helper	⟶ Problem	⟵	Receiver	Values
Feelings					Feelings

8. The receiver's needs, values, and feelings, and his perception of them as well as his perception of the situation (including the problem and the helper) cause the receiver of help to have certain objectives in the interaction which takes place.

9. The helper's needs, values, and feelings, and his perception of them as well as his perception of the situation (including the problem and the receiver of help) cause the helper to have certain objectives in the interaction that takes place.

10. Both helper and receiver of help have power, i.e. influence, in relation to the helping situation. Except for surface conformity or breaking off the interaction, however, it is the receiver of help who controls the questions of whether in the final analysis change takes place.

III. It is not easy to give help to other individuals in such a way that they will be strengthened in doing a better job of handling their situation. Nor is it easy to receive help from another person, that is, the kind of help that makes us more adequate in dealing with our problems. If we really listen and reflect upon the situations in which we adopt either the helper or helping role, we not only are impressed with the magnitude and range of the problems involved in the helping situation, but also realize that we can keep on learning as a helping person or a person receiving help as long as we live.

IV. Let us reflect on some of the things about ourselves that make it difficult to receive help.

1. It is hard to really admit our difficulties even to ourselves. It may be harder to admit them to someone else. There are concerns sometimes whether we can really trust the other person, particularly if it is in a work or other situation that might affect our standing. We may also be afraid of what the other person thinks of us.

2. We may have struggled so hard to make ourselves independent that the thought of depending on another individual seems to violate something within us. Or all our lives we may have looked for someone to depend on, and we try to repeat this pattern in our relationship with the helping person.

3. We may be looking for sympathy and support rather than for help in seeing our difficulty more clearly. We ourselves may have to change as well as others in the situation. When the helper tries to point out some of the ways we are contributing to the problem, we may stop listening. Solving a problem may mean uncovering some of the sides of ourselves that we have avoided or wished to avoid thinking about.

4. We may feel our problem is so unique no one could ever understand it, certainly not an outsider.

V. Let us reflect upon some of the things that make it difficult for us to give help.

1. Most of us like to give advice. Doing so suggests to us that we are competent and important. We easily get caught in a telling role without testing whether our advice is appropriate to the abilities, the fears, or the powers of the person we are trying to help.

2. If the person we are trying to help becomes defensive, we might try to argue or pressure him—meet resistance with more pressure and increase resistance. This is typical in argument.

3. We may confuse the relationship by only responding to one aspect of what we see in the other's problems by over-praising, avoiding recognition that the person being counseled must see his own role and his own limitations as well.

VI. To be fruitful the helping situation needs these characteristics:

1. Mutual trust.

2. Recognition that the helping situation is a joint exploration.

3. Listening, with the helper listening more than the individual receiving help.

4. Behavior by the helper that is calculated to make it easier for the individual receiving help to talk.

VII. "Feedback" is a way of helping others to consider changing their behavior. It is communication to a person (or a group) that gives that person information about how he or she affects others. As in a guided missile system, feedback helps an individual keep his behavior "on target" and thus better achieve his goals.

Some criteria for useful feedback:

1. It is descriptive rather than evaluative. By describing one's own reaction, it leaves the individual free to use it or not to use it as he or she sees fit. By avoiding evaluative language, it reduces the need for the individual to react defensively.

2. It is specific rather than general. To be told that one is "dominating" will probably not be as useful as to be told that "just now when we were deciding the issue, you did not listen to what others said, and I felt forced to accept your argument or face attack from you."

3. It takes into account the needs of both the receiver and giver of feedback. Feedback can be destructive when it serves only our own needs and fails to consider the needs of the person on the receiving end.

4. It is directed toward behavior that the receiver can do something about. Frustration is only increased when a person is reminded of some shortcoming over which he or she has no control.

5. It is solicited rather than imposed. Feedback is most useful when the receiver has formulated the kind of question that the observers can answer.

6. It is well-timed. In general, feedback is most useful at the earliest opportunity after the given behavior (depending, of course, on the person's readiness to hear it, support available from others, etc.).

7. It is checked to ensure clear communication. One way of doing this is to have the receiver try to rephrase the feedback he or she has received to see if it corresponds to what the sender had in mind.

8. When feedback is given in a training group, both giver and receiver have opportunity to check with others in the group the accuracy of the feedback. Is this one person's impression or an impression shared by others?

Feedback, then, is a way of giving help; it is a corrective mechanism for individuals who want to learn how well their behavior matches behavior intentions; and it is a means for establishing one's identity—for answering "Who am I?"

ENDNOTES

1. Hannah Arendt, *The Human Condition* (Chicago: University of Chicago Press, 1958), pp. 188 ff.

2. Ralph M. Stogdill, *Handbook of Leadership, A Survey of Theory and Research* (New York: The Free Press, 1974).

3. Eugene E. Jennings, *An Anatomy of Leadership: Princes, Heroes, and Supermen* (New York: Harpers Brothers, 1960), Chapters 1–6, 11. Used by permission.

4. Niccolo Machiavelli, *The Prince and the Discourses* (New York: Modern Library, 1950, p. xxxvii), cited in Jennings, p. 42.

5. Thomas Carlyle, *On Heros and Hero Worship and the Heroic in History.* 1901, cited in Jennings, pp. 71 ff.

6. Edwin A. Burtt, *The English Philosophers from Bacon to Mill* (New York: Modern Library, 1939), p. 99.

7. Ralph W. Emerson, *Representative Man.* Cited in Jennings, p. 85.

8. William James, *The Will to Believe and Other Essays in Popular Philosophy* (New York: Dover Press, 1956), p. 218.

9. Sidney Hook, *The Hero in History* (Boston: Beacon Press, 1943), p. 151 ff.

10. Cited in Jennings, *Anatomy of Leadership,* p. 91.

11. *Ibid.,* p. 128.

12. See Alfred Adler, *Individual Psychology* (New York: Harcourt, Brace, 1932). Cited in Jennings, p. 134.

13. Otto Rank, *Will Therapy and Truth and Reality* (New York: Alfred A. Knopf, 1940). Cited in Jennings, p. 136.

14. Erich Fromm, *The Sane Society* (New York: Rinehart, 1955). Cited in Jennings, p. 139.

15. David Reisman, *The Lonely Crowd* (New York: Doubleday Anchor, 1952), cited by Jennings, *Anatomy of Leadership,* p. 123.

16. Jennings, *Anatomy of Leadership,* pp. 140–146.

17. Ordway Tead, *The Art of Leadership* (New York: McGraw-Hill & Co., 1935), pp. 83–257.

18. Emory S. Bogardus, *Leaders and Leadership* (New York: Appleton-Century Co., 1934), 325 pp.

19. Stogdill, *Handbook of Leadership,* pp. 62–65.

20. *Ibid.,* pp. 72–82.

21. Emory S. Bogardus, *Essentials of Social Psychology* (Los Angeles: University of Southern California Press, 1918).

22. Clarence Marsh Case, "Leadership and Conjuncture," *Sociology and Social Research* 17 (1933): 510–513.

23. Frederick Herzberg, *Work and the Nature of Man* (New York: Thomas Y. Crowell Company, 1966), pp. 92 ff. Used by permission of Harper & Row, Publishers, Inc.

24. Douglas McGregor, *The Human Side of Enterprise* (New York: McGraw-Hill, 1960); Douglas McGregor, *Leadership and Motivation: The Essays of Douglas McGregor* (Cambridge, Mass.: MIT Press, 1966); Douglas McGregor, *The Professional Manager,* edited by Caroline McGregor and Warren G. Bennis (New York: McGraw-Hill, 1967).

25. Examples of these authors' works are: Chris Argyris, *Personality and Organization* (New York: Harper & Row, 1957); Warren Bennis, *Changing Organization* (New York: McGraw-Hill, 1966); and Abraham Maslow, *Motivation and Personality,* 2nd ed. (New York: Harper & Row, 1970).

26. Robert R. Blake and Jane S. Mouton, *The New Managerial Grid* (Houston: Gulf Publishing Company, 1978).
27. Ernest G. and Nancy G. Bormann, *Effective Small Group Communications*, 3d ed. (Minneapolis: Burgess, 1980).
28. Max Weber, *The Theory of Social and Economic Organization*, trans. A. M. Henderson and Talcott Parsons (Boston: Oxford University Press, 1947).
29. Eric Hoffer, *The True Believer* (New York: Harper, 1951).
30. Tead, *The Art of Leadership*, pp. 25–28.
31. Kurt Lewin and Ronald Lippitt, "An Experimental Approach to the Study of Autocracy and Democracy: a Preliminary Note." *Sociometry* (1938): 292–300, and in Stogdill, pp. 365–385.
32. Stogdill, *Handbook of Leadership*, p. 364.
33. *Ibid.*, p. 366.
34. *Ibid.*, pp. 365–370.
35. Robert Tannenbaum and Warren G. Schmidt, "How to Choose a Leadership Pattern," *Harvard Business Review* 36, no. 2 (March-April 1958): 95–101.
36. Warren G. Bennis, "Post-Bureaucratic Leadership," *Trans-Action* (July-August, 1969): 44–51, 61.
37. *Ibid.*
38. Hans Gerth and C. Wright Mills, trans., *From Max Webber: Essays in Sociology* (New York: Oxford University Press, 1946), p. 190.

SUGGESTED READINGS

Blake, Robert, and Mouton, Jane Srygley. *Building a Dynamic Corporation Through Grid Organization Development*. Reading, Mass.: Addison-Wesley, 1969.

Cartwright, David, and Zander, Alvin. *Group Dynamics: Research and Theory*. New York: Harper & Row, 1968.

McGregor, Douglas. *The Professional Manager*. New York: McGraw-Hill, 1967.

Ross, Murray G., and Hendry, Charles E. *New Understandings of Leadership*. New York: Association Press, 1957.

Chapter Three

THE NATURE AND FUNCTION OF GROUPS

The amount of material on groups is enormous. It is one of the major concerns of sociology, a discipline established in the nineteenth century to facilitate the study of the human being as a social animal. We are born in groups, live in groups, and are buried by groups. People's existence is a social existence. It behooves students of recreation and parks to have a working knowledge of the nature and structure of group behavior.

Fundamentally, groups are collections of individuals, bound by time and space, interacting and supporting each other. Families, communities, and nations are forms of groups. They establish patterns of behavior, techniques of control, and means by which individuals can obtain satisfaction while contributing to the continuation of their social structures—society and its institutions.

All groups have certain characteristics, including a definable membership, some sense of purpose or awareness, a pattern of interaction, and a common or agreed-upon goal or goals and system of order. But social groups are more than this. Missing in this general definition, which is very appropriate for describing communities and nations, is the element of recognition. That is, social groups are characterized by people recognizing others as members of their group and interacting accordingly. Sociologists take this into account. When they refer to small groups or group dynamics, they are normally describing social groups.[1] They reserve terms such as *community, neighborhood,* and *audience* to describe other group formations. Our primary concern is for social groups.

Recreation and park specialists are constantly dealing with groups since, for a great many of us, most of our leisure is spent in a group setting. Social behavior and conditioning are affected by the group experience; therefore, the approach to the provision of recreation services through agencies and organizations is group-oriented.

Of course, not all recreation groups are social groups. Remember, the essential difference between a group of individuals and a social group is the interaction and recognition of the members of the group. For example, a boat show may attract thousands of people from a community. Many of those attending the show attend with others, but, as a collection of persons, they are not a social group. They are at the coliseum looking at the boat show with little concern for the behavior of others or awareness of the larger audience. Their primary focus is on their own social group and the boats and motors they are there to see. On the other hand, the West Side Club's picnic outing is a social group function. Those in attendance are aware of the West Side Club's membership. They can call each other by name, and much of the satisfactions they derive from the outing stem from their social interaction, not just the food, environment, or activity, even though these elements are important to the total experience. In the first illustration there are few shared goals, only individual goals, few boundaries for interaction, and a minimal consciousness for the group as a group. In the second, the lines of interaction are strong, the group is aware of itself as a group and its functions as a single body, a collective unity.

Several indicators show when a group has become a social group. One is the calling of members by their first (given) names. This is the ultimate act of identification, the specifying of species. Other signs are (1) the degree of cohesiveness the individuals exhibit when working together, (2) their sense of shared purpose and goals, and (3) their need and acceptance of others, so critical to their own satisfactions and accomplishments.

Recreation specialists can add to the quality of recreation experiences for people by capitalizing on these natural qualities of group membership. This can be done through mottos and slogans, monograms and logos, credos and songs. Anything that reinforces the group's consciousness of itself and gives members a sense of identity and pride adds to the recreation experience. Athletic programs have long recognized this and have used it to its fullest. Many athletic contests would be boring were it not for the cheerleaders, pep bands, half-time shows, and impromptu posters and signs.

These same techniques of group reinforcement and identity can be used in any group situation. Of course, the basic values of individual group members may determine how these methods are used, but they are available in one form or another for the recreator's use. They also apply to the development of morale and team spirit among the professional staff of a recreation agency or the furthering of the identity of the recreation profession through our various professional associations and societies.

LEVELS OF GROUP FUNCTIONING

All social groups share a similar history or pattern of behavior regardless of their reason for being. They progress through various stages of action and share common elements of structure. Because each stage and element has its own characteristic and purpose and all are important to the health of the group, students of group dynamics need to be aware of them. Essentially the stages or levels of functioning are stroking, organizing, producing, and creating.

Stroking. When people get together, the first thing they do in a group situation is *stroke.*[2] Stroking is nothing more than exchanging social amenities. It may take the form of kidding, shaking hands, smiling, or doing anything that sends the message: "I recognize you and it's good to see you again. I'm okay; you're okay." The more familiar members are with each other, the more time they devote to stroking. New groups often seem cold and indifferent because members have not developed enough commitment to each other to stroke. The stroking period is formal and minimal. Well-established groups need lots of stroking time. It is important to allow for it.

Organizing. Every group has some form of organization or structure. Its rules of behavior may be conscious or unconscious, but its members are aware of them. Since leadership is a shared responsibility, certain members of the group may spend more time working on the group's organizational activities than other members. They are concerned with procedures and structures. They understand that organization is basic to production. When the group's need for stroking is filled, someone gets it moving with organizational statements like "Okay, let's get down to business." Groups may be formally organized with by-laws and officers who carry out its procedures, or they may function on some loosely structured, informal process. In either case, groups must organize in order to act.

Producing. Producing is doing. It is what happens when a group moves toward fulfilling its objectives. When the panel members are debating a point, they are producing. When the team scores points, it is producing. When a staff makes decisions, it is producing. Production takes many forms, and it is both the process of achieving as well as the achievement itself. For groups to continue, they must have a sense of movement, and that is producing.

Creating. Some groups are creative. They have little difficulty in moving toward this level of performance, an extension of producing. When groups are creative, they are usually unaware of time and space. They are caught up in the experience and are totally involved in it. To some degree, the statement "Where did the time go? It seems like we only got started, then suddenly it was time to leave" best characterizes the creative experience. For some, achieving creativity is the highest form of the recreative experience. Of course, some groups never achieve this level of production, yet they remain as groups. Creativity is not a prerequisite for group maintenance, but it goes a long way in keeping a group vital and fulfilled.

Although we have described these levels of functioning as a series of steps, they need not always be ascended in order. They are dynamic, and groups move from one level to another, back and forth, just as a child playing on steps may skip from one to the other and back again. Frequently groups, especially in their producing stage, become very tense. Conflicts may develop; when they do, they may be handled by dropping back to a level of stroking (joking) or organizing. Someone may make a kidding remark, the group laughs, and then it's ready to go back to work. The working stage (producing) is again introduced by someone who makes an organizational statement or action that gives it direction.

Some groups get locked into one level and have diffculty moving to the next. When this occurs, the recreator needs to assess why the group is meeting and why it has become static—spending all of its time on stroking or organizing. For example, if a teenage club is having difficulty maintaining interest in its club meetings—its members would rather spend time joking and kidding with each other (stroking) than doing the meeting task assigned it—then the meaning of the meeting should be questioned. Are the tasks relevant? Has proper organizational structure been developed to move the group from its stroking to task (producing) levels? Maybe there are differences between the goals of the club officers and recreation specialist (club advisor) and those of the members. The members may feel left out of the decision making process and consequently use the club meeting time as time for "fooling around." By carefully analyzing where the group is and what it is doing, proper action can be taken to make it dynamic again. Skill in recognizing this and acting to help the group produce are what recreation and park professionals must develop to be effective leaders.

The shifts from one level of functioning to another are similar to the shifts that occur when driving an automobile with automatic transmission. When the car slows down or extra power is needed, the transmission automatically moves to a lower gear. When extra power is no longer needed, it shifts to another level. The same is true for groups. Stroking is the first gear; it is as necessary for movement as is organization. When a group gets bogged down with its task (producing), it automatically shifts; if not, then the group is under strain and the results may be damaging. The key is for the recreator to recognize which level the group is in and the importance of all for the total group experience.

GROUP PROPERTIES

A second universal set of characteristics of the group are its properties. Regardless of the group's structure, complexity, or purpose, all groups possess these properties. They have their purpose, their procedures, their patterns of communication, their organizational structure, their cohesiveness, their patterns of interaction, their tone or social atmosphere, their degree of internal commitment, and their history.

Purpose

For a group to exist there must be a purpose that meets the needs of its members, or the group will cease to function as a group. Some groups formally state their goals or purpose, such as the recreation department goal "to provide recreation opportunities for the citizens of a community." Others, like the family, have implied goals, such as the continuation of the species, the educating of the young, and/or the protecting of the group from others or from natural disasters. Group goals may be verbalized or unspoken (simply understood), but in all instances they are necessary to the group's functioning. In the recreation setting, it has been observed that when group members understand the group's purpose and clearly state the group's goals, they tend to have a better tone and a high probability of reaching their objectives.

Tone or Social Atmosphere

Groups give out "vibes" just as do individuals. When group members are in harmony, the tone or social atmosphere is one of warmth, freedom, and conviviality. It is best illustrated in the following manner: When you walk into a room where people are enjoying themselves and are at ease, you *feel* the climate. On the other hand, when groups are tense, threatened, or anticipating conflict, the social atmosphere is quite different. They tend to be hostile, formal, and restrained. Like taking one's temperature, an observer can read the tone of the group by sensing its atmosphere. The more positive the atmosphere, the more productive the group.

Cohesion

To a great extent social tone of the group is directly related to the commitment individual members make to each other and to the group. If there is a sense of team work, of commitment and a "we feeling," then the atmosphere is going to be positive, even when the group is experiencing conflict. Cliques, factions, and egocentric individuals erode the group's spirit and negatively affect its ability to pull together. When they are present, there is little group cohesion. One of the best indicators of group cohesiveness is the members' reference to themselves as a group, such as "our gang," "my team," "our staff."

Organizational Structure

Every group has both a formal and informal organizational structure. There are acknowledged leaders or positions of responsibility, and tasks are delegated to those who hold these positions. These are formal leaders in the formal structure. Some organizations are quite complex with various levels of responsibility, while others are simplistic. For example, the formal structure of the recreation department may take a pyramidal form with the director at the top and the activities leaders at the base. Between these two may be several levels of authority and a variety of subgroups (departments) with varying structures. On the other hand, the formal structure may be as obvious as the baseball manager and his players. The informal structure reflects the interaction between leaders and followers. In it group members know to whom to go to get certain jobs done regardless of their position or formal duties. In some groups the two, formal and informal, are one and the same. The group's power structure and communication patterns are intertwined with the organizational structure. (See Fig. 3–1.)

Patterns of Communication

To facilitate group functioning, a communications network of "sending and receiving" messages is established. It takes many forms, such as a specialized vocabulary or jargon, body language and facial expressions, particularly among key group members, and the establishment of network focal points. We learn to whom to listen, whom to ignore, which messages are important, and which ones are "window dressings." Problems develop when communicational links break down and we act on what *we think* is being said rather than what is *being* said. Successful groups develop good feedback mechanisms and a well-defined network of information exchange. This is discussed more fully in the chapter on group problems (Chapter Seven).

Patterns of Interaction

Closely related to communications is the group's pattern of interaction. In time there develops an expected pattern of communications and responses—a particular sequence of who speaks, after whom, to whom, and when. For example, when *A* speaks, *B* and *C* respond, but when *C* speaks, no one responds. Patterns of interaction vary according to many factors, such as the seniority and status (position) of the speaker (research shows that leaders tend to speak to the group as a unit, whereas followers tend to speak to specific individuals), the length of time the group has been together, and its tone. Patterns of interaction can be charted; these charts can help in determining the key communication linkage and decision

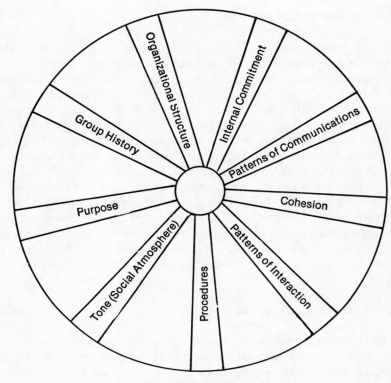

Each spoke supports the whole

FIG. 3–1.   Group Properties

makers. This technique is discussed more fully in the chapter on evaluation. Sociometric patterns, such as those found in Chapter Ten, and interaction patterns are closely related.

Procedures

Every group develops its way of getting things done. The range is
from a highly structured obedience to Robert's Rules of Order with a set
agenda and order of business to an informal pattern of dealing with issues
as they develop according to the feelings of the group. What is essential is
the members' recognition that some procedure for getting things done is
necessary and that groups do modify their procedures as they develop
their structures, interaction patterns, and history.

As groups develop procedures, standards are established. How things
are done becomes as important as what is done. Certain subjects and actions may be taboo while others are encouraged. In many ways procedures

and standards are the ground rules by which the group game is played. Irritation, frustration, and inaction occur when these rules are not understood or are disregarded by members "who should know better." The choice of procedure is directly related to the group's history, the issues involved, the nature of the group and its meeting, and the styles of its leadership.

Internal Commitment

It is axiomatic that the more involved the members of a group are in determining their goals and direction, the more committed they are to carrying them out. Since the degrees of personal investment may vary from goal to goal, the degree of commitment members have to the group varies according to the issues involved. Fluctuations in commitment occur both within the group as a unit and within individual members. It is difficult to get excited about very long-range goals. Those which demand immediate action tend to get our attention and commitment. That is why it is important for groups to have a set of intermediate tasks that sustain interest while the group moves toward the accomplishment of its long-range objectives. A favorable social climate and communications pattern can strengthen the commitment of members to the group in general, even when their commitment to a specific program is not great.

Group History

Groups are comprised of individuals with a history of group experience. Each group also has a history of its experience as a group. These two facts play critical roles in determining the success of any group endeavor. When the recreation administrator meets with his or her advisory board for the first time, it may not be the first time the advisory board has met with a recreation director. The history of their past experiences sets for them their expectations—they want the director to act a certain way and expect a procedure much like that followed in the past. Similarly, the recreation director comes to the meeting with a personal bias, based upon previous experiences with recreation commissions and advisory boards. The success of the relationship between the two parties may hinge critically upon their ability to overcome their past history and develop a history unique to their relationship.

The more frequently a group meets, the better acquainted the members become with each other, expecting certain roles and functions to be performed. Members take on certain behaviors and patterns of interaction, not all of which are positive. In some instances, groups come to expect arguing and bickering over points; it is a part of their past. Consequently, they may misuse their opportunities and time without recognizing what is happening. They have become accustomed to "poor" performance.

It is healthy for a group periodically to pause and reflect upon its past and its present behavior to see if it is consistent with its ideals, particularly as its past relates to its present performance.

THE SIGNIFICANCE OF GROUPS

Groups tell us who we are, what we can do, and how we are to behave. We are members of many groups simultaneously. In each we have a function, derive some strength or support, and perform some acts. Some groups are more critical to our emotional and physiological development than others; some are short-lived; some are a part of us throughout our lives. In their attempt to describe the role played by groups, sociologists have divided them into two major categories, primary and secondary.

Primary groups are essential to the development of our personality, our value system, and our patterns of response. The family is the basic primary group. From it and its members we learn to react in specific, predictable patterns to various situations and stimuli. Our response to family members is both intellectual and emotional. Subconsciously, we model much of our behavior after our parents, the way they perform their roles and responsibilities. Primary groups are long-lasting in their effect and are characterized by an emotional interdependency, one for another.

Secondary groups are more numerous than the primary ones. Membership in them may be temporary or long-term; responses to other members of the group tend to be more intellectual than emotional. Secondary groups provide us with opportunities for achievement and recognition and become avenues for meeting many of our basic social needs. They usually form around some task or social function, such as work or worship. Whereas the primary group experiences shape our personality and emotional character, secondary groups polish our behavior and socialize us. Most organized recreation experiences occur in a secondary group setting.

Groups both condition and stimulate our behaviors. In them, we learn what to do and what is expected of us; in other words, we assume certain roles and perceptions. In each group we have status, and our perception of that status dictates our performance. Of course, the way we act is conditioned by previous group experiences that we tend to use as references. We continually monitor and modify our behavior depending on the way those we respect respond to our performance; they become our "critical others." Take for example the child who enjoys "clowning." In school, with his classmates, he is expected, or thinks he is expected, to be the class clown. When he is with those same people in other situations, he may continue to perform that role, feeling it is expected of him. Yet, when placed in a group of strangers, such as those at a summer camp, he may reject the "clown role" for a more serious one. However, if some of his "critical others" friends come into his new group, he may immediately revert to his clown behavior, rejecting his new status and role expectations.

The way we carry out our role varies according to our experiences and feedback. For example, the recent college graduate goes to work for a recreation department and although her position may be "down the line," in terms of the organizational structure, she assumes that it requires her to act differently than in the way she acted in her student days (student role). She may change her wardrobe, hair style, and social group affiliations. She wants to act like a professional. If she discovers, however, that the other full-time recreation employees do not have her concept of the professional (image and action), she may reject her ideas as idealistic and adopt their pattern. She does this to be accepted, to become one of the group.

Status is simply the position one holds in a group. Certain positions carry higher status. For example, being a supervisor is more prestigious than being a playground leader. Status usually reflects the number of persons holding a similar position; the more people in a given position, the lower the status of position. Frequently, status is related to the skills required to carry out a certain role. If a position requires unusual skills, and if the position is critical to the function of the organization, those in that position have a high status. Every group and everyone in every group has status. Training and responsibility, as well as public recognition of the importance of a given skill, are essential to the status.

With status comes role. Role is the performing of one's position; it is the acting out of one's status. Each of us has our perception of the way we are to perform, and that is why there is such diversity in action. Being able to recognize the key positions in a group is essential to students of group dynamics. Also, understanding the role expectations and role performance of each position is critical. For example, what is the status of recreation therapy in a psychiatric hospital, what role do other mental health personnel (doctors, nurses, occupational therapists) expect of recreation, of the recreation therapist? The answers to these and similar questions about status can determine, to a great degree, the success of the recreator in that situation. It certainly determines the role he is *allowed* to play. Prior experiences, one's value system, membership in a particular social class, and training shape role expectation and role performance.

ESSENTIAL GROUP ROLES

Although certain roles, such as director, captain, or quarterback, are identified with specific groups, Benne and Sheats feel that general roles are present in every group. These roles are classified according to their function: group building and maintenance roles, and/or group task roles.[3] The former are necessary for a group to maintain itself as a group by meeting individual and personal needs, while the latter are essential to the group's achievement of its goals. Among the major *group building* or *maintenance functions* are:

- *Tone setting*—encouraging members to participate, praising performance, being fair in response to others, and encouraging and accepting others' opinions.
- *Harmonizing*—mediating and conciliating differences of viewpoint, smoothing troubled waters, and working toward a group feeling of "we-ness."
- *Gatekeeping*—making sure that all members have their chance to participate, asking for feedback and the opinion of others, and suggesting a time limit to make sure everyone has his or her chance to be heard. (See Fig. 3–2.)

FIG. 3–2.   Gatekeeping

- *Standard setting*—making sure that all members adhere to the agreed-upon roles of conduct and ethical standards, and preventing "cheap shots" and special interest pleading.
- *Tension reducing*—encouraging stroking and other forms of expression that relieve tension and drain off negative feelings, and accentuating positive rather than negative points of view.

Among the *task* functions are:

- *Opinion Seeking and Opinion Giving*—asking for or stating one's view about something the group is considering.
- *Information Seeking and Giving*—asking for or providing relevant facts or critical information pertinent to the group's task.
- *Clarifying and Elaborating*—asking for and building upon previous comments by restating what has been said, and enlarging upon it so that the issues become clearer and better understood.
- *Coordinating*—putting together the ideas and suggestions of various members so that a unified view can be established, and demonstrating the relationship of various ideas in such a manner that unity is encouraged or achieved. (See Fig. 3–3.)
- *Testing*—checking with the group to see if it is ready to take some action or make a decision.
- *Initiating*—asking for new ideas or ways of acting, being the first to introduce a concept or begin a discussion which has relevance to the goals achieved, and proposing new actions or activity.
- *Summarizing*—restating the highlights of the discussion, identifying the points developed by the group, and verbalizing the consensus reached or decision made by the group.

Although different individuals play different roles at different times in the group process, most become comfortable with certain roles and tend to play them more often than others. Consequently, groups tend to look to certain members for certain activity. They expect John to initiate the discussion, Mary to gate keep, and Fred to summarize.

All of the above-mentioned roles are essential to good group performance, but if they are performed inappropriately, they may interfere with the group's operation. There is also a danger of stereotyping people in certain roles, thereby negating their potential contribution in other roles. Who expects the clown to initiate or give pertinent facts? Although leaders may play several of these roles, it is not necessary for them to play all of them. However, it is necessary for them to make sure someone plays each of them for all are important to the group's health and success. Likewise, it is critical that the leader avoids or helps the group avoid the emergence of negative roles.

FIG. 3–3.   Coordinating

Negative Roles

Occasionally groups fail to achieve their desired objectives because of the negative roles some individuals play. They are called by some "individual roles." People join groups for many reasons. Among them is the personal satisfaction derived from being a part of the group activity. When the motivation of the individual is selfish—that is, when it contributes not to the functioning of the group but only to the satisfaction of one's personal needs—it may destroy the group's morale or prevent the group from accomplishing its task. Among the more frequently identified self-oriented roles or negative roles are:

- *Aggressive Behavior*—acting in a way that lowers the status of other members by criticizing or blaming them, attacking the motives of others, and generally being hostile towards the group and its activity.

- *Blocking*—preventing the group from making decisions by irrelevant digressions, going off on a tangent, arguing a point too long, rejecting the ideas of others without proper consideration, and keeping the group in a holding pattern rather than seeking to make a decision. (See Fig. 3–4.)

- *Dominating*—having to have a say on every item, pulling rank, seeking the final word, calling for a decision before everyone has had a chance to speak, and running roughshod over people and decisions.

- *Special Interest Pleading*—introducing and supporting personal ideas and projects, seeking to win support by making the group feel guilty about not acting on behalf of a "pet" project, and seeking special favors and considerations.

- *Withdrawing*—remaining silent, becoming indifferent and passive, engaging in side conversations, and doodling or exhibiting other forms of apathetic and disinterested behavior.

- *Clowning*—disrupting the group through various joking and attention-getting mechanisms, or calling attention to oneself as the "entertainer."

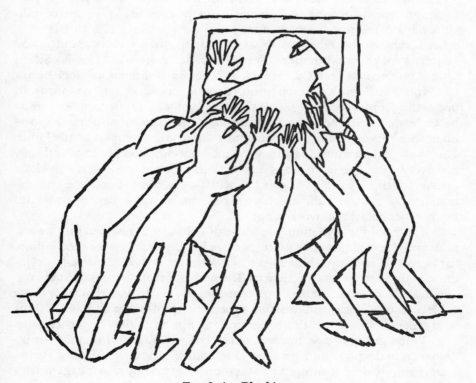

FIG. 3–4. Blocking

To some extent, these negative behaviors are a natural extension of group maintenance and task function roles. For example, opinion giving can become special pleading or recognition seeking; relieving tension may evolve into clowning. When these behaviors occur, they may irritate other group members, possibly causing them to assume negative roles. Negative roles are destructive and must be dealt with in a positive manner. Since participation in the recreation setting is voluntary, nothing will turn participants off more quickly than the negative acting of group members. Many a teenage club or senior citizens group has been disrupted or even destroyed by the special pleading, dominating, or blocking behaviors of some of its members.

SOCIAL NEEDS

Groups exist because of a human need for affiliation. People want to be with others. According to developmental psychologists, the ability to relate, to understand, and to cope with others is the highest state of social development. It would be rather difficult for us to gain a sense of worth and achievement if it were not for the presence of others to give us feedback and to acclaim our performance. Even the most avid pursuers of individualized recreation, such as hiking and backpacking, like to talk with other hikers and backpackers about their discoveries, understandings, and concerns for the environment. Were it not so, there would be no Sierra Club, Appalachian Trail Conference or other environmental associations.

Individuals seek different group experiences for different reasons. In one setting it may be recognition through competition; in another, it may be to belong and live vicariously through the exploits of others. Sports boosters clubs and athletic associations are prime examples of the latter. They have chapter meetings, their members wear school colors, and they live every game the team plays as if they themselves were on the field. Of course, for those participating in the activity, the competition and recognition for their effort suffices, though recognition value carries over into many other social and work groups.

The need for affiliation, the sense of belonging; the need for new experience, the testing of one's interpersonal skills; the need for recognition, the sense of accomplishment—all of these are provided directly or indirectly through group experiences. The recreation professional should understand this and maximize the potential of the group experience for these achievements. This is true whether it be in the professional's relationships with other staff or in creating programs and opportunities for participants.

When groups cease to meet our needs, we abandon them. Poor attendance and apathetic members are "telltale" signs of a failing group. People simply do not support those groups that do not provide them with satisfaction; they choose to seek other settings, other groups, and environments that do meet their needs.

RECREATION GROUPS

Successful recreation leaders are able to provide positive group experiences for the participant. They create situations in which people can interact with those of a similar interest, value system, and level of performance. They are constantly reminded that recreation groups exist because of the satisfactions their participants derive and experience, and that all participation is voluntary, entered into freely by the players. Since there is such a multitude of different groups, recreators cannot rely on any one style of leadership or group organizational structure to develop and maintain them. They must adapt to the group and help it establish its own patterns of interaction and functioning. The only constant with which they work is the group process: the dynamics at work, the interaction of followers, leaders, and the environment as people seek satisfaction through activity. Among those groups one encounters most frequently in a recreation setting are the recreation staff, including volunteers; the recreation advisory board; recreation clubs; recreation teams and classes; leisure education and leisure counseling groups; neighborhood recreation associations; and professional recreation societies. Briefly, here is a description of each of these in terms of purpose, membership, stability, organizational structure, and most commonly practiced leadership style.

Staff

The recreation staff is a social group. Its members interact in order to provide opportunities for the recreation expression of the citizens. It is a formal group with many subgroups, and, like all formal groups, it has a variety of informal structures and patterns of communication. It is relatively stable with its members deriving satisfaction from their work, their interaction with participants, and with other staff members. The director is the acknowledged head and should provide the basic leadership. Two settings in which the principles of group dynamics are highly apparent are (1) staff meetings and (2) supervisory conferences. Providing opportunities for staff members to contribute to the planning and decision making of the department or program unit is critical.

Volunteers

Although not a formal group, volunteer workers require treatment as a unit. Developing a system of rewards and recognition for their participation is fundamental. With the professional staff, rewards come in the form of money and recognition; with volunteers, money is not a factor. Consequently, public and peer approval and recognition are fundamental. Involving the volunteers in program decisions and establishing some procedure for recognizing their contribution are basic leadership tasks.

Recreation Boards

Whether advisory or policy making, recreation boards have a similar function. They exist to give direction to the activities of the recreation department by providing a platform for community thinking (input) and evaluation (review). These bodies are composed of volunteers who serve for a specified period of time. The membership is fairly stable, but the interaction between members is periodic rather than continuous, as is the case with the recreation staff. Because recreation boards are relatively small (seven to thirteen members), the principles of small groups can be easily applied. Their meetings are generally formal in structure, with the board chairperson providing the leadership. The recreation professional is generally involved in the leadership process but more in a consultant or expert role than in a headship capacity. Avoidance of negative group roles is critical to the success of recreation policy in advisory boards. Since members come from diverse backgrounds and often represent specific vested interests, the tendency for special pleading must be guarded against. Helping board members understand their function as a board increases the potential of positive group interactions and the board's usefulness in achieving the objectives of the recreation department.

Recreation Clubs, Teams, and Classes

These groups constitute much of the recreation service. They exist because of the interest of the participants and require a variety of leadership styles since they are created for different reasons and attract a wide range of members. Clubs usually form around some commonalities, such as the age of the participant or interest in a specific activity. They remain vital as long as the members derive pleasure from their associations. This is especially true with such general interest groups as senior citizens and teenagers. Activity classes and recreation teams may require a more autocratic leadership style than do general interest clubs. The participants come because of their desire to learn a particular skill or take part in a sport or contest. The activity, rather than social relationships, attracts them. Consequently these groups tend to have a more stable membership than do recreation clubs. All three types normally have a well-defined organizational structure and formal leadership pattern with designated heads: instructors, team captains, club officers, etc.

Leisure Education and Leisure Counseling Groups

Leisure education and leisure counseling groups are ideal for the application of group dynamic techniques. By using them the facilitator is able to draw upon the views, information, and values of all involved rather than imposing personal ones on the group. Value clarification and understanding are enhanced; learning and attitudinal changes and insight are promoted. In these environments, the participants become both the teacher and the learner; the group becomes the medium of growth.

Neighborhood Recreation Associations

In some communities recreation services have encouraged neighborhood recreation associations. Generally, these associations are composed of area residents operating on some membership plan. The association functions as a semi-autonomous body, programming for its members with the aid of professional staff. The association is often an organizational structure to accommodate many subgroups with specific interests. To coordinate the activities of these many elements, a well-defined organizational structure evolves with identifiable leaders and heads. Both formal and informal communication patterns are discernible and a power structure develops. Recreation professionals working with this type of association often find themselves assuming the same role as the professional recreator working with a larger community. A diversified leadership style is necessary since various subgroups require different approaches and have differing expectations of the service. To facilitate a sense of belonging, recreation associations often create their own special events, celebrations, and slogans. Although there is turnover in the membership, the formal group remains rather stable.

These are but a few illustrations of the types of groups with which recreation specialists must deal. Common to all are the process of group functioning, the presence and need for certain roles to be performed, and the interaction between leadership and followership. All are products of the human desire to share experiences with others. All are molded by the members' value system. It is important that recreation professionals understand both their own value system and those of the groups with whom they work, or else there may be little communication and cooperation. A community recreation agency, by definition, works with all the public, and that public is composed of many different groups and subgroups with various value systems.

ORGANIZATIONAL THEORY

The application of group dynamics to the everyday functioning of an organization similar to a recreation department is well documented. Leadership development programs and sensitivity training evolved primarily because business organizations wanted to improve communications among their employees, strengthen employee commitment to the organization, and enhance the workers' morale. Robert Townsend, in *Up the Organization*,[4] was actually advocating the use of group dynamics and group work concepts when he suggested that organizations be humanized; that is, he recommended involving those affected by decisions in the decision making process and minimizing or eliminating bureaucratic controls. He did not, however, advocate disregarding good organizational practice. A particular set of theories and understandings have given rise to organizations; it is advantageous that the recreation practitioner understand those concepts.

We create organizations to accomplish those tasks that individuals cannot do alone. Organizations are extensions of individual efforts. To maximize these efforts, certain practices and behaviors develop; they have become the art and science of management. We have learned a great deal about the value of lines of authority, chain of command, and standard operational procedure.

Like most good things, abuses and excesses occur within organizational structure and have a negative effect on their functioning. When an organization relies too heavily on a set procedure—a single way of doing something—and discourages open communications between various levels of the organization, an insensitive bureaucracy develops. Workers cease to have a sense of accomplishment and participation; they do their task, sometimes halfheartedly, and go their way. Work becomes drudgery. Even recreation workers might find their jobs becoming irksome. This need not be the case, however. It is possible in the recreation setting to blend good organizational theory and practice with good practices of group principles.

Group principles are most appropriate in the planning and decision making phases of organization life.[5] Since planning and decision making occur at all levels of the organization, all employees should have an opportunity to participate. On the other hand, it is essential that when decisions are made, the principles and practices of good organizational structure are implemented. Some of the more essential ones are: (1) each employee has a well-defined description of his or her role and responsibility; (2) each employee is responsible to one specific supervisor who, in turn, knows those employees for whom he or she is responsible; (3) authority is equal to the responsibilities assigned to the employee; and (4) those given the authority and responsibility for carrying out the tasks are held responsible for carrying them out.

When people understand their roles, they feel more secure about their responsibilities and positions with the group. A good organizational structure facilitates that understanding. Groups may be involved in decision making but individuals carry out responsibility. Organizations are nothing more than a series of positions that have specific responsibilities assigned to them. It is important that those assigned the responsibility of expediting the assigned tasks do what is expected of them and also that those responsible for seeing that these tasks are done monitor the performance of their workers.

The two systems—group dynamics and organizational management— are interrelated and quite compatible. The former is critical to the decision making process and the satisfactions that come from being involved in that. Workers need to feel they have significant input in the decisions that affect their roles and satisfactions. The latter, organizational practices, are necessary to ensure the expediting of responsibilities, the accomplishment of tasks, and the accountability of performance. To illustrate, the recreation specialist may involve the participants in determining what game they want to play. This is the application of group dynamics. But once the group has decided on the games and enters into the contest, the principles of organization take over. Baseball becomes chaotic unless it is played by the rules that all players understand and agree on.

In this chapter we have described the characteristics of social groups, made a case for their importance, and demonstrated how the application of group dynamic principles relates to them in the recreation setting. Also, we have described some of the roles individual members play in groups and the importance of these roles in the functioning of the group, in maintaining its quality as a group, and in carrying out its agreed-upon plan of action.

EXERCISES AND STUDY SUGGESTIONS

To help get your group into the mood and to build group spirit and identity, the following activities are suggested.

1. Create your own group (class) logo, motto, and "in-group" name. This might be done by dividing the class into work (task) groups of three to five members. Each group would work on all three elements since the group's motto and name may appear in its logo. Each group can then present its materials to the entire class. The class may wish to choose one of the subgroup's (task group's) materials to be its own, or it may choose to take elements from all and create a logo, motto, and name of its own. From then on and throughout the life of the group, use this name, logo, etc., to reenforce group identity and purpose.

2. Have individual class members conduct a survey to see how many and what types of groups in the local or their home communities have logos, mottos, initiation ceremonies, and the like. Have the group discuss its findings and its opinion on the value and significance of these identification modes to the life and tone (social climate) of the group.

Here are a couple of ideas (assignments) that can produce a lot of information about group/individual functioning and test your skills of observation.

1. Attend a public group meeting, preferably one of a recreation or policy making group (recreation advisory committee or town council). Chart the action and interaction of the group members and note how various group properties (tone, organizational structure, procedures, history, etc.) influenced or affected its performance. The following questions may aid you as you determine the influence each of the factors had on the group:

GROUP OBSERVATIONAL GUIDE*

I. Group Characteristics
   A. *Background*
      1. Premeeting observations and reconnaissance
      2. Physical setting
         a. Is the seating conducive to accomplishing the group purposes and goals?
         b. Will room conditions help accomplish these?
   B. *Participation*
      1. Does the discussion seem to bring out what the various members might be able to contribute?
      2. Does overparticipation by some keep others from participating?
      3. How much of the talking is done by the leader? by various members?
      4. To whom are questions or remarks usually addressed?
      5. How appropriate are contributions in relation to the topic?
   C. *Communication*
      1. How clear are the members in expressing their ideas?
      2. How clear is the leader in expressing his or her ideas?
      3. How well does everyone understand what is going on?
      4. What factors, if any, contribute to misunderstanding?
   D. *Cohesion and groupings*
      1. How well does the group work as a team?
      2. What subgroups exist and how do they work together?

* Adapted with special permission from *Human Relations Training News*, Volume 4, Number 1, pp. 7–8, 1960, NTL Institute for Applied Behavioral Science.

3. How willing are members to accept and act on group goals?

E. *Atmosphere*

1. How free do members feel to express themselves?

2. How willing are members to share personal feelings?

3. How would you rate the group on: friendliness? informality?

F. *Group standards*

1. Has the group developed a code of ethics for its own operation (sense of responsibility; appropriate response to needs of group; self-discipline)?

2. How does the individual's beliefs regarding groups affect group process?

II. Group Process

A. *Setting of goal(s)*

1. How does the group choose its goals (group consensus, leader dominated, or strong member dominated)?

2. What kinds of goals does it choose?

a. Content goals

b. Skill goals

c. Immediate goals

d. Long-term goals

3. How clear are the goals to the group?

4. Level of aspiration—How realistic (achievable) are the goals to members? to the observer?

B. *Steps toward goal*

1. How does the group plan steps in achieving goals? How well-defined are these steps?

2. Is the whole group moving in the same direction toward the goals?

3. How clearly does the group recognize its position in relation to goals?

4. How efficiently does the group move toward its goals?

5. Does the group recognize how different goals are related?

C. *Procedures for group progress*

1. How are the group procedures related to the type and achievement of goal(s)?

2. How informal or formal are the procedures?

3. How flexible are the procedures?

4. What kinds of procedures does the group use (e.g., note taking, subcommittees, evaluation, role playing, etc.)?

5. How clear is the group in using its procedures?

6. How well does the group handle its routine?

7. How able is the group to make decisions?

D. *Feedback and group self-evaluation*

1. Does initiative for feedback and evaluation come from group, leader, or observer?

2. How is the feedback accepted by the group?

3. Is the feedback simply tolerated or is it used constructively?

4. Are the sources of resistance to feedback due to: timing? content? method of presentation?

III. Behavior of designated leader

A. *Social sensitivity and characteristics*

1. Does the group understand him/her and does he/she understand the group? (This has reference to communications problems.)

2. How sensitive is the leader to the wishes and feelings of the group?

3. How adaptable and flexible is the leader in responding to group needs?

4. How sensitive is the leader to individual needs? How responsive is the leader to these needs?

5. How does the leader reconcile conflicting individual and group needs?

B. *Leadership skills and techniques*

1. Does he or she "sell" the group into accepting essentially autocratic decisions and procedures?

2. How well does he or she set the stage for decision making?

3. Does the leader state problems clearly?

4. How does the leader cope with people when they assume roles that hinder efficient group functioning?

5. How does he or she help the group to provide the necessary functional roles?

6. Does the leader function as group evaluator or stimulate evaluation?

7. Does the group seduce the leader into accepting some decisions against his or her better judgment?

2. Select a group of six to nine people who meet periodically and do an analysis of the role(s) each member of the group tends to play. If several of your class attend the same group meeting, have a group discussion about what you saw. Compare analyses to see if you are all working with the same definition and perceptions of roles. The charting device in Fig. 3–5 may help you with this assignment.

In addition to the discussion topics already mentioned, consider these:

1. What role does laughter play in a group? Or, how is laughter used personally? in a group?
2. What roles and group properties do you see emerging in this class or group? When did you first become aware of them? Why?
3. Of what value are advisory groups to recreation agencies? What are their limitations and negative effects (if any)?

Here is an exercise that has good group building potential. Try it.

*Left Out**

Objective: To allow participants to experience being consciously excluded and included in a group.

Time Needed: 1 to ½ hours

Setting: A room large enough for groups to work together without disturbing each other.

Process: Divide the group into subgroups of five or six members; each group is seated on the floor with some distance being between groups. Each subgroup is asked to develop some criteria that they will use to exclude some group members. This should take no longer than 15 minutes. When the group has decided which member to exclude, the excluded member is sent to a predetermined place in the room. There he/she meets with the members excluded from the other subgroups.

All those not excluded are told to take a 10- to 15-minute break but not to talk to the excluded group members. They remain apart. When they reassemble after the break, they continue to exclude the excluded members.

* Johnson/Johnson, *Joining Together: Group Theory and Group Skills,* © 1975, pp. 185–186. Adapted by permission of Prentice-Hall, Inc., Englewood Cliffs, New Jersey.

	Members' Names						
Roles							
Task Roles							
Initiator							
Coordinator							
Clarifier							
Tester							
Information Seeker							
Information Giver							
Opinion Seeker							
Opinion Giver							
Summarizer							
Maintenance Roles							
Harmonizer							
Gatekeeper							
Standard Setter							
Tone Setter							
Stroker							
Negative Roles							
Blocker							
Dominator							
Special interest seeker							
Withdrawer							
Clown (Playboy)							
Aggressor							

FIG. 3–5. Role Observation Chart (Instructions: for each member, place a check mark in the column corresponding to the role played. Check each time the role is assumed. The total number of times each person plays a role gives you a picture of that person's role(s) preferences.)

The excluded group is then asked to locate in the center of the room and the non-excluded groups are asked to form clusters around them. Once this is done, each member of the excluded group is asked to tell why he or she was excluded, whether the exclusion was justified, how he or she feels about it, about that group, and the new group of other excluded members.

After each excluded member has spoken, each original group is asked to select a spokesperson who will then share with all what they used as criteria for exclusion and why that excluded member had been left out. When all spokespersons have talked, the original groups are reassembled (including excluded members) and are asked to react to the content of the various phrases used by both their spokesperson and excluded member.

Finally, all form a large group to discuss what has transpired, what they learned about rejection, how "stigmatized" individuals form their own group for support, how important social identity (being accepted) is, and how one feels when the social tone is negative or "cold."

To develop insight into organizational structures and functioning, have each student select a small organization (ten to thirty employees) to study. Interview the various members of that organization and ask each to whom they report and for whom they are responsible. On the basis of this information, develop an organizational chart; then check with the chief administrator to see if it is a valid representation of the organization's actual structure. Discuss any discrepancies that might exist between the two views and the reasons for these differences.

ENDNOTES

1. George A. Lundberg, C. C. Schrag, and O. N. Larsen, *Sociology* (New York: Harper & Row, 1963), pp. 66–76. Ely Chinoy, *Society* (New York: Random House, 1961), pp. 81–87. H. Lawrence Ross, *Perspectives on the Social Order* (New York: McGraw-Hill Co., 1963), pp. 204–206.

2. Eric Berne, *The Structure and Dynamics of Organizations and Groups* (New York: Ballantine Books, 1963), pp. 215, 327.

3. Kenneth D. Benne and Paul Sheats, "Functional Roles of Group Members," *Journal of Social Issues*, vol 4, no. 2, 1948, pp. 41–49: excerpts.

4. Robert Townsend, *Up the Organization* (New York: Alfred A. Knopf, Inc., 1970).

5. Daniel Katz and Robert Kahn, *The Social Psychology of Organizations* (New York: John Wiley and Sons, Inc., 1966), pp. 336–389.

SUGGESTED READINGS

Gibbard, Graham S.; Hartmann, John J.; and Mann, Richard O., eds. *Analysis of Groups.* San Francisco: Jossey-Bass Publishers, 1974.

Shaw, Marvin E. *Group Dynamics: The Psychology of Small Group Behavior.* New York: McGraw-Hill Co., 1976.

Shepherd, Clovis R. *Small Groups.* Palo Alto, Calif.: Chandler Publishing Co., 1964.

Zander, Alvin. *Motives and Goals in Groups.* New York: Academic Press, 1971.

Chapter Four

FORCES AFFECTING THE FUNCTIONING OF GROUPS

An amazing experience for human beings is to become aware—*really aware*—of the communication that goes on between themselves and others. A large number of forces are constantly at work when two or three or more persons interact. Few people realize that these forces are in effect; even fewer perceive that the forces can be used for the good of all persons involved. In this chapter you will be introduced to a variety of the forces that are at work when people get together and that affect their functioning as a group. As you become increasingly aware of these forces, through reading and by observing and participating in groups, it can seem like putting on glasses to see better, or cleaning away successive layers of dirty film on a window pane. You may be amazed at the things you "see" that you had not "seen" before.

In this chapter we will examine several kinds of forces that can have impact on a group. We will identify these forces, examine them, and cluster them in natural groupings. We will try to understand each force or group of forces so that you can become increasingly aware of each in the groups of which you are a member. Try to "see" them as you read about them. The more you relate these ideas or concepts to groups in which you naturally participate, the more you will come to recognize these forces. As a student or as a professional in a recreation or a park position, you will be able to use them more effectively.

How can you use knowledge and awareness of these forces? Another way to phrase this question is to ask, Of what value is the study of group dynamics? One value is a kind of forced introspection. People become more aware of themselves as they study and become aware of the forces operating in a group of persons. Long ago through Socrates, Plato said

"Know thyself." A step, perhaps many steps, in self-understanding can result from the study of group dynamics. Better awareness of "what makes me tick" allows a person to be more effective in interpersonal relationships—one-to-one and one-to-group.

The above leads to a second value of studying group dynamics. By studying and understanding these dynamics, one becomes more aware of, and better able to react to, the behavior of other persons. You can in many cases anticipate the response of others. This ability can give you a great edge to plan your behavior advantageously if you can anticipate, with some certainty, the response of others to a particular behavior pattern. This knowledge can be put to constructive use by a park or recreation professional. Of course, in focusing on these forces, we presuppose the professional is a person of good will, acting out of the highest values of the profession for the good of the people he or she serves.

A third value (as suggested by Elton T. Reeves) in understanding group dynamics is that one develops a greater capacity for more effective interpersonal relationships.[1] When you know yourself and have some ability to predict how others will react to your behavior, then your interpersonal style should become smoother and more efficient. Communication is more complete; messages are sent, received, and more often understood.

A BRIEF HISTORY OF GROUP DYNAMICS

People have been interested for some time in what happens when people get together in groups. Individuals seem to act differently when with other people than when alone. Certain groupings of people will bring about different reactions from a person than other groupings. Some of the history of how writers have examined groups of people is helpful to the student of group dynamics. Malcolm Knowles presents a good summary of that history, some of which is adapted in the following two paragraphs.*

Early students of groups, such as Spencer and Comte in the nineteenth century, focused on mobs, crowds, and mass publics. Phenomena such as hysteria, fads, and fashions were examined. Emile Durkheim became interested in the process of interaction. Around the turn of the century he theorized that individual ideas can be altered by the process of "psycho-social synthesis" that goes on in groups, resulting in a group dynamic that cannot be rationally explained in terms of the mental processes of individuals. Hare, Borgatta, and Bales indicate that much of the early experimental research of groups in the early twentieth century dealt with the element of "social control"—an area still subject to regular research.[2]

* From *Introduction to Group Dynamics* by Malcolm S. Knowles and Hulda F. Knowles, Copyright 1972. Used by permission of Follett Publishing Company, a division of Follett Corporation.

Early in the 1920s, Eduard Lindeman suggested that functional groups be studied by a more empirical method. The result was the first large scale research on the processes of groups. "The Inquiry," reported in Lindeman's *Social Education*, described conferences and small deliberative committees, and the processes they followed when working on large scale social problems.[3] Following John Dewey's analysis of the act of experimental thought, students of groups, using the discussion method, developed a concept of group process as problem solving. They went so far as to suggest descriptions of effective group procedure based on the problem solving concept. Others put considerable effort into the examination of leadership and its sources and styles (as described earlier in Chapter Two).

The Field Theory approach to the study of groups, the theory most closely associated with group dynamics, was begun by Kurt Lewin. He came to the United States in 1932 to lecture at Stanford, and the Nazi coup made impossible his return to Berlin. In 1935 Lewin began work with a group of dedicated graduate students on a series of classic studies on group behavior at the University of Iowa in their Child Welfare Research Station. Later his research efforts and most of his colleagues moved to Massachusetts Institute of Technology. After Lewin's death in 1947, his assistants, including Gordon Lippet, continued intensive research at the University of Michigan Research Center for Group Dynamics. The real broadening of application of the theory began to take place in the Bethel, Maine, programs, which, after 1947, became known as the National Training Laboratories (later renamed the NTL Institute of Applied Behavioral Science). These experience-based programs, which took place in the 1950s and 1960s, served as intense personal training experiences for leaders at middle and upper levels in business, industry, education, political, and social institutions. From their initial efforts, several networks of skilled trainers or group leaders have spun off training programs that are widely infused in one form or another (organization development, team building, "T" groups, communication skills training, etc.) into almost all administrative, business, and educational training centers and programs in the country.

The influence initiated by Lewin was due to three major factors. He held to the unusual—in the 1930s—phenomenological position. For him this meant that a psychologist should focus his attention on what the individual perceives subjectively, consciously *or* unconsciously, rather than what the observer saw as "objective reality" from the outside. From this position the source of psycho-sociological phenomena is within the person rather than within the environment in which the person is located. Secondly, Lewin had considerable ingenuity in research design. His study of the leadership climate found in three different styles of leadership with three different groups of children is a classic in findings as well as in design. He and his students investigated phenomena that were until then largely ignored. The laboratory became then a viable setting for important human research. Finally, Lewin developed a theoretical system that used topology to represent his findings mathematically.[4]

The application of Lewin's theory of the phenomenological field of the individual was soon applied also to groups of individuals. Thus was developed what is now called "field theory" as it is applied to group dynamics.

The five basic assumptions of field theory as developed by Lewin are simple, yet functional. They can be applied mentally (internally) and behaviorally (externally) to both the individual and the group. These assumptions are: (1) The examination or study of the phenomena you perceive as your environment. This leads to the concept of the *psychological field* or the *life space* of the individual. (2) You have a position in that life space in regions which make up the life space, and consist of your activities, group membership, etc. (3) You are oriented toward *goals* for some component regions in your life space. These goals ordinarily involve some change in the position or relation of the person from one region (activity) to another. (4) You—and each other person—behave or act (Lewin, in his Germanic style, used the verb "locomotes") in ways designed or calculated to achieve the goals you have for that object. (5) In your goal directed activity, you may encounter *barriers* that must be overcome or circumvented. When this happens, you may change your goal, or your relationship with the object in your life space, or both.

You can better understand human behavior, your own as well others', when you use these five assumptions and think in terms of goal-oriented behavior. "All behavior is purposive." In simplistic terms our goal can, in nearly all cases, be either to gain a benefit or to avoid a loss (or avoid something seen to have a potential hurt or fear).

When Lewin and his colleagues began to apply this basic psychology as social psychology—the study of individuals in groups—it was quickly seen that a group has a life space, it occupies a position relative to other components in the life space, it is oriented toward certain goals, it behaves to achieve those goals, and it may encounter barriers as it acts to reach goals. Certain other realities of groups, as opposed to individuals alone, cause the field theorist to introduce several other concepts to facilitate understanding. Among these are *norms*, or rules of behavior among group members, *roles* of group members and the duties and rights of each role; *power* and *influence*, or the control each member of the group may exercise over the group or other members of it; and *cohesion*, which refers to the belongingness, attachment, or involvement individual members exhibit for the group. Among the additional basic concepts for the field theorist are *valence* (borrowed from hard sciences such as physics or chemistry) showing the strength of goals for the objects in life space; *consensus* or agreement on roles, norms, goals, or other group life components; and *interaction* or the degree and kind of communication patterns between group members.

While the psychologist focuses on the life space of the individual, the field theorist appropriately focuses on that dynamic that holds together the group—*cohesion*. The close relationship between cohesion and such group issues as productivity, style of communication, leadership style, and control cause us to state that the *key concept* for field theory as applied to small groups is *cohesion*.

In the study or analysis of the dynamics (energy, vibrations, patterns) of groups, the field theorist puts much attention on two areas: (1) concepts associated with producing greater or lesser cohesion, such as agreement on norms, goals, membership, or roles; (2) concepts that tend to be the *result* of greater or lesser cohesion, such as satisfaction, effective interaction, and problem solving, efficient movement toward goals.

Some of the key indicators of cohesion in a group include how members value or relate to each other, how decisions are made, the trust or openness level of members during group sessions, humor or the lack of it, and whether or not disagreement or conflict can be dealt with openly and directly.

With this background, admittedly only a small portion of the considerable history of group dynamics and its development, we move now more directly to examine group dynamics.

FORCES ON THE PARTICIPANTS

A group is composed of two or more individuals, each of whom is unique and separate, a psychology unto himself. Within him and acting on him, thus affecting his behavior in the group, are personal forces that are part of his own life space or his personal milieu. Examples are personal drive, expectations, confidence and maturity, ego strength, introversion/extroversion style, passivity or aggressiveness, and openness or closedness to personal interaction with others. Additionally, social situation, family, work responsibility, and successes or failures in other groups affect him in the group. Psychological togetherness or dissonant internal conflicts, "dependency" toward authority persons, and willingness to enter into "interdependence" with others affect how he will participate in the group.

Each of these individual forces influence the person as he or she participates in the group. Thus her style of relating to other individuals and her response to their personal styles affect the dynamics of the group while the group meeting is in progress.

The individual (and also the group as we shall see later) is affected also by the stage of the group's development. Initially most groups are rather immature in their skill level. They go through a *process* of development, often cyclically and with increases in their maturity. The level in the development of the group—somewhere between immaturity and maturity—affects individuals and the way they relate to persons in the group.

External Forces

A considerable variety of forces external to the group affect the group as a whole. These external forces also affect the individual participant in ways which vary from person to person. All have some effect on the dynamics of the group as a whole.

Some examples of external dynamics would be:

- The amount of *time* formally or informally allotted for the group to meet (begin at 8:00 p.m.; close no later than 10:00 p.m.) or the length of time devoted to each item on the agenda.
- The *space* in which the group meets. Is there plenty of space to move around, or are the walls close and the members of the group crowded together?
- Is the *lighting* sufficient for people to see each other and any visuals used for the meeting?
- Are the *acoustics* such that what is spoken by each person can be heard by each other person? Do sounds carry from outside the group?
- Is there *openness* in the meeting area, or are pillars, compartments, or corners jutting into the room?
- Are the *seats* comfortable? "The mind can absorb no more than the 'sitter' can endure!"
- Is the *seating* around a *table or tables?* Advantage to lean on or write upon, but physical barrier. It is a research-based fact that furniture between persons is also a *barrier* between persons.
- Is there *isolation* of the group either in a closed room or without interruption, or do people pass through the room occasionally, or enter the room to get something or perhaps deliver some message?
- Is isolation for *extended periods of several days*, or are there interruptions of phone calls, visits from family or friends, trips home or to sightsee, etc.? (See Fig. 4–1.)
- If several *meetings are in sequence*, does the group recreate and eat together or separately? Does the order in which things occur (the sequence of events within a meeting) affect the process?
- In the *meeting room* are sufficient electric plugs available? TV screens? TV equipment and extension cords? Paper and pencils? Tape, felt tip markers, and newsprint?
- If *smoking* is planned, are there ashtrays for each smoker? Is there provision for smokers to leave the room if group consensus is opposed to smoking?
- Are *refreshments*—coffee, tea, cola, cookies, or fruit—available in the room?
- Are *restrooms* proximal or located behind doors leading from the room?

FIG. 4–1.   Group Bombarded by External Forces

- Will there be any *observers* who, though they do not participate in the meeting, can reduce trust and increase threat to openness of the group members?
- Is the *temperature* of the room consistent and comfortable to all members?
- Are the *colors* of the walls and other decor components attractive and comfortable for the group members?
- Are the *physical properties* of the room surrounding the group attractive and neat, or are they distracting?

The effect of the external forces upon the individual members and upon the group as a whole is too often unrealized or overlooked. That these external forces can have a significant impact on the internal dynamics of the group could hardly be doubted after scanning the list of possible external forces listed above.

Internal Forces

Within the group also a number of forces can exist. Some or all of those that follow can profoundly affect the dynamics of the group as a whole and the individual members who contribute to the group's dynamics.

Internal dynamics are numerous in both cause and kind in relation to a group. Some are highly visible, such as group size, dress, attendance, sex, and ages of group members, participation, skills in human relations, and agenda content for discussion or communication. We shall call these "Cluster A." Other internal dynamics are less visible and are more forces or energies. A person skilled in the process of groups can often "read" or "feel" or "sense" a number of these less visible internal dynamics and put them to good use. The more knowledgeable you are of the individual members of the group, the more your skills are compounded in effective "reading" and use of these dynamics for the good of the group.

Some of the less visible or invisible dynamics that affect the ongoing nature of the group and communications within the group would include motivation, perceived status of various group members, definition of roles, atmosphere or emotional tone, energy flow, heterogeneity or homogeneity of the group interests, and leadership style. Others are the group's cohesiveness, norms and standards, participation patterns, relation to other groups in the system of which this group is a part, and the phases of group development or maturity of the group. Still others are the identity of individuals and of the group as a whole, the power and influence of the group and group members, internal pressures to conform, group motives and aspirations, and the desire of individual members to achieve. We shall call these less visible forces "Cluster B." "Cluster C" is composed of feelings, the feelings of the individual group members toward each other and the group, and the general openness or lack of openness of the group members.

Cluster A—Visible Internal Dynamics.   Most of these "visible" internal dynamics are generally visible to the human eye. Of course, we do not actually perceive or consciously compute all that is visible to us. The result is that while much is visible, it is not seen. Remember, one of the purposes of group training is to increase one's capacity to see, understand, and make constructive use of the dynamics of groups.

Group Size.   This term refers to the number of members in a group. Size of the group may limit the quality and the amount of participation for each person as well as his or her communication with other group members. As each additional person enters a group, each member has a more complicated set of social relations on which to spend energy, and proportionally less time to give to the social relationship with each person. This is especially true when the time for the group is limited.

Each additional member in a group brings more knowledge, experience, points of view, strength and energy, skills, and "bodies" for the work of the group. For problem solving groups this can be advantageous. However, as more interesting, verbal, and attractive persons become available, thereby increasing energy in the group, shy persons can more easily find greater anonymity.

Increasing group size causes more group members to report feelings of threat, frustration, inhibition, and tension. There is a tendency to move to more formal procedures or techniques, such as parliamentary procedure. Decisions and conclusions are reached with less exploration of the feelings or ideas of each member. A person has less "air time" to share with each additional person in the group. There is less concern for whether or not persons agree with a decision or a solution. The group strives less for consensus and for unanimity. A few members will be more apt to dominate as group size increases.

As group size increases, so does leader responsibility and the difficulty of her job. A definite leader is more apt to emerge in larger than in smaller groups (say, in twelve- rather than three-member groups). The leadership role will be increasingly assumed by one to the exclusion of others, and the one leader has more data to compute, more names and facts to process, and remember, more recognition and stroking for the maintenance needs of individuals.

Members of larger groups report less satisfaction with the group, less attraction to and interpersonal relating with other members, and greater tension as group size increases. Deleterious effects of larger groups upon the members can result in more absenteeism and more negative comments about and to the group, and can reduce trust in the atmosphere or tone of the group.

Group performance varies with increasing size. Added resources (abilities, opinions, etc.) can contribute to effective group performance. On the other hand, increased problems with organization and meeting individual needs cause inhibition and reduced member participation. Thus, the effect of size on performance is the result of both positive and negative dynamics, and will depend on whether additional resources can be utilized and the kind of processes these various forces cause to take place.

Ideal size will vary with the task. Some experts say four to six members, with five being best for small task or committee work, is the ideal size for a problem solving group. Others say up to eleven or twelve members can function well as a total group if there are sufficient time, shared leadership, and maturity of group skills present.

Age, Sex, and Other Physical Characteristics.[5]   These characteristics will have some impact on the group, but not necessarily the "obvious." Age is not highly significant in interaction except with preteenagers. Preschoolers often exhibit isolated or paired interactions, while rivalry tends to develop after age six. As people become older, they interact with others with greater selectivity of contacts and in a more complex pattern of interaction. In peer groups, children are more apt to conform to the group up to age twelve and decrease conformity beyond that.

Little evidence exists that age is closely related to leadership; skills and practice of leadership can be effectively developed and used by all persons. Increasing experiences with age in a variety of social situations often facilitate group participation.

Women and men have tended, until the recent past, to behave differently in groups. The differences likely have been imposed by cultural training. Traditional sex roles for males have taught that men should be aggressive, task-oriented, domineering, and assertive. In contrast women's roles have tended to be nurturant, person-centered, passive, and submissive. The Women's Liberation Movement has contributed to increasing freedom for both sexes from these stereotyped role structures, at least among the persons involved in that movement and those with higher educational levels. Little careful research has been done to identify the consequences of sex differences for group interaction. Some evidence suggests that in regard to eye contact as non-verbal interaction, more females engage in visual interaction than do males.

When participating in mixed groups, more females have tended to conform to the norms of the group than have males. College men have tended to be task-oriented, conforming more to get the task accomplished, while college women have been more inclined toward interaction and the establishment of harmonious relations.

Some existing data indicate that the conformity situation is more complex than merely "males are more dominant and females more passive." For example, in groups with a task perceived as more appropriate for masculine roles, females are more conforming, but men conformed more in groups where the task was feminine in role.

Physical characteristics—weight, height, general size, and robustness—influence how people in a group react to the individual and how the individual behaves. Larger size among equals in other charcteristics may aid one in becoming a leader. Fortunately, performance as a leader is related more to ability than to size.

There is a definite variability in physical attractiveness and group participation. It is obvious that the taller, more handsome male or the more beautiful female draws more positive response from others than a man or woman less physically gifted. An individual who is too thin, too overweight, or physically disfigured will not initially find a favorable response in a group. It is a well-known fact that a winning, confident personal style will enhance or counterbalance whatever physical characteristics one may present to the group. Again, performance is the measure of effective leadership.

Attendance.   This is another variable that definitely influences a group. The person who is faithfully present, on time, and stays through each meeting will have a more positive impact than the member who arrives late or leaves early consistently or is often absent. Physical presence—as well as absence—indicates to other group members how you value the task of the group as well as them as persons.

Participation.   One who is physically present but is a low participator will not normally have as much effective input into the life of a group as the person who speaks up more. Comments that are appropriate and effective in the group task, whether from a low-verbal or a high-verbal participator, will bring more positive response than ineffective or inappropriate comments.

We can think in terms of frequency of participation and also of intensity and of quality of participation. Generally speaking, the group member who participates frequently, who is "on target" with comments, and who communicates in his comments that he is trying to help the group reach its goals will show an identity with and positive concern for the group. Even when one's ideas are not in full agreement with the final decision of the group, he is much happier and the group more sound and mature if both have taken the opportunity to participate openly. It is a compliment to fellow group members, which they receive and respond to positively, when a person trusts himself and others enough to risk sharing opinions and ideas, and especially feelings, about an issue before the group.

Agenda.   When printed and visible to the group members, an agenda has a definite positive impact on the group. When the agenda is crowded and time limited, people tend to reduce their participation in all but the most important and/or emotional items on the agenda. One's intensity of desire to move a group along in accomplishing its task is referred to by some as "agenda anxiety." This is especially true when some participation by members seems too social or irrelevant to the point or goals of the group.

Of equal importance to what is on the agenda is what is *not* on the agenda. Items omitted because of their potentially explosive nature must be dealt with sometime, though a wise group member will not force a group to deal with an issue of this nature until the time seems right, the group ready.

A third area deals with "personal agenda." One member may feel a strong need to continue discussing a dead issue, perhaps to get back at someone in the group, or even to confirm his own "favorite feeling" of a lack of worth when the group explodes all over him with resentment at his taking more than his "fair share" of time. When a personal or "hidden" agenda is brought into a group, it is desirable to share it "up front" and clearly to all members so that it can be dealt with openly.

Individual Abilities.   Intelligence, information about an item under discussion, skill in leadership, ability to read the mood of the group and introject an appropriately timed comment to clarify a logjam or move the group toward its goal—all of these are welcome abilities that can assist the effective work of a group. Human relations skills that help the group both work on tasks and also maintain the personal needs of the group members and the atmosphere of the group are desirable. These skills in human relations are a science rather than a clump of generalizations about "personality." When a person is willing to work at it, she can learn and develop a high level of human relations skills.

Communication Pattern.   Examples of this are who is included, to whom do most eyes glance in important times of the group's conversation, and who is listened to or who can speak yet have little effect on the group. The patterns of communication within a group are visible and can be charted as by Bales' Interaction Process Analysis Profile.[6] The variability of the time the group gives to positive and negative comments, to questions and answers tell a trained observer much about the nature and life of the group. Equally visible is the sociogram drawing that shows the number of comments made by each member, and whether to the group as a whole or to specific individuals. This graphic picture clearly shows high and low verbal participators. It is, however, of little use in judging such areas as the nonverbal participation or the effectiveness of leadership or even the progress toward goals. (See Chapter Ten.)

Group Goals.   A well-developed goal has six characteristics. It is: (1) written, (2) visible (on chalk board or the agenda sheet), and (3) concretely specific. It is also (4) realistic or attainable in the time and circumstances given and (5) shared by the group as a whole with each member having opportunity to speak about wording and content. Finally, a good goal is (6) *measurable*—that is, it is quantified so that when the task is completed, the work of the group can be measured or evaluated in terms of the goal.

A well-written goal has four components: (1) person or group; (2) action or behavior; (3) results when completed; and (4) quantifier or means of measurement. Some examples of well-written goals could be:

1. "Our staff will plan the budget by January 15, so as to develop funds and staff for two new playgrounds next year."

2. "We will consider three major problems involved in our task and by the end of our meeting develop two viable solutions for each problem."

3. "By May of next year William J. Brown will be graduated with a B.S. in Recreation Administration by Clemson University with a grade point ratio of 3.3 on a 4.0 scale."

4. "Our committee will discuss and list five or more community resources and agencies with which our department can cooperate in the city's centennial celebration the year after next."

5. "Our task force will develop three stategies by which accidents requiring medical attention in our park can be reduced next year by 15 percent." (See Fig. 4–2.)

Goals are not the same as objectives. A goal is long-term while an objective is short-term. Goals are for a month, a semester, a year. Objectives are for a shorter time period and are steps to a goal. Several objectives could be successive parts of the process of accomplishing a goal. For example, the second and fifth examples above could be objectives for a specific meeting.

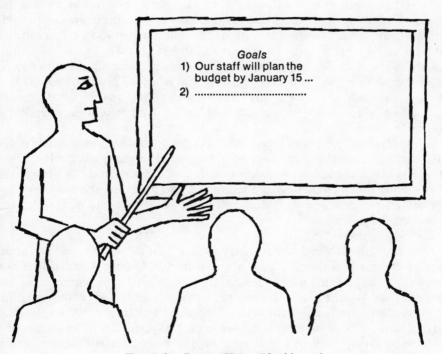

FIG. 4–2.   Person Using Blackboard

Goals have several values or uses. They form targets toward which activities of the group are aimed. They are a basis for common interest and activity, for identity and "we feeling." They are a means to measure progress, and they provide a framework for rational decisions.

When a goal is formed, a tension system tends to develop that motivates action until the goal is achieved or changed via conscious decision or some form of psychological closure or satisfaction. Stopping effort to accomplish a goal or getting sidetracked tends to develop internal frustration in individuals and in the group. One who feels and expresses these tensions is recognized both as task-oriented and as a positive value in the group, provided the expression is done in a way that enables forward movement toward the goal without limiting or destroying the maintenance needs of other members and the effective atmosphere of the group.

There is a difference between individual goals and group goals. When not recognized, this difference can disrupt the group process. Individual goals that have nothing to do with the group ("external goals" for other groups or personal situations outside the group) can upset a person and emotionally limit his or her participation in the group. Some external personal goals come under the term "hidden agenda." Recognizing the "external goals" frees one to concentrate energies in the group for its progress.

When a group is working on setting its goals, it is important that the group leadership and emotional climate encourage and draw out participation from each member. Questions to elicit participation are helpful to the group. If a member has a chance to put her ideas into goal formation, she is much more apt to put her energies and skills consciously to work to accomplish that goal. It becomes "our" goal when all group members feel this. A leader should "check out" when a goal is being set by asking something like "does everyone agree?" before the goal is written in its final form.

Individual members have their own goals for the group. Their goals are meshed with those of other members until group goals evolve. Then these goals become formal, operational, and explicit, and the group will work with more efficiency to accomplish the goals. In the manner suggested above, group goals become effective guidelines and motivators for good group process.

Cluster B—Invisible Internal Dynamics.   In this cluster will be found several forces less tangible than those found in Cluster A. This does not mean that they are in any way lesser forces in affecting the dynamics of the group. They are of equal or greater strength in most cases. Their intangibility nonetheless may allow them to be forces of which the skilled or trained group member can be readily aware as they happen. By being aware, one is able to "read" and to use them constructively for the progress of the group.

Motivation.   Motivation is an exceedingly complex matter, on which research has been done from ancient Greek times and through all sorts of employing agencies, companies, and industries today. A group can perform a task as well as member resources meet demands of the task. How well a group actually performs a task depends additionally upon how group members contribute and coordinate their resources to the task. Only when there is no loss due to non-optimum motivation does actual production equal potential production.

The presence of others, imagined or in reality, usually has some definite effect on one's participation or work. Not only in groups is this true, as the large percentage of team or group recreational activities attests. However, one person alone will usually perform differently when in the presence of others. Social facilitation can be one result, as can social inhibition. Whether others are co-workers, fellow group members, or observers may make some difference in motivation.

The presence of others can arouse more efficient participation and is more likely to have positive results when well-learned behaviors are natural in participation. New behavior or responses can inhibit participation in the presence of others. Personal confidence, the presence of trust as opposed to threat in the tone of the group, and the positive encouragement of other members all increase the chance of positive participation.

Persons who are present can arouse more or better effort in a participant if those persons are seen as ones who can reward or affect the results of what the participant does. A secretary may type more efficiently, or a maintenance caretaker work harder at getting a ballfield ready for a game, when the supervisor or director is present.

In contrast to this, persons with low confidence level in a situation may experience "evaluation apprehension," the fear of being hurt, rejected, or reprimanded in the presence of persons seen to be in authority. This apprehension will often reduce efficiency or inhibit participation. Stuttering, saying the "wrong thing," or damaging equipment are all examples of this kind of result. Even more, withdrawing to limited participation or even to non-participation can be more damaging to a group effort.

The presence of others can cause a sense of competition. If persons feel there is a limited commodity, such as "air time" to speak, money for raises, or words of appreciation from a boss, the sense of competition can motivate a stronger effort. Competition can be turned to cooperation, especially when purposes and goals are shared by persons formerly seen as adversaries.

The presence of others can provide the advantage of modeling for us. Most of our behaviors are learned from others. When persons in a group provide role models for efficient or productive behaviors, we are likely to follow their good lead. In fact, efficient leadership training in groups often results from this kind of behavior and opportunity to learn from the modeling of others. In this manner a discussion leader, a professor, or a director can model group participation and leadership styles that motivate the emulation of participants in the group, class, or staff.

People tend to act in ways that will bring desired rewards. We are generally more intensely motivated by more valuable than by insignificant or less valuable rewards. In many cases one will work better when the payoff or reward is linked positively with the reward of another group member. While this internal reward system is important, research shows external or group-to-group rewards can influence or motivate behavior of members also.

One major motivating reward is appreciation from others together with a sense of accomplishment. The more significant the goal and the task, the greater the sense of accomplishment, and thus the stronger the motivation. When participants receive positive strokes, verbal or nonverbal, from other group members, they tend to be more highly motivated for performing the task or accomplishing the goal.

In the case of each, strokes and success, cohesion in the group is increased. With greater cohesion comes greater motivation, more efficiency, more maturity, and greater satisfaction in the group participation.

Motivation from outside a person, whether by rewards and incentives or by fear of loss (for example, a loss of job, promotion, status, or opportunity) depends on another person or persons developing and providing the reward or incentive or else causing the fear. In this sense the motivation is both temporary (when incentive or reward is achieved or fear removed) and external (when dependent on being provided by another person). It seems obvious, then, that the development of motivation internal to the person is more to be desired. This is achieved when the attitude of the participant is changed and the motivation is consciously within the person. This most likely comes about when an individual's goals are strongly felt personally, when these goals are in harmony and agreement with the goals of the group as a whole, and when "hidden agenda" are few or nonexistent in the person. He feels cohesive with the group, and bends his energies and efforts toward accomplishing or achieving the group goals. A highly successful leader is apt to be able to assist the group in defining clearly and agreeing closely with the goals of the group. His skills and style, coupled with the atmosphere and tone of the group, can cause him to increase the internal and personal motivation of the individual members of the staff or group. Thus, the leader is aware of and consciously uses these internal, often invisible dynamics for the effective and efficient operation of the group.

Perceived Status.   Status can be either *achieved* (earned and possessed in the group) or *ascribed* (awarded because of rank, title, reputation, handsomeness or beauty, age, sex, or other arbitrary characteristics). Ascribed status often has to do with personal attributes, and frequently is due to circumstances largely beyond the control of the individual. Achieved status on the other hand is earned by virtue of the individual's record of successes or failures within the group as an effective leader or participant. Both ascribed and achieved status are real; they actually exist. However, achieved status is usually more lasting and more effective in the work of the particular group.

If one has relatively high status in a group, she can have a bigger influence on the effective operation or production of the group than can a person of lower status. The person of higher status usually selects or is accorded a spatial position of importance—e.g., sits in a physically important location such as the head of the table in a formal, structured, or autocratic group. In a democratic or informal one, she might sit in the middle or in any location for that matter.

Of greater importance is the effect of status on communication pattern and content in a group. One's relative status in a group will influence the amount of communication she initiates, the amount of communication she receives from others, and the particular group members with whom she communicates most frequently. The content of messages sent to a person of higher status tends to be more positive and less aggressive than messages sent to persons relatively lower in the status hierarchy. In other words, the more power and influence people believe a person has, the more they will talk to and listen to that person, or nod or look at or speak to that person for affirmation of their participation. A person of relatively higher status will tend to communicate more with others of relatively higher status in the group than he or she will with others of relatively lower status in the group. One can also, from a higher status position, help the group move more efficiently and effectively toward accomplishing the tasks and goals of the group than can a person from a lower perceived status position. Part of the responsibility of persons with higher status, power, and influence is to facilitate and encourage more participation by those members who have, or feel they have, lesser influence, power, or status.

One's title can have considerable effect on the group's invisible dynamics. A suggestion such as "we should quit messin' around and get on with the job" will have a different effect when spoken by a person whose title is of lower perceived status than when spoken by one of more highly perceived status. Certain types of role behavior are expected of persons with certain higher status title roles. That this is so is seen by the power and influence that certain roles seem to possess and exert within the group. In general it can be said that the higher the relative amount of status associated with a specific title role, the greater will be the power and influence on the group by the person with that title.

Recreation and park professionals with higher status roles need to be aware of their relatively higher power and influence and use it appropriately, with both caution and wisdom. If not, these persons with higher status roles will likely end up with authoritarian styles, bulldozing the group in the direction they want the group to go. General results will include reduced cohesion and lower member satisfaction. While meetings will likely be shorter under this style, members will also likely experience frustration and suspicion, and creativity will be reduced. The "yes, sir, boss!" syndrome will increase.

This can be summed up by saying: If a person has a relatively high status role position, she should know the implication of the power and influence she wields in the group. Using power and influence wisely and consciously within the parameters of one's personal style can help your group (staff, class, team) to be more productive and more satisfied with what all are doing. (See Fig. 4–3.)

Group Norms.   Norms (also called "the normative system") are a set of standards for acceptable and unacceptable behavior by members when the group is together. Norms are usually set and enforced by the group, though they can be set and enforced by outside forces or groups. Group members are generally expected to conform to group norms. Some form of sanction usually exists to encourage conformity to norms and discourage deviation from the norms.

Some examples of group norms are:

- Dress—every man is expected to wear a tie to meetings but coats are optional.
- Sex roles—women in this group may support opinions of others but are not expected to initiate ideas.
- Uniform codes—coaches will wear billed baseball caps and coaches' shorts at every practice.
- Personal expressions—smoking is not allowed in our meetings, but we will break five minutes of every hour for those who wish to smoke.
- Status privileges—the rangers must be on time for staff meetings, but the superintendent will show up ten minutes late, and the agenda does not begin until then; or only the assistant director and center directors are allowed to differ in meetings with the opinion of the director.
- Public behavior—we make public statements of unity and togetherness about our group; differences are to be aired and resolved in the privacy of group meetings.
- Sexual expression—no physical contact or expressions of affection other than the most perfunctory and casual between the sexes are allowed while on duty.

Included in the list above are several kinds of norms. *Formal norms* are encoded in policy manuals, bylaws, or similar written collections. All in

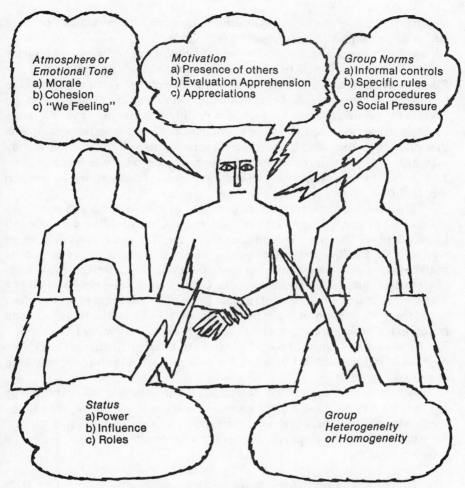

FIG. 4–3.   Person Bombarded by Various Forces

the group have access to them, are expected to know them, and behavior is to be governed by them. At times a formal norm is tacitly ignored though it is still in writing. For example, a club's constitution may state that the latest edition of Robert's Rules of Order will govern its meetings, but in practice it uses other rules, such as the casual nodding of the heads, with no spoken words or raising of hands to signify agreement on an issue.

Explicitly stated norms may not be in writing formally, but they are stated from time to time and the group generally follows them. Examples would be "Be at work on time" or "Our Monday staff meetings begin promptly at 9:30 a.m." Other norms may be explicit and stated, but the actual norm is a different behavior—as in the latter example, the meeting's agenda discussion does not begin until 9:45, after fifteen minutes or so of late arrivals and social conversation (stroking).

Other norms are *nonexplicit* or *informal*. Group member behavior can be strongly affected by these. For example, the chairwoman of the Recreation Commission may state that she expects items for the agenda to be only those received two days before the meeting and thus printed on the agenda everyone receives. In fact, she readily accepts new agenda items verbally presented each time the Commission meets. Another example is that players on the church basketball league teams will not cheat and may play only when regularly attending the church on whose team they play. This is the kind of informal norm that becomes formally stated only when it is broken.

The group brings pressure to conform to the norms. The process by which this pressure is applied is called social control. "Every player will know his plays" is an accepted team norm, and the put-downs and angry rejection are familiar to us all when applied to the casual player who does not study the playbook and who loses the game on a broken play. Less obvious but still real sanctions or social control can be seen in "Don't bring it up if it will cause us to be kept in class longer" or "Bill gets emotional and explodes if we press him too hard on certain touchy subjects such as pay raises, extra program equipment, or hiring women. Stay away from them!" The most obvious kinds of social control are fines, suspensions, rejection, or even being transferred or fired if a person does not go along with the norms of a group.

Group norms then often determine what behavior is acceptable or not. Transgressing these norms causes a swirl of invisible, or sometimes highly visible, dynamics that affect the group's cohesion and productivity. Pressures, stated or implied, encourage conformity to these norms by group members.

Heterogeneity and Homogeneity.   We tend to group ourselves with people of similar interests and backgrounds, similar abilities and status. This occurs both in formal and informal groupings, and we are relatively homogeneous in our groupings.

The effective leader will be aware that in even the most homogeneous group there is a considerable amount of heterogeneity, of differences in specific knowledge or special skill areas, of moral standards and life styles perhaps, and differences in levels of creativity or ability to synthesize and harmonize the input of other group members—skills in the practice and leadership of group dynamics. With this awareness a skilled leader will use the potential and actual knowledge and talents of each of the various group members. He will welcome the heterogeneity with the awareness that each is unique and has unique offerings to the group, so that each can be enabled to contribute his or her uniqueness to the group for its positive and ongoing life and successful goal accomplishment and task completion.

Atmosphere, Emotional (Hedonic) Tone.   The group's emotional tone plays a large part in its successful productivity. Internal dynamics are directly and inevitably linked to the group's emotional or hedonic tone. Have you ever entered a group (such as a family, a club, or a class) where the prevailing mood was one of distrust, fear, apathy, aggression, or suspicion? If so, you recall that you could almost feel the negatively charged atmosphere. In such a situation most people withdraw and say as little as possible, or else attack ideas and remarks in a hostile manner. Morale of group members, as well as creativity, is generally low in this kind of group. "Let's get this over with" seems to be the unwritten norm, and facial expressions reenforce the mood. Negativity and apathy prevail. That any progress toward goals of task is possible in such a situation seems unlikely, though it can happen. When progress is made, it is slow going; it seems as if "the brakes are still on." It takes extra effort and energy from informal and/or formal leaders to turn this atmosphere around, to set a productive tone and process.

In a group where the general atmosphere is friendly, warm, cooperative, and positive, you can feel a positive tone or mood. When it is present, leadership is generally shared and democratic, people look at each other and use first names, there is a sense of movement toward goals, there is levity at appropriate places, and both the group and community share success. A feeling of "we-ness" prevails—"we are producing together, and we can and will meet and solve any problems together." People tend to speak freely, yet responsibly, in this setting. They tend to listen and understand each other, as illustrated by such comments as: "I really care about what you mean, the facts and the feelings of what you are trying to say. You accord me the same respectful style of dialogue in interpersonal communication." Trust is high in such a group, there is openness about opinions and feelings and differences are faced honestly and with little, if any, defensiveness.

In this kind of group creativity and morale are high, friendliness and cooperation prevail, progress is definite toward goals, and tasks and production are consistent. Group members show their satisfaction by being present, on time, involved, and sharing leadership roles. Frequent use of maintenance roles is shown almost spontaneously, and motivation, confidence, and participation are high. In a sense everyone is perceived and feels a kind of high status in the group; a genuine interdependence of needing the participation of everyone seems evident. People seem to feel good about themselves and about the others in the group as well as the progress of the group. The level of cohesiveness is high—and the confidence of dealing adequately with whatever comes up keeps cohesion at a high level.

When you are a participant in this kind of group, you *know* it! You sense or feel it, and it feels good. The practice, learning, growth, and maturity of a group like this are attained only by effort, awareness, and positive energy on the part of nearly everyone, and by wise and considered leadership from those who have the skills; this enables those who want to grow and learn to develop these skills for themselves. Such shared leadership leads to shared satisfaction from shared success in the group's goal accomplishment and task completion.

Developing this kind of atmosphere begins with careful planning by aware, trained, and practiced leadership. The leader has confidence in his or her abilities and in the group process, coupled with a basic belief in the worth, dignity, and value of each individual. This leads to relating to each individual in a positive expression of beliefs and builds confidence and skills.

Cluster C—Emotional Components of Internal Dynamics.   Earlier we indicated that, according to Kurt Lewin, all behavior is goal-oriented or purposive. Each participant in a group, if this "field theory" is accurate, behaves in a particular way because of some reason or cluster of reasons, many of which have emotional components. They have to do with emotions we call feelings. These emotional components can be powerful motivators of human behavior. Many times they result from direct reaction to other internal or external dynamics operating in the group environment.

Everyone who participates in groups should know of the existence of these emotional forces. Awareness of these forces allows a professional to operate more effectively in interpersonal relationships. Skillful use of this awareness leads to better leadership and human relations.

Along with beliefs, values, and attitudes, *feelings* are what accentuate the humanness of people. Feelings are the emotional expressions of "what is going on inside of us." Though we may not recognize or be aware of them, feelings are real. Feelings exist both within you and within other people with whom you associate. They are powerful forces that must be acknowledged and dealt with.

The fact of feelings is emphasized here because so often now they are de-emphasized. For years we have (especially in academic environments) put much—perhaps too much—emphasis on the intellect, on clear logical thinking. "Don't get angry. It won't do any good." "Hey, now, control yourself. Don't lose your head!" Commands such as these betray our emphasis on the head, the intellectual or cognitive aspect of our interpersonal relations, and deny the reality of emotions. Both are important and need to be developed and expressed. How often have you heard such expressions as: "Don't cry. It doesn't do any good." "Will you shut up! Everybody's looking at us." "Be a man. Suck up your gut and fake it." Messages like these from parents, coaches, teachers, and other adults lead us to cover our feelings with layer after layer of "control" as we grow. As babies, we had the full range of feelings and could spontaneously express joy, obstinancy, fear, sadness or any other emotion that arose in us. We had to learn from our culture that when we lost or got hurt, we were not to reveal what we felt; to cover up and hide our anger or pain. Some of us, to protect ourselves, expended a great energy repressing our feelings. We denied their existence, fearing that if we expressed them, others might know how we felt and would manipulate us. We've paid a terrible price in that many of us "over-control" our feelings and do not express them. We keep them bottled up inside where they can and often do cause or contribute to physical wear and tear (ulcers, cardiovascular damage, etc.). At times we explode and express these repressed feelings by overreacting to situations or people. The price is, in fact, that many of us are either unaware of or else unable to control our feelings.

Fortunately, in the past decade or so we have begun to recognize the need for accepting feelings as a fact of life. It is more widely accepted now that all feelings can be felt and expressed by each sex. In doing so, we become more human and, consequently, less dehumanized. When we know that we do feel, can recognize specific feelings, and are free to show or express these feelings when we choose, we grow. This realization and freedom allows us to be more natural, more whole, more human, and more in touch with ourselves and with others. When we feel, we are also more free to risk, to savor more of the richness and fullness of life, and to know that our feelings are real and OK.

In dealing with groups of people, or merely relating to others individually, a wise and sensitive person will listen for the feelings expressed in or behind the words. More importantly, look at the nonverbal body and facial language, for even more than words these communicate what a person is feeling.

The challenge is two-fold: to recognize the feelings in yourself and others and to accept those feelings. See them as legitimate concerns. If you have insight into a person's emotion, you can then be better able to interact honestly and effectively with that person. To do this requires that you know and accept your own feelings; if you do not, you will spend far too much time and energy dealing with your own cover-up strategies and defensive systems.

One surely will be less effective as a professional in the field of parks and recreation if he is stumbling over his own feelings when he wants honest and effective relationships with others—his co-workers, customers, users, and other professionals. Take, for example, the low participator or person who sits back quietly with little or nothing to say and who is probably feeling one or more of these: bored, inadequate, or incompetent in the topic area. He may be afraid of being rejected, embarrassed, laughed at, or argued down if he does speak up to make a point. On the other end, the high participator or person who speaks up a lot may be feeling a need to control or manipulate, a self-assurance in the topic area, a fear he will be "left out" if he doesn't speak up, or a sense of worth, confidence, and value in the leadership and goal striving efforts of the group.

It is up to each participating leader to think about what sort of feelings might be going on in the other participant during that person's verbal or nonverbal participation. It helps to think in terms of his or her goal—to gain recognition, approval, inclusion, or goal attainment for the group. Perhaps the goal is to avoid being rejected or laughed at. Much of our behavior comes from efforts to avoid feelings we dislike, and to obtain feelings we like. We may not think in just these terms because we look at the surface behavior that is expression of feelings, or at the very least, is accompanied by feelings. And the behavior has some purpose, some goal or combination of goals behind it. Realize the goal, and then deal more effectively with the person.

EXERCISES AND STUDY SUGGESTIONS

1. To reinforce your use of goals, the importance of setting goals, and your skill in writing goal statements, develop five or more personal goals for your own growth and skill development in these areas:
    Observation of group processes and group dynamics;
    Leadership of groups;
    Awareness of external and/or internal forces affecting the functioning of groups;
    Awareness of your interpersonal skills; and your
    Development of sensitivity to the feelings of others.
    In writing these goal statements, be sure to follow the form suggested in this chapter (the identification of six characteristics and four components). Ask a friend to critique the goals for components and characteristics—not as goals you should establish for yourself as personal objectives. The critique should comment on your ability to write goal statements, not on the intent of your goals.

2. Divide your group or class into small groups of five. Assign to each group the problem of developing a detailed outline of a speech called "Motivation in a Group." Be sure to include in your outline the role group processes and leadership play in motivation, especially for those who are inhibited. From each group choose one person to represent his group on a panel of judges who will review the quality of the outlines. The panel should make its deliberations in front of the total class; the panel will announce its decision as to which group developed the best outline. Once the panel decision is announced, have the panel discuss the pressure it felt when deliberating a judgment decision in front of those being judged. Have the class discuss its feelings about the panel's process, the roles played by various members, the communication patterns observed, and the forces which seemed to be most dominant in shaping the panel's behavior and

decision. Finally, discuss the validity of the winning subgroup's outline—did they really home in on the factors which motivate individual and group behaviors?

3. Here is an exercise which involves cooperation during competition, factors which tend to be present in most group situations.

The Million Dollar Giveaway*

Objective:	To look at the role competition and cooperation play in group functioning, particularly when the group is involved in a decision making process where the winning group gets all the rewards.
Time Needed:	Forty-five to sixty minutes.
Setting:	Divide the group into three smaller subgroups of five or more members. For each subgroup, have a designated observer who will chart the group's process.
Process:	Once the group is divided into the three small subgroups, each subgroup is asked to choose one of its members to represent it. They are told they will be given a common task to work on with the other subgroups. This phase of the exercise should take no longer than ten minutes. Once the representatives have been selected, seat them in the center of the room in such a way each representative can clearly see the members of his subgroup. The following role play situation is then explained.
Situation:	The recreation commission has just received a one-million dollar grant from the Humanities Endowment Foundation for a recreation project of the community's choosing. There is one condition: The recreation commission must agree on a single project which will use the entire sum of money. The representatives are told to go back to their respective subgroups, each subgroup representing a particular neighborhood or ethnic interest of the community, and to develop with them a project of their choosing which will be presented to the other two subgroup representatives. The subgroups have fifteen minutes in which to develop their projects. Only the representative for the subgroup can present his subgroup's proposal.
	After fifteen minutes of planning, the three representatives again meet in the center of the room. Tell them they are to present their proposals and that they must come to an agreement on the one that will be acceptable to all three subgroups to present to the Humanities Foundation.

* Johnson/Johnson, *Joining Together: Group Theory and Group Skills*, © 1975, pp. 95–96. Adapted by permission of Prentice-Hall, Inc., Englewood Cliffs, New Jersey.

After all three proposals have been presented, the representatives of the subgroups return to their subgroups for a five-minute briefing before returning to the center of the room.

The representatives reconvene in the center of the room and discuss for five more minutes their proposals; during this period of time, members of each subgroup can communicate with their representatives through notes. This process of having the representatives of the subgroups meet with the other representatives in the center of the room for five minutes and then returning to their own subgroups for a five-minute briefing is repeated three times or until agreement is reached.

Discussion: Once the representatives reach an agreement, have both the representatives as a group and each subgroup discuss their feelings. In the discussions, be sure to have each consider the role competition played in their decision making, their loyalty to the community as well as their loyalty to their own vested interest, the techniques used to negotiate a settlement, the transference of loyalty (for group representatives) from their subgroup to the representative's subgroup, their sense of power and responsibility, and the factors which ultimately influenced their decision.

If you like, have those observing each subgroup's functioning report on their observations: the role played by various members in influencing the group's view and the role of their representative, the communication patterns, the effects of time and other external dynamics, etc. To facilitate these observations, the observer may wish to use one of the observation charts used with previous exercises (Chapters One and Three). Divide the group or class into two equal groups. Using the fishbowl technique, have one group serve as discussants; the other group will be observers. Let the discussants talk about which of the external forces suggested in this chapter are currently operating on the members of this discussion group or on the class as a whole. They should not be limited to the forces identified in the chapter; they may add others if they wish. Be sure the discussants describe how these forces are at work. No one should be appointed as leader of the discussion but the discussion should last for no longer than twenty minutes. At that time, the facilitator should have the two groups switch roles.

The observers now become the discussants and enter into the inner circle. Those formerly serving as discussants become the observers and move to the outside. The new discussant group now has its go at things. For twenty minutes, it should talk about those visible and invisible dynamics which they have seen or sensed to be operative in their group or class. Specific examples should be given as verification of the role of these internal dynamics. Then, have the entire class discuss the insights, learnings and surprises they have had from these discussions.

Using the same procedure described above, have the group discuss the norms operating in the class or group and the goals, conscious, unconscious, visible or invisible, which seem to be a part of the behavioral pattern of the group.

4. Finally, have the class, as a group, attend a public meeting such as a recreation commission, a city council meeting or a planning board meeting. Have each individual critique the meeting in terms of the external and internal forces affecting the group's functioning. It may be advantageous to have the class work in teams so that more comprehensive critiquing can occur. Specific attention might be focused upon communication patterns, interaction patterns, roles played, time sequences, etc. Have each observer write a report of his observations. These reports should not be shared with other class members until the class reconvenes as a group. When the class does reconvene, have the group discuss its observation (anyone of the small discussion group procedures mentioned in Chapter Five may be used), critiquing the role played by the various external and internal dynamic factors. Then have the class discuss the insights and learnings it had as a result of this assignment.

ENDNOTES

1. Elton T. Reeves, *The Dynamics of Group Behavior* (New York: American Management Association, Inc., 1970). p. 18.

2. A. Paul Hare, Edgar Borgatta, and Robert Bales, *Small Groups: Studies in Social Interaction* (New York: Alfred A. Knopf, Inc., 1955), pp. 2, 3. Cited in Knowles, p. 19.

3. Eduard Lindeman, *Social Education.* Cited in Knowles, pp. 19, 20.

4. Kurt Lewin, "Experiments in Social Forces," Chapter 5 in *Resolving Social Conflict* (New York: Harper & Brothers, 1947), pp. 71–83.

5. The research findings supporting this section is cited in Marvin E. Shaw, *Group Dynamics: The Psychology of Small Groups* (New York: McGraw-Hill, 1976). Used by permission of McGraw-Hill Book Co.

6. Robert F. Bales, *Interaction Process Analyses: A Method for the Study of Small Groups* (Chicago: University of Chicago Press, 1950).

SUGGESTED READINGS

Gibber, Graham; Hartmann, John; and Mann, Richard, eds. *Analysis of Groups: Contributions to Theory, Research, and Practise.* San Francisco: Jossey-Bass, Inc., 1974.

Luft, Joseph. *Group Processes: An Introduction to Group Dynamics.* Palo Alto, Calif.: The National Press, 1970.

Tubbs, Stuart L. *A Systems Approach to Small Group Interactions.* Reading, Mass.: Addison-Wesley Publishing Co., 1978.

Wood, John. *How Do You Feel? A Guide to Your Emotions.* Englewood Cliffs, N.J.: Prentice-Hall, Inc., 1974.

Chapter Five

SMALL GROUP TECHNIQUES*

Recreation professionals' work requires that they, and those with whom they work, find methods for developing staff, for resolving social problems, and for interpreting, predicting, and controlling group behavior. This chapter presents seven small group techniques that may be helpful when such needs arise requiring an issue or concern to be discussed or decided upon. In style, it is a "how to" chapter, offering information on how and when to implement each technique. Examples of the application of each technique are given, as well as models and examples of materials that can be given to each group member. Keep in mind that the particular setting and situation will ultimately determine which technique will be appropriate or which ones must be modified to meet your needs and objectives. The intent of this chapter is *not* to suggest that small group techniques are a surefire way to accomplish any and all group goals. Rather, the intent is to present tested and acceptable techniques that can be used in conjunction with other strategies for group action, such as the large group techniques discussed in Chapter Six.

Each technique should be viewed in light of its acceptability by group members, its adaptability to a particular situation or issue, and its credibility in eliciting pertinent information for group action. Moreover, since productivity is the focal point of group work, evaluations should be ever present. Such questions as "Are we getting the answer?" and "Is the group satisfied with the results of its efforts?" will aid the group leader in getting feedback. As will be noted in Chapter Ten, these and other questions often can be answered by observing what is, has, and should be taking place in the group. All group members should be involved in this process.

There are a variety of small group techniques that may be used by recreation students, academicians, and practitioners. We do not pretend to

* This chapter was prepared by Cynthia J. Hampton, Lecturer, University of North Carolina at Chapel Hill.

offer an exhaustive collection of the techniques available. Instead we have chosen those that can be easily learned and applied without a great deal of professional training. They are the Small Group Discussion, Role Playing, Buzz Group, Brainstorming, Case Study, Fishbowling, and the Committee techniques.

THE SMALL GROUP DISCUSSION TECHNIQUE

The small group discussion technique is widely accepted as a basic means of enhancing the democratic ideal, to give group members an opportunity to engage in a free exchange of ideas and opinions under the guidance of a leader. The basic principle of all small group discussions is the same: each member should have a clear understanding of what the group plans to accomplish and should feel free to enter into its activities. Furthermore, each member should feel his or her equal share of responsibility for the success of the group's effort. When these conditions exist, the group can immediately begin functioning as a unified body and set to work toward a common cause.

The first step in conducting a group discussion using the group discussion technique is to make sure that all members understand the group's responsibilities and goals. When people do not know, do not care, or have been misinformed why they are members of a small group discussion, they are usually less prone to act and therefore stifle or hamper other group members who are aware and want to be productive.

Once a group has established its goals, it can begin to organize its membership toward a productive end. There are specific characteristics of a small group discussion which set it apart from other small group techniques. These characteristics include its size, the group-centeredness of the discussion, the role of the leader, and the attitude and interaction of those participating.

Group Size—The size of the group should be small enough to allow for maximum participation of all group members. Operating on the principle of the least group size, you should have from eight to twelve members when using this technique, although up to twenty persons can be accommodated with it. Not only does a smaller number of participants allow for everyone to take part in the discussion, it also assists in the efficient expenditure of time and energy, two critical factors in productivity.

Structural Design—Participants should be arranged in a fashion that allows for eye contact by every other person. This is usually done by having the participants in a circle or a square (see Fig. 5–1) with the

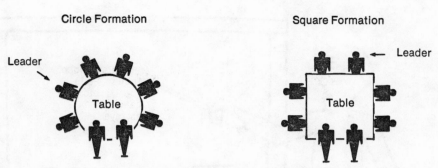

FIG. 5–1.   Sample Arrangements for Small Group Discussions

leader being a member of the group, not sitting to one side or apart from the group. The chairs shold be sturdy and comfortable, but not so comfortable that participants become too relaxed. If a table or tables are used, the physical arrangements should allow all participants to sit around them, but they should not be so large as to cause the participants to shout from one end of the table to the other.

Time, Setting, and Atmosphere—The discussion should be held at a time and place agreed upon by all group members. It should be as convenient as possible for all. If, for example, it is known that some group members have elementary school children who must be met after school, it would probably be unwise to schedule a discussion during this time. The best rule is to place the question before the group members and have them reach a consensus for time and place. Let them, not you, decide. Of course, if the small group discussion is a part of a regularly scheduled class or meeting, there should be no conflict along these lines.

Secondly, the leader should work carefully to establish a positive social atmosphere, one in which the participants feel friendly, relaxed, informal, and free to talk and act. This social climate is most important to the successful application of the small group discussion technique. You will have to rely on your senses to decide what the atmosphere should be within any given small group discussion. Be mindful that the way a group "feels" will definitely affect the outcome of its working together as a unified body.

Materials—It is the responsibility of the group leader to have available all the necessary materials—pens, pencils, paper, chalkboard, chalk, ashtrays, trash cans, tape recorders, handouts, and books—that might be used by the group members during their discussion period. (See Fig. 5–2.) This does not mean the leader must bring these items himself, but it is his responsibility to see that they are

Materials Needed
Pencils Pens
Paper   etc.
Chalk
Ashtrays

FIG. 5–2.   Use of Chalkboard

there (each member is alerted to bringing these items or several members are assigned this task). This kind of preparation helps avoid delays or possible cancellation because the needed materials and data were not accessible.

Participants—Each member of a small group discussion has a specific function. The three most common roles are group leader or moderator, group member, and group recorder. The discussion leader should have a basic belief in democratic principles and must be one who demonstrates this by his or her own behavior. He or she should believe in the group as a means of individual development; have a knowledge of, and skill in, handling small groups; hold a high regard for the rights of every individual member to be heard; and have a good understanding of the discussion environment made up of people, feelings, things, and events. The group leader's role is crucial to the smooth flow of the dialogue and interchange between group members. While not necessarily the expert opinion giver, the leader should always be mindful of his or her position as one who constantly filters out the nonproductive elements, such as random conversations, that tend to pull the group away from its intent and established goals. In their book *Leadership and Dynamic Group Action*, Beal, Bohlen, and Raudabaugh cite various tasks the group leader should do in the small group discussion situation. Among them are:

1. Assist the group in defining clearly its problems or objectives.
2. Aid the group in establishing the necessary structure to accomplish its objectives.
3. Refer questions to the group and see that facts are made available when needed and are free from prejudice and opinions.
4. Establish and maintain an informal, cooperative, and permissive group climate.
5. Ask questions and make summaries without letting personal views intrude; make suggestions rather than give directions.
6. Stimulate and maintain a spontaneous exchange of ideas and thinking.[1]

A good small group discussion leader has a strong commitment to produce a good discussion through participation as well as direct the group's actions. She is the communication supervisor within the group and should provide "air time" for all who request it verbally or non-verbally, while simultaneously summarizing, restating, clarifying, and injecting humor and new ideas throughout the course of the discussion. The leader should keep a smooth flow of discussion going, but with a light, nondefensive style.

Group members are equally vital to the overall effectiveness of the small group discussion. It is their task to help produce clearly defined goals and select the group's methods of reaching these goals. If ground rules are to be established and followed, it is up to the group members to decide what the ground rules are and who is to enforce them. For example, the group should decide how each member is to be addressed (if everyone will be on a first name basis) and if, when, and on what issues experts will be called in. Other tasks of group members include operating within the democratic process and allowing every member the right to give freely of his opinion or facts; participating as a member and avoiding becoming self-centered and rigid in regard to one's personal viewpoint when the group's information shows that point of view in error or of little use in achieving the

group's goals; being available to accept leadership responsibility if
the occasion arises; and being willing to contribute a share of energy,
time, and thought equal to other participants in the discussion. In all,
the good group member in a small group discussion is intellectually
alert, prepared for the discussion (has researched the topic when it
has been previously announced as the basis of the discussion), and
sees himself as a part of an efficient and effective operation bent on
working as a productive total unit.

The third and final important role is filled by the group recorder.
This person is often seen as a kind of recording secretary, but the
recorder's tasks go beyond the "note taking" function. He or she
serves as a type of referee. One responsibility is to notify the group
when the discussion has gotten off the track. This can usually be accomplished with a summation of "where we are" and "where we appear to be heading." It should not be necessary for the recorder to
write every word that is spoken; recording the main points should be
sufficient. The recorder is responsible for presenting the summary at
the close of the discussion, thereby allowing the group to respond to
his or her record keeping. If possible, especially if the group meeting
is on a critical issue that will result in having some document developed, the recorder should prepare copies of the discussion notes and
distribute them to the group so that the group can edit (if it wishes)
what has been written, in light of what was discussed.

Other assigned roles that are often used by groups employing
discussion technique are the observer and the group consultant. The
latter role is also referred to as the "resource person role." The group
observer normally sits outside of the group and takes notes on the
progress the group is making and its interaction patterns. He may use
a variety of recording techniques to assist him with this responsibility. Among those techniques are the use of flow charts, interaction
charts, and audio-visual tapings. At the close of the meeting, the
group observer is responsible for reporting on the internal dynamics
of the group, how well members worked together, and what, if any,
problems they had in reaching their productive state. Also, the group
observer may offer suggestions for more efficiency in operating toward and within group goals.

In a similar manner, the group consultant or resource person
assists the group on an "as needed" basis. The group consultant
should be prepared to speak as a group member only when she feels
that her information may be pertinent to those involved in the discussion or when invited by the group to give them subject matter input.
These two group members, the group observer and the group consultant, will likely not be necessary for groups convening for a short
period of time or when this kind of feedback is not required. The

group members should decide what the makeup of the membership should be, what roles are required, and respond accordingly.

Procedures—Once all group members have been identified by roles and know what they are expected to do, the next step is, through group discussion, to move toward goal accomplishment. We recommend this be done by having the group build an agenda—that is, develop a list of ideas or assumptions that the group wishes to discuss. To deal with them according to their importance, have the group rank them first, second, and so on. Brainstorming, a technique described later in this chapter, may be one way of accomplishing this. You can expect quite a bit of discussion when you start the rank ordering process. Identifying and ordering these items must be done openly and honestly if the decisions to be reached are produced out of rational, reflective thinking.

In order to sound and sort out the ideas and reasoning of the group members, it is suggested the following sequence of action be taken for selecting a topic: (1) look closely and critically at each fact and anticipate its ramifications; (2) consider each item seriously in light of the evidence and proof offered; (3) decide and act on critical items. The problem, issue, or action to be taken should lend itself to reflective thinking; if there is no solid foundation upon which to base one's beliefs, no amount of deliberation by the group is likely to solve the problem. Information must be available to, and obtainable by, the group members if a realistic discussion is to be had. This is especially true if the topics are so controversial that they do not normally permit rational, objective thinking to take place. In choosing a discussion topic, consider its suitability to the group. Is it timely, significant, interesting? Does it fulfill the group members' needs? Consider, as well, if it is a clear issue, open to alternatives, unbiased, concise, worthy of action. A good discussion topic is usually not answered with a "yes" or "no." Ideally, a good topic, such as the ideal leisure behavior (say for a leisure education discussion group), presents more than one solution to the problem, thereby causing the group to analyze critically a variety of alternatives that may be in the best interest of all participants. If the group knows that additional resources and/or expert advice will be needed in order for it to act responsibly, it should seek out this assistance from the outset. This is where having a process observer and a subject matter expert is vital.

Two aspects of the small group discussion should be viewed with particular caution. First, effective listening is paramount for good discussion—listening not only with one's ears but also with one's mind and heart. All group members should keep alert to what is being said, what is being implied, and what is occurring between group members. Vital discussion time can be lost when members do not stay "in touch" with the discussion. Listening exercises can improve one's ability to listen. The second point is to make sure adequate time is available. If not, then do not begin the discussion. The group needs to feel it has time to deal with the issues and with its feelings and emotions. Since the group leader has the directive role, the potential problem of structuring the discussion within the specific time frame rests with him. A possible strategy for keeping things together is for the group leader to encourage all group members to develop an outline of their discussion points so that everyone will be prepared to provide input. This should stimulate active involvement and should help keep the participants task-oriented. Secondly, if the results of the small group discussion call for the implementation of ideas, as is often the case, the membership can respond by delegating responsibilities in a democratic fashion, and thereby ensuring that this closing phase of the discussion is as vital as were the steps leading to it.

ROLE PLAYING

Role playing is the enactment of a real life situation in order to provide human relations data for a group to analyze and discuss. It is not a drama or a skit in the true sense of acting. Rather, it should be a spontaneous portrayal of a real situation or problem that occurs or might occur in everyday life. It is a simulation experience. Therefore, the role play is based on reality and gives the participant the opportunity to identify with the situation so that the feelings and points made can be discussed and serve as a reference for future behavior toward others and their reactions to him in a similar situation. Role playing is not to be thought of as a game or amusement to do at a party; it is a very serious learning technique that should be entered into thoughtfully and directed by someone skilled in the dynamics of the technique. It is first cousin to psychodrama, a valuable tool in therapeutic recreation. Feelings and emotions may run high or be at the raw edge in role playing. Therefore, plan and use role play judiciously.

The following are some of the basic steps for implementing a role play:

1. Define the problem
2. Define the solution
3. Identify the role players
4. Enact the role play
5. Analyze and discuss the role play
6. Evaluate the role play

Defining the Problem

The first step in using the role play technique is to determine exactly what situation (the learning objective) the group wants to consider. As the group leader, you may be called upon to assist in defining the problem; however, it is best to have the group assess its own needs and interests and decide what problems or courses of action it wishes to analyze with this technique. For example, if the meeting is a training session or a staff meeting, the group may wish to use the small group discussion technique to determine how it wants to deal with the problem, say the planning of the summer playground schedule. Perhaps it decides to use the role play technique; the discussion method is ideal for developing the situation and for discussing the results of the role play.

A second technique for defining the problem (e.g., eligibility rules for youth sports), would be to have each person write down what he or she thinks the problem is and what can be done about it. Once this is done, the group can develop a composite list and brainstorm possible solutions. The most important fact to remember is that the problem must be real and should result from a need for a solution. One possible problem that affects many recreation agencies is the relationship of staff members to volunteers. A role play involving staff members functioning as volunteers and trying to get insight as to why the volunteers act as they do would be most helpful in developing the professional's appreciation of the volunteer's point of view. Likewise, if the volunteer plays the role of the professional, he or she might better understand the views of the professional and the frustrations the professional has when the volunteer does not function according to the professional's expectations. This exchange of roles for emphasis is called a "reverse role play."

Defining the Situation

Once the problem has been defined, it should be placed in the context of the situation that is specific and clear to those involved. The situation should fit the problem and, in the case of a role play, provide the players with latitude in which to react safely and comfortably. Caution should be taken not to design a situation so tightly that the role players are unable to express themselves freely and explore the problem creatively. It should place the group in the mood for the learning experience and inspire action. All members of the role play should be equally aware of the situation. For example, the situation might be one of having to interview prospective staff members. All persons playing in the role play—the interviewer and those to be interviewed—should be informed about the setting of the interview, the actions to be taken, and other essential facts. The situation statement sets the scene for action.

Identifying the Role Players

Ideally, the role players should want to be involved in the role play. It is recommended that players not be forced, coerced, ridiculed, or begged to take part. It is up to the individual group members to decide if they want to participate or wish to be observers. Some people do not feel comfortable in some roles because they fail to identify with the problem, the situation, the roles themselves, or all three. Also, there are some instances of over-identifying with the role to the extent that it becomes too real or too personal, and therefore participation is ineffective and sometimes dangerous to the success of the role play. This is especially true with groups that have not been working together or have not been together long enough to really get to know each other.

If at all possible, rely on those who volunteer to participate unless, as sometimes happens, all the group members have agreed to do so. You should find that group members who have established a sense of trust and security between themselves will be more willing to experience a role play without being prodded. A good idea is to begin the role play with a simple and nonthreatening problem or situation of little real significance to the group except to demonstrate how a role play is conducted. Another method is to use those persons who volunteer readily and when the role play has been done once, switch the roles with those who chose to observe, thereby involving all.

Roles can be tightly or loosely structured. If they are tightly structured, they are written with a personality and behavior for the role player to assume, such as:

> You are a recreation center directer, 40 years of age, flirtatious, disciplinarian, quick to resort to tears to get your way, demanding and prone to argument, etc.

> You are a businessman, easygoing, nervous, clock watcher, daydreamer, puritan, etc.

If the roles are loosely structured, the role players react to the problem and situation by their own design and choose whatever role they feel is appropriate, such as: "you are a college student" or "you are an older sister" with no elaboration on the role.

Enacting the Role Play

The key word is spontaneity. The role play should be allowed to unfold naturally in a permissive and relaxed atmosphere. This is enhanced if the role players are given an opportunity to "warm up" and "digest" their roles, to reflect upon them and internalize them. This is not to suggest that they be permitted to rehearse, but rather that they read the roles, ask clar-

FIG. 5–3. The Steps in a Role Play

ifying questions or have questions asked them by the leader to get them "into" the role. In some role plays players may offer suggestions to one another on how the role might be portrayed. In other role play situations it is important that the role is not discussed until after the role play is completed; only the role players know the specific posture they are to take in the role although everyone knows the roles—business executive or school teacher—that they are playing.

Once the role players are secure in their understanding of what is to take place, the action can begin and progress should not be interrupted except when the role players are not being heard or have been stopped because of some external factor such as laughter or someone entering the group unexpectedly. The observers should be cautioned *not* to laugh, for laughter, more than any other factor, can cause the role players to cease their emotional involvement with the role and become "actors," playing to the audience.

It is usually up to the leaders to keep the role play running smoothly. They may have to step in and "cut" if:

1. The role play has become so emotional that strong, emotional conflict is threatened.
2. The role play has gotten off track and is not speaking to the problem.
3. The dialogue slows down or the role players are not "into" their roles.
4. The role play reaches a particular point or incident that needs discussion or clarification.
5. The role play is operating within a certain time frame and time is running out.

This last point calls for clarification. To be a useful technique in problem solving, a role play should not be locked into a rigid time frame that allows little or no time for analyzing and discussing what took place. Timing becomes an important part of the overall success of the role play technique. Sufficient time should be available for the role players to react to the problem and not to feel pressured to reach a speedy closure. Of course, some role plays may have the time element as a problem in itself in order to make more vivid the effect of time as a dynamic.

Finally, it is the responsibility of the leader to know when the role play has run its course and should be stopped. The action should be stopped when the role play has reached the extent of its usefulness, when the purpose is clearly in the minds of the participants, including observers, and all are eager to discuss and analyze what has happened. Sometimes this happens naturally because of the dialogue or when one or more role players step out of the situation. Avoid letting the role play run long enough to agitate, bore, or confuse the role players. Be mindful, also, of stepping in before the role play has reached its logical conclusion. After a few experiences, timing will be more apparent and certain cues—such as long lapses of silence, repeating and restating points, fighting, or possibly a role player saying "I think we have said all there is to say"—will alert you to the need to stop the action.

Analyzing and Discussing the Role Play

Once the action has been stopped, the role play should be analyzed and discussed by the players and observers alike. Generally, the role players are first asked to respond to their feelings and reactions as they moved through the role play. This is referred to as the de-roling process. This permits the role players to step out of their roles, defusing any intense feelings, and speak about what they have experienced, not what others thought they had experienced. Also, since the observers tend to be more critical of the role players in their roles, having the role players immediately respond to what they have experienced assists the observers in focusing criticism on the characters rather than on the participants who played the characters.

The leader should discourage unnecessary criticism focused on a particular role player by reminding the observers that people react differently according to their understandings and feelings about a particular situation and problem. This step by the leader could lead to having different groups of people participate in the same role play to show how different opinions and behaviors do develop.

Most helpful for purposes of analysis and discussion is the use of a "briefing sheet" (a brief, printed summary of the situation) for the observing audience. It should assist the observers in becoming psychologically involved with the role play and allow them to make notes about specific actions and the events surrounding those actions. The discussion of the observers should provide new insights into what occurred and why it happened.

The leader should have a series of discussion questions ready to assist the players and observers in this analysis. Questions should focus on what occurred and why it occurred; they should stem directly from the learning objective set for the role play. In this way, the group takes on more responsibility for its learning and understanding.

Evaluating the Role Play

To determine the success of the role play, ask the group members to look back at the problem statement and determine if they have produced adequate solutions. Ask them to explore the consequence of the solution, then have them discuss what could have been done differently. If the problem or situation was not presented realistically and thereby failed to stimulate the group to discuss alternative courses of action, this technique of forcing the group to look at alternatives is useful. Coupled with the use of the briefing sheet, it can broaden the basis of the group's discussion regardless of what happened in the role play *per se*.

Summary

We began this discussion of the role play technique by stating that a certain amount of skill is necessary to direct a role play adequately. This skill can be acquired through repeated experiences in conducting a role play and in carefully taking note of what occurred in each instance. Do not be afraid to let the group operate independently of your leadership. It is the task of the group to solve its own problems, and you, as director, should not interfere with the group as it examines, questions, considers alternatives, refines its discussion, and reaches some kind of group consensus as to the total outcome of the role play experience.

Remember, role playing is a small group technique that can be applied to problem solving. It is useful in helping to develop insight and to learn in practice interpersonal skills. One of the best resources for learning more about the role play technique is Alan Klein's work on role play.[2] According to Klein, role plays can be used to: (1) stimulate discussion; (2) develop skills; (3) develop sensitivity and insight into how one might solve social and human relations problems; and (4) deal effectively with certain emotional problems that tend to block group productivity.

THE BUZZ GROUP

While the buzz group is basically a small group discussion technique, it can be used effectively with large groups. Its purpose is to allow everyone an opportunity to participate in a relatively short period of time, usually five to ten minutes. By design, any large audience can be divided into two- to six-person subgroups and given the responsibility to discuss the question, problem, or issue that has been placed before the larger body. In doing so, the audience participates actively and is given an opportunity to air its feelings and reactions to what has been said. By having one member of the subgroup summarize the general feelings of the subgroup's discussion, the entire audience has the benefit of the thinking of each of its members.

If the recreation commission, for example, is conducting a public hearing on some recreation issue, it might find it most appropriate to use the buzz group technique. After the commission has presented its information, it would divide the audience into small groups and charge them with the responsibility of discussing what they have heard and posing questions that the commission might consider. In that way, the commission would receive immediate feedback from the audience, and the individual members of the audience would feel that they were heard and had had an opportunity to participate in the discussion.

It should be remembered that the larger the buzz group, the more time it should be given for discussion. A two-member group might need five minutes while a six-member group might need ten.

Choosing the question or questions for the group to discuss is an aspect important to this technique. The questions should spur the participant's immediate interest. They should not be vague or misleading or create frustration. For example, when using this technique with teenagers planning for a spring dance, you might say: "Help us identify some specific means for funding our spring dance. We need some realistic solutions. If each subgroup could come up with one or two solid solutions, we would be in business."

The mechanics for using this technique are simple. If the audience is seated in chairs attached to the floor, members might be encouraged to group in twos or fours by talking to the persons next to them or immediately behind. If the audience is seated in portable chairs, then it is a matter of designating subgroups and asking them to cluster.

It is critical that each subgroup be responsible for having someone report the feelings and thoughts of the group so that the whole group can have the benefit of their exchange. Two immediate benefits accrue from the use of this technique: one, the leader and audience are immediately aware of the thinking of the total group; two, a set of concerns and/or solutions can be generated, thereby giving the group an agenda for discussion and further action.

BRAINSTORMING

Brainstorming is designed to stimulate group interaction to develop a large number of suggestions about a specific topic or problem. Sometimes called "idea inventory" or "free-wheeling," brainstorming elicits suggestions and ideas in a rapidfire presentation without criticism, evaluation, or limiting comments on any idea presented. Spontaneity of thought and free association are the central thesis of this technique.

The technique works best with small groups of five to eight people. For a stated period of time, generally from three to ten minutes, the group is to develop and record, on the blackboard or by designated recorders using note pads, as many ideas on the subject as possible. All ideas are accepted without criticism or elaboration. Imaginative, creative, and even seemingly ridiculous suggestions are encouraged and accepted. *Quantity* of ideas is valued above quality; the quality control occurs at a later stage when an evaluation of all ideas is made. At the end of the brainstorming period, all ideas are made available to all group members by listing them on the board or by having the recorded list of the note takers duplicated and distributed. Once the free idea association phase is completed, the group moves into the evaluation stage.

It is imperative that the leader set the ground rules for the brainstorming session. Brainstorming is best done when the leader creates a nonthreatening environment, free from the traditional limitations of evaluation. It is a task-oriented technique, yet one that tends to build group cohesion since it encourages all to participate. The leader should encourage all members to say what comes to mind and inform the group that it will be working within a specific limited time period; that it should try to get as many ideas generated as possible; that no one will be allowed an opportunity to elaborate on or question an idea until the brainstorming is over;

that no laughter or any form of an evaluation should be made until after the group has generated all ideas; and that creativity and spontaneity are encouraged. Recorders should be appointed; both the recorders and the leader should not participate in the idea generation phase since it is their responsibility to record and monitor the process.

Once the idea generation phase is completed, the leader can move the group into the evaluation stage where the small group discussion or buzz group techniques are most appropriate. In the evaluation phase, the group should be asked to discuss and evaluate all the solutions and decide upon the best ones. At this time, the group should be given time to reflect collectively upon the ideas that have been generated. They should seek to:

1. Eliminate those that are clearly irrelevant or impractical.
2. Clarify, restate, combine, or expand ideas that have potential.
3. Establish, by consensus, a priority of those ideas the group wishes to take or explore further.
4. Deliver a plan of action for implementing solutions and actions based upon the ideas generated and the priorities set.

CASE STUDY

Another technique that may be used to stimulate group discussions is to present the group with a case study. The goal of the case study is to involve the participants in analyzing and resolving a real life situation. The leader or moderator should be familiar with most aspects of the case. The case may be drawn from experience or be hypothetical; more frequently than not, the leader prepares the case for the group.

Each member should be given a copy of the case history. It should contain all the necessary elements and facts that the participants would need in discussing and solving it. The case information should include the historical background of the situation and events leading up to the crisis; the people involved, including their sociological, ethnic, economic, and educational backgrounds; and the action the group took in resolving the issue. The last piece of information may be omitted if the leader wishes the group members to project what they think the group did in resolving the problem and what the consequences were. The leader can have the group members work either individually or in small groups on the solution of the case. Regardless of the technique employed, ultimately the leader should have everyone share his or her solutions and participate in a general group discussion of the situation and its application to similar situations.

The case problem should be like some issue facing the group so that the group can identify with it. For example, if a recreation staff is dealing with the issue of fees and charges, it might be given a case study dealing with the implementation of a fee system in another community. By discussing what happened in another situation, one in which the individual members were not emotionally involved, the group might be led to explore alternatives that would give direction for solving its own problem. The leader may later tell the group members what actually did occur so they can measure their projected solutions against the realities of the situation. The case history should be brief and complete, between 500 and 3000 words in length.

When using the case study technique, use those solutions about which enough information is available to permit analysis by the group at the time of its meeting. Be practical and realistic about time, interest, and abilities of people participating in the case study. If possible, have copies of the case history reproduced and given to all members prior to the meeting to give them ample time to think about the solution. The small group discussion technique is ideal for dealing with the discussion phase of the case study.

THE FISHBOWL TECHNIQUE

The fishbowl technique is designed primarily to aid group members in becoming more effective observers. It can be used for purposes other than group training since it is a modification of the small group discussion technique. The uniqueness of the fishbowl is that one group discusses the topic or exercise under consideration while members observe, take notes, or in other ways identify with the participants. Small groups may be assigned to sit behind individual members and quietly coach or encourage them as they operate in the fishbowl. (See Fig. 5–4.) By having periodic recesses, the discussion member can meet with those assigned to observe him to receive their coaching and encouragement. At some point in the discussion, it may be well to reverse the position of the observers and participants. This increases the participation and insights of both groups.

A variation of the fishbowl is to have designated seats in the fishbowl left unoccupied. (See Fig. 5–5.) Observers are allowed to participate in the fishbowl activity but only by moving into the unoccupied seat. They should be recognized and their input encouraged as soon as possible by the group. Persons who enter the designated empty seats should remain there only as long as their individual input is under direct action by the group. They should then vacate the seat and return to the observer status so that others outside the fishbowl may occupy the open seat as the issues or areas of particular interest stimulate them to participate.

The fishbowl technique is normally used with all participants on the same floor level. Planners should consider the size of the group when using this technique, since it is absolutely necessary that the observers be able to

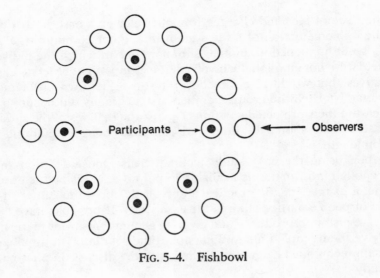

FIG. 5–4.   Fishbowl

see and hear clearly what is being said by those in the fishbowl. When the leader feels the group has thoroughly discussed the assigned issue or topic, he or she may wish to open the total discussion to both the fishbowl participants and observers or may wish to restrict all comments to the group's process alone, that is, what happened within the group and which roles were instrumental in the discussion.

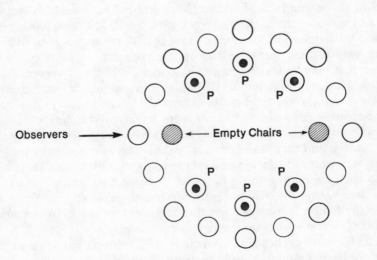

FIG. 5–5.   Open Fishbowl

THE COMMITTEE TECHNIQUE

A committee is two or more people elected or appointed to investigate, deliberate, sponsor, act, or report on matters that have been assigned to them on behalf of a larger body of which they are a part. The word committee comes from the Latin term "committare" which means "to entrust." Committees are groups entrusted with the responsibility of acting on behalf of others. For our purposes, the term is used to include a variety of recreation groups—such as recreation councils, advisory boards, commissions, and task forces—that use the committee process in the normal conducting of their action. Membership in a committee is usually limited to those who have been appointed or elected because of their singular and/or collective ability to contribute to the assignment before the group. By its nature, it is a subgroup to some other authority or larger body. A joint committee represents two or more authorities and/or organizations. Occasionally, a self-appointed committee emerges when a group of persons identify among themselves a common interest and come together to deliberate and act upon the matter. In doing so, they serve the interest of the larger group or community.

The committee technique allows for an orderly discussion and resolution of a task by a small group; it is a laboratory for democratic leadership. Once the committee is charged with its responsibility, it should be given the necessary freedom and autonomy to act collectively on behalf of the larger body. Because it should be accountable for its actions, it should periodically report its activities and findings to the parent body that established or appointed it. In such instances where committees are appointed to explore an issue and make a recommendation to the parent body, the parent body is not bound by the decision of the committee. In other words, it may receive the report of the committee and its recommended solution but not act upon those recommendations if it feels the committee's choice was not in the best interest of the parent body. A committee should never exceed the authority given it.

The committee chairperson may be selected by the parent body or chosen by the committee membership. If the latter course is pursued, the parent body should only appoint a convener of the committee, one who serves to bring the group together until such time as the committee chooses its own chairperson. Like the moderator, the chairperson's role is one of supervising and facilitating the group's action. Basic to this is the organizing of the group to achieve its goal, to structure the activities of the group in such a way that it can effectively carry out its assignment. Once formed, the committee should assess the skills of its members, develop its plan of action, and act accordingly. In this way, the group experiences the benefit of shared leadership through a mutual commitment and freedom to achieve its goal. It may use any one or all of the small group techniques previously mentioned in this chapter as it proceeds with its assignment.

MAJOR FUNCTIONS OF COMMITTEES
1. To make decisions on matters of policy, program, or action.
2. To make recommendations regarding policy, program, or action.
3. To give advice to an executive or perhaps to some policy-determining body.
4. To direct or supervise an executive, subexecutive, or staff member.
5. To effect coordination among the members and the departments, groups, or other units which they represent.
6. To study, make inquiries, or carry on fact finding.
7. To visit or inspect.
8. To educate the committee members.
9. To promote sound public relations.
10. To carry on administrative or service activities.
11. To select, appoint, or approve personnel.
12. To render judgment or to arbitrate in cases of conflicting claims or interests.
13. To sponsor or endorse an agency, program, or undertaking.
14. To assist in a ceremonial function.[3]

The size of the committee depends on the task assigned. The nature of the assignment and the need for representation determine the parameters of the size. Most committees are small, three to seven members, and are task-oriented. This is especially true with committees given policy responsibility or working on some investigatory assignment. Occasionally committees have communitywide responsibility and are involved in a fund raising or public relations activity. Needless to say, large committees necessitate more structure and subgrouping (subcommittees). Commonly, the discussion method is used in conducting committee business.

A committee is no better than its individual members. Important criteria for selection are interest and knowledge of the matters to be considered, past experience with any aspect of the assignment, and knowledge of the committee process. Since the committee is generally task-oriented, its membership should be composed of persons committed to "getting the job done." High interest in the assignment coupled with some knowledge of the specifics involved is a motivating factor that moves the group toward its goals. The designated authority, be it a person or sponsor, has the responsibility of selecting committee members who have demonstrated a willingness to "be involved" and who have some general knowledge of the area to be investigated. Of course, some committee members are selected because of the groups they represent or because of their particular status in the community.

As an illustration of the above comments, consider the creation of a capital improvements committee by the recreation commission. The committee is responsible for successfully planning and conducting a recreation bond election. The choice of committee members is critical. There must be representation from the various interests and neighborhoods of the community, or else their support will not be assured. There must be individuals who know how to organize a community for a bond election, as well as those who can interpret or legitimize the actions of the committee to their constituents. It is important to have both workers and "named" people on the committee. The chairperson must be a competent organizer, and the committee must very early in its life develop its organizational plan and calendar of action. Once the bond election is completed, the committee will be disbanded; it will have done its job.

The chairperson's responsibilities are similar to those of the moderator. He or she is responsible for the committee's general work plan, scheduling its meetings, moderating its discussions, appointing subcommittees, summarizing its accomplishments, and reporting its findings, actions, and recommendations to the parent body.

Committee members are responsible for attending committee meetings, making sure the objectives of each meeting are clearly stated, actively participating in the decision making process of the committee, accepting responsibility for following through on those tasks assigned by the chairperson, and assisting in maintaining a sense of commitment to achieving the special purpose of the committee's work.

The committee's records are important. At the completion of each meeting, minutes should be prepared, under the general supervision of the chairperson, and made available to the committee members. The minutes serve two purposes: they are a history of the committee's action and a reminder of the committee's future activities and individual responsibilities. The minutes should indicate which members have been given assignments and the proposed date of their report. In that way, individual committee members, when they read the minutes, may be reminded of their obligations to the committee. The minutes should be distributed to the committee members before the next meeting. Three to five days before the next meeting, members should receive minutes of the previous meeting, the agenda of the next meeting, and any reports that must be made at that meeting. The agenda should be prepared by the chairperson and/or an agenda subcommittee. Each committee should have a procedure whereby individual committee members can make sure their concerns are placed on the agenda.

Most committees using the small group discussion technique decide by consensus. Occasionally some large group parliamentary procedure may seem desirable, particularly when there are strong differing opinions within the committee, where resolutions seem impossible using the consensus approach, or when the committee is too large to use the small group discussion technique effectively. Some knowledge of the fundamentals of parliamentary procedure is essential for the conduct of committee meetings. It may not be necessary to follow strictly *Robert's Rules of Order,* but some basic underlying principles of good parliamentary procedure should be adhered to. It is recommended that:

1. An orderly procedure be followed;
2. Every proposal presented for consideration is entitled to a full discussion;
3. The rights of all members are equal;
4. The rule of the majority prevails;
5. The rights of the minority must be respected;
6. The needs and interests of the represented organization is of more importance than are the needs and interests of individual committee members. The important consideration is that which is in the best interest of the group as a whole.

SUMMARY

In this chapter we have examined several techniques that can be applied to small groups. The dynamic process of small groups can be more effectively guided by a recreation or park professional who is familiar with these techniques: their values, structure, procedure used, and leadership roles. Each of the seven techniques examined—Small Group Discussion, Brainstorming, Buzz Group, Role Playing, Case Study, Fishbowl, and Committee—has its unique value and ideal use. They should be used selectively and in the appropriate relationship to the group situation.

EXERCISES AND STUDY SUGGESTIONS

Although desirable, it is difficult to provide an exercise for each of the small group techniques discussed in this chapter. Since many are similar in form, we have elected to include a representative grouping. For additional exercises, we highly recommend you review the exercises in the several, annual books by Pfeiffer and Jones, *A Handbook of Structured Experiences for Human Relations Training.* See also Johnson and Johnson, *Joining Together.* Both these resources were mentioned in earlier chapters.

Listening Triads: Building Communication Skills*

Goal:	To develop skills in active listening and to identify and overcome barriers to effective listening.
Time Needed:	Thirty to forty-five minutes
Setting:	A room large enough to allow an unlimited number of triads (groups of three).
Procedure:	This is an exercise to aid in the development of listening skills so fundamental to small group discussions. To begin the exercise, divide the group into subgroups of three. Assign the following roles. For each subgroup there will be a discussant (participant A), a listener (participant B), and a referee (participant C). List on the chalkboard topics of controversy or interest from which the group may choose one for discussion purposes. Have the speaker (participant A) discuss the topic. Both the listener and referee should remain silent. The listener and discussant should work to establish nonverbal cues so that discussion can be properly paced. Once the discussant has finished his topic, the listener (participant B) must summarize, in his or her own words and without notes what the discussant said.

If the summary is felt to be incorrect, both the speaker and the referee are free to interrupt and correct any misunderstanding. The referee (participant C) should make sure the listener does not omit, distort, add to, respond to, or interpret what the speaker has said. The listener is simply to summarize what he or she has heard. The total process of speaking and summarizing should take no more than seven minutes for each round.

When the first round is completed, the roles are reversed, the listener (participant B) becomes the speaker, the referee (participant C) becomes the listener, and the speaker (participant A) becomes the referee. A new topic for discussion is chosen and the group repeats the exercise. The exercise should be repeated once more so that all have a chance to participate in each role.

Situation:	Have the group develop a general list of topics that might be of interest to all. Place these on the chalkboard. The brainstorming technique might be used to generate these

* Reprinted from: J. W. Pfeiffer and J. E. Jones (Eds.), *A Handbook of Structured Experiences for Human Relations Training*, Vol. I (Rev.), San Diego, CA: University Associates, 1974. Used with permission.

topics. Previous groups have found some of the following topics interesting:

Drug Use and Abuse

Women's Liberation

Interracial Marriages

Homosexuality

Competitive Athletics

Preservation of the Environment

Discussion: After the third round everyone should have had an opportunity to function in each of the three roles—listener, speaker, referee. Have the subgroups discuss the difficulties they experienced in each of those roles, what they learned about themselves as listeners and observers, and the general value of this exercise. Make sure the discussion includes an identification of those barriers that inhibited listening and the general applicability of the paraphrasing techniques to other discussion situations.

Role Playing

There are many types of role plays. We've just completed one by having each of you assume the role of discussant, listener, and referee. No instructions were given to you as to how to play your role. That decision was based on your own perception of the responsibilities required when carrying out the task inherent in each of these roles. Normally, when one is involved in a role play, the limits of the role are well-defined in advance, and the experience becomes one of simulation. We try to get into a role set—that is, become someone else or carry out a responsibility that involved several roles—such as husband, father, recreation director—simultaneously.

Here are two role playing exercises that involve a multiple role assumption. They are typical of what we normally assume a role playing exercise to be when somebody mentions role playing.

The Informal Role Play Exercise.   Decide if you want to design each of the following situations for role playing either in a tightly structured manner (with a background statement for each person in which some of the basic information about that person's role such as "wife of athletic director, married three years with no children, teaches fourth grade, enjoys swimming, sewing and jazz music, well-traveled since father was military officer, etc.") or in a loosely structured one with no role data given other than the role term "wife." If you structure it tightly, privately give each role player the facts of his or her role before presenting the situation. The facts might be written on a card to be given to the players, or they may be given verbally in a private conversation. If you choose a loosely structured role play, you need only describe the situation and let the participants feel their own way into the roles. In either case, the role play begins with a reading of the situation.

Situation 1. The recreation commission for Smithfield, a city of 23,000, is composed of seven members plus the director. Some questions have come up about the assistant director's social behavior—his way of dealing with female staff and volunteers, his "hands-on" style, and some inattention to work hours. These complaints have been taken to the recreation commission chairperson. The director knows the assistant director as a good worker; he gets his job done well. The director and the seven commission members are meeting to discuss the situation; a decision must be made.

Situation 2. A parent has discovered that the members of her child's soccer team have been smoking marijuana after practice and at some team meetings. The soccer players are between the ages of twelve and fourteen. She is incensed and has asked for an appointment with the recreation director and the athletic director. The role play begins with the mother's arrival at the recreation director's office.

Situation 3. The park superintendent is giving a quarterly evaluation and feedback to a staff member who is fifty years old and who has been doing a "so-so" job. The staff member has just entered the superintendent's office.

For each of these situations, you (the facilitator) should feel free to cut the role play when you feel the players are involved enough with the situation to really talk about their feelings, what is going on, and what might have been other appropriate ways of handling the issue. After the role players have had a chance to discuss their feelings and views, it would be well to invite other members of the group (the observers) to talk about their perceptions and ask for their suggestions as to how the situation could have been handled. In fact, it might be well to role play the same situation using one of the alternative suggestions with a different set of "actors" assuming the same set of roles.

The Formal Role Play. In the formal role play situation the group is not told the objective of the role play. The exercise begins with the distribution of the roles and the reading of the situation. The role play, however, does have a specific objective that will be revealed once the role play is completed and the discussion phase is over. In fact, the last question asked by the facilitator should be "What do you think the purpose of this role play was?" The facilitator should have the goal statement written before beginning the role play since the questions asked by the facilitator are directly related to the goal statement.

A Status Role Play*

Goal: To explore the effects of status differences on the feelings and interaction among the group members.

Time Needed: Forty-five minutes

Setting: A committee meeting with chairs for six to twelve participants. If the room is large enough, two or more groups can "perform" this role play simultaneously.

Process: The role play begins with the formation of the role play group. The group members, six to ten participants, are told they are the planning committee for a student organization. The organization is meeting to plan its annual spring outing. The choices of location have been narrowed to a very popular beach resort (i.e., Fort Lauderdale, Catalina Island) and a popular ski resort (i.e., Aspen, Mount Washington). The final choice is to be made by the planning committee today. Two members of the committee are new and have not met with the group before. The group arranges its chairs in a circle leaving two chairs for the new members. One of the chairs will be designated for the faculty advisor; the other chair is designated as for a new student. At this point, the facilitator should ask two people to be the new group members and have them leave the room for a briefing. Once they are out of the room, the facilitator should level with the group about the actual objectives of the experience. He should say, "The two new members of your committee are very different in terms of prestige and power. One is a very popular faculty member who will serve as advisor on this trip. He loves the coast and has written several poems about the seashore. He is enthusiastic about his selection as faculty advisor. The second new member of your committee is a sophomore who spent last winter ski bumming and is an accomplished skier. He was selected to take the place of another sophomore who dropped out of school. Your by-laws dictate that at least one member of the committee must be a sophomore."

The facilitator should then say, "This is important. The new members of your committee will be told only that they are new members of your committee. They will not

---

* Reprinted from: J. W. Pfeiffer and J. E. Jones (Eds.), *A Handbook of Structured Experiences for Human Relations Training*, Vol. II (Rev.). San Diego, CA: University Associates, 1974. Used with permission.

know that one is a faculty member and the other is a student. It is essential that you do not reveal this to them by using such titles as professor or doctor or by asking such information as a faculty member might be presumed to have. Just call them by their given names."

Once this is done, you (the facilitator) should meet with the new members away from where the others can hear them and brief them in the following manner:

"You remember my description of the committee whose job is to choose a location for the spring trip. You are to be the new members of the committee. You have not met them before. When the meeting is over, I will ask each of you how you felt about the reception the committee gave you." The facilitator should then ask one of them to support the beach trip; the other is to support the ski trip. The new members then join the committee, sitting in their respective chairs, and the discussion phase begins. It should last for ten to fifteen minutes with the group honestly seeking to make a decision about the location of the trip.

Discussion: When the committee discussion period is over, the facilitator should ask the new members how they felt about the reception they received. After the interviews, the facilitator should ask the group to share with the new members the real intent of the exercise and the magic of their roles. The discussion should center on the effects power and prestige have on the decision making process, the attributes we ascribe to people based upon their title or "expertise," the group's feelings about the role play, and what they learned from it.

Brainstorming

With groups of ten, brainstorm other situations that could be used for role plays. After developing the list, polish the situations in a manner that would allow them to be duplicated and used in this or some other succeeding leadership course or training session. Try to identify situations that involve various specialties and branches of the park and recreation profession.

Another interesting brainstorm is to select a group of five class members and have them arrange themselves in a semi-circle. The facilitator should join the group and pose the following problem: "We have been asked by the Brick Manufacturers of America to develop new markets for their product. Let us see, in the next three to five minutes, how many different uses of bricks we can generate. Based on our ideas, the Brick Manufacturers of America will enter into a national advertising campaign titled *The Many Uses of Bricks*." Be sure to have a couple of class members record the ideas developed. Also, the facilitator should remind the group not to elaborate or make value judgment remarks while the exercise is in progress. The facilitator should apply as much pressure as she can to make sure all members participate. She should be firm and somewhat autocratic as she solicits opinions.

Once the group has generated its ideas, the facilitator can involve them in a small group discussion to see which of their ideas really have a merit. She may wish to involve the entire class by dividing it into buzz groups of five members, charging each to discuss and evaluate the ideas generated.

Case Study

Another technique that allows for the use of two or more small group techniques is the case study. By dividing the large group into buzz groups of five persons, each group can be assigned the responsibility for developing a case study that might be duplicated and used by other small groups as a basis for study and discussion. The case studies might be developed around such issues as the relationship of job performance and job description; marriage problems (a couple with poor communications); a supervisory training session; roommates in conflict; an employee stealing from the agency; a management training session; and a human relations situation involving sexual or racial discrimination. Your buzz group may want to select a situation close to its own experience, rather than deal with one of the suggested areas. In either case, the written case studies should not exceed two pages. All the pertinent facts and problem elements should be included. The outcome of the case studies should be omitted, thereby forcing the group to consider alternative results and consequences.

Committee

Rather than simulate a committee experience, the group can experience this technique by visiting committees in action. Assign each class member, individually or in pairs or trios, to observe a committee in the community and report on observations. Each should examine carefully the committee's leadership structure, participation patterns, ability to problem solve, subgroups, conflicts, norms, social climate, decision making processes, and other relevant areas critical to the committee's functioning. Also, each should pay particular attention to the small group procedures and techniques employed and offer suggestions on how the committee could improve its functioning. Each may wish to share its observations with the committee. A written report based on these observations should be prepared and submitted to the instructor. The written report would serve as an excellent practice in report writing based upon direct observation.

Small Group Discussions

The democratic discussion group style can be used when discussing any topic or when using any one of the small group discussion techniques identified in this chapter. It stresses group involvement and interaction with no dominant leader. Using this approach, have your group work through this exercise of establishing a New Society.

New Society

Goal: To provide practice and small group functioning using various small group discussion techniques. The exercise should (a) increase interaction of participants, (b) increase mutual interdependence and group consensus seeking, and (c) enable reexamination of basic personal and social values.

Time Needed: Sixty to ninety minutes

Setting: Create groups of seven to twelve persons. It is preferable to have a mixed group and to assign one member of the group the role of process observer.

Assignment: Your task is to create a new society. Establish the objectives for your group, the only living people on earth. To do this, basic values must be considered. Any ground rules for future behavior should be established and consideration should be given to how these will affect the persons in your group. Remember, the society you establish determines the future of the human race. Your discussion should touch on group values, society rules, support systems, leadership styles, public policy, child bearing and child raising practices, etc.

Situation: The facilitator should say: "You are the sole survivors of a total disaster holocaust. This disaster could have been caused either from within or beyond our planet system. Source or cause is not relevant to your problem. By some means you have discovered each other and come together here in a rural and undevastated area. Plan your society."

Discussion: Have each subgroup share with the class its process and plan. It is suggested that one of the small group presentation techniques, such as fishbowl, be used when presenting your plan. Have the process observer for each group share with the class his/her evaluation of the group's process. Particular attention might be given to the interaction patterns of the group members as well as roles played. The process observer should not deal with the validity of the group's plan, only its process. The group's presentation to the class should deal only with its plan, not its process. Have the entire class discuss the significance of this exercise, what they learned about themselves and the task of building a new society.

ENDNOTES

1. George M. Beal, Joe M. Bohlen, and J. Neil Raudabaugh, *Leadership and Dynamic Group Action* (Ames, Iowa: The Iowa State University Press, 1962), pp. 185, 186.
2. Alan Klein, *Role Playing* (New York: Association Press, 1956), p. 21.
3. Arthur Dunham, *Community Welfare Organization* (New York: Thomas Y. Crowell Company, 1958), pp. 390–96, 399–411.

SUGGESTED READINGS

Bergevin, Paul, and McKinley, John. *Participation Training for Adult Education.* St. Louis: Bethany Press, 1965.

Bradford, Leland P. *Making Meetings Work.* La Jolla, Calif.: University Associates, 1976.

Klein, Alan F. *How to Use Role Playing Effectively.* New York: Association Press, 1959.

Leypoldt, Martha M. *Forty Ways to Teach in Groups.* Valley Forge, Penn.: Judson Press, 1967. See Chapters 1 and 3.

Potter, David, and Anderson, Martin. *Discussion in Small Groups: A Guide to Effective Practice,* 3rd ed. Belmont, Calif.: Wadsworth Publishing Co., 1976. See Chapters 8–11.

Chapter Six

LARGE GROUP TECHNIQUES

The last chapter focused on small groups, both in theory and in exercise. Now we turn to larger groups and expand upon those concepts and principles. To carry out their responsibilities effectively, recreation and park professionals need to be familiar with the characteristics and techniques of larger groups. From the annual National Congress of the National Recreation and Park Association to the monthly meetings of the community Parents' Boosters Club, from the state professional societies to the training clinic for clients enrolled in a scuba course, recreators are in contact with large groups. The effective planning and leadership of large group meetings are therefore necessary tools.

Basic to our understanding is a definition: "Small groups" include up to twelve to fifteen people, with twenty as a maximum. In many cases, especially formal learning situations, any group of over fifteen could be considered a "large group." Also basic to our understanding are the settings in which large group techniques are employed. On the one hand, it should be recognized that many large group meetings are for such groups as parents of little or pony leaguers, teen representatives, or persons in a neighborhood interested in backing development of a particular recreation program or facility. These kinds of large group meetings are generally one-time meetings and should be carefully planned. On the other hand, large group techniques are used in continuing education and training programs. In our rapidly changing society it is necessary that the knowledge and skills of both professional and volunteer workers in the park and recreation and leisure service fields be upgraded regularly and consistently through clinics, congresses, conventions, conferences, institutes, learning laboratories, retreats, workshops, and similar large group meetings. Most of these will last two or more days.

Following are descriptions of these techniques for large groups.

Clinic. The emphasis here is on problems: their diagnosis, analysis, and solution. In the clinic, the effort is directed toward recognizing existing problems in a community or an organization. Through the use of selected techniques, examined in another section of this chapter, problems can be studied in a lifelike or realistic way that can lead to solutions and strategies to effect solutions. Examples of clinic study areas could include: "Vandalism in Our Parks"; "Developing a Steady Flow of Volunteers"; and "Broadening the Leisure Opportunity Awareness of Our Citizens." A limited and select number of representatives are invited to participate in the clinic.

Congress or Convention. This is perhaps the largest group method, with participants numbering from a hundred or so to several thousand; examples include the National Recreation and Park Association Congress or your state recreation and park society's annual convention. Many kinds of large group meetings, involving many kinds of techniques, would be involved in each of these programs. Multiple divisions within a congress— such as Therapeutic Recreators, Board and Committee Members, and Professional Recreation Educators—would each have their own series of meetings, banquets, and training programs. In addition, general sessions and large banquets can be held for the entire membership present at the convention or congress. Clinics, institutes, and workshops may be a part of the convention format.

Conference. The term *conference* means "a bringing together." Some confuse "conference" with congresses or conventions. However, a conference should include people brought together to confer about a particular informational area. It is not a term applied best to an annual meeting of a professional association, unless participants are dealing with conferring or with pooling knowledge, experiences, and opinions in efforts at fact finding, problem identification, information exchange, inspiration, or decision making. A term recently applied to some smaller conferences is "task force" when a particular problem is addressed.

Institute. Usually a series of meetings in consecutive or sequential manner forms the institute. It is designed to convey specific information and instruction in particular work areas. Participants usually learn in groups, but individual study can also be emphasized. Examples would be "Communication Skills," "Coastal Estuary Problems," and "Coping with Drugs in Recreation Programs."

Learning Laboratory. The laboratory or lab meeting is usually conducted in continuous residence. Specialized training is provided in personal skills, such as personal growth, conflict resolution, experimental education, life and career planning, systems approach to institutions, and organization development. In the laboratory program, considerable emphasis is placed on case study or other "live world" exercises in which participants involve their total selves and skills, cognitively and effectively. Laboratory learning was mentioned earlier as having begun at Bethel, Maine, directly resulting from teaching and research by Kurt Lewin and his followers.

Retreat. This large group meeting term has been borrowed from religion groups. It means, quite literally, retreat from the normal environment. The parallel is retreat *to* another environment, usually in a rural and natural setting such as a camp. Away from office phones, daily work demands, and the people with whom most work days are spent, participants are more emotionally free to concentrate on the learning experience. Here also a variety of techniques can be applied to the meetings, as in the other methods. Isolation, concentration, focus, and development of closeness among the learners are key values of the retreat method.[1]

Workshop. In the workshop setting the emphasis is on the individual learner and improving his or her skills and knowledge. Ideally a workshop lasts two days or longer, thus allowing all participants to be involved in planning, working, and evaluating. Participants should be involved for the entire time and should not arrive late or depart early. In a workshop techniques are chosen to minimize lectures and maximally involve participants actively in the learning experience. The program of study in a workshop should develop from the needs and interests of the participants. Examples of workshop study areas could be "Maintenance Skills for Park Personnel," "Operating City Swimming Facilities," and "Preparing and Obtaining Grant Monies for Your Recreation Facilities."

PLANNING FOR LARGE GROUP MEETINGS

Three groups of people are usually involved in large group meetings: (1) the audience or participants, (2) the leaders or platform personnel and other resource people, and (3) the planners. Those who plan, either as individuals or as a planning committee, have a most important job. How many times have you heard people complain about sitting through a boring meeting? How many meetings have you yourself attended and could hardly wait until it was over? Untold dull hours are wasted because those who planned the meeting did not do their job as well as they might have. There is no acceptable excuse for a boring or ineffective meeting if it is properly planned and the participants and leadership are carefully prepared for their roles. The following may assist you in carrying out your responsibilities.

I.   Be aware of the problems you may encounter so that constructive actions can be taken in the planning process. Among the major problems are:

   A.   In many meetings with large groups of people, the audience remains mostly passive. People listen but are not active participants.

   B.   Audience members may understand and even identify with content presented by the leaders. However, they are not led to plan the steps necessary to put new ideas into action.

   C.   Audience members remain individuals rather than members of a group. The lack of reinforcement or "sparked" ideas from others in the audience causes information from leaders to filter through their minds and be lost.

   D.   When not led to participate, audience members tend to feel they are less able or more uninformed than the leaders. For many, it is easier to accept noninvolvement passively and leave early for the "happy hour" or other social activities, than to make the effort to listen and learn.[2]

II.   Remember that much of the same body of basic truths applies to large group meetings as applies to small group meetings. In addition to the basics in the philosophy of learning:

   A.   Examine carefully the interests and needs of the potential audience participants for they are the primary purpose of the meeting.

   B.   Select the most appropriate physical resources and consider seats, lights, temperature, visibility, hearing, and the emotional atmosphere set by the physical environment for the group and for the topic or theme.

   C.   Give extended consideration to leadership and resource persons. Never get somebody who is simply familiar with the topic. Aim for the best leaders and try to "hook" their interest in the group. The better they are, the more likely they are to be heavily scheduled, so plan far in advance. Write details to them, and follow with a phone call in a week or so.

   D.   Make sure your audience participants participate! With leaders and topic set, choose the techniques and methods that will best accomplish the goals. The methods used must be consistent with the audience's background and needs, the topic under consideration, and the leaders employed.

III.   Develop an agenda. The following is a six-step agenda for the planning session:

   A.   Find out as much as possible about the population for whom the meeting is planned so as to determine their *interests* and *needs*.

B. Develop the *topic* or *theme* based on their needs and interests.

C   Set the *goals* and *objectives* to meet the topic or theme.

D. Select the *resources* to be used in the meeting, including leadership and physical environment.

E. Select the *methods* and *techniques,* combined with resources, to reach the goals.

F. Outline the *meeting schedule* tentatively so as to determine the most effective progress and timing for the meeting.[3]

IV. *Keep in mind these other consideratons for good planning.* The success of the large group meeting, whether it lasts for one hour or several days, depends to some degree on several dynamics:

A. *Size of the Group.* The number of participants will affect choice of room, seating, and all physical arrangements. Techniques are selected with some consideration for the size of the group. The number of resource and leadership personnel will also be affected by the number of persons in the group.

B. *Age and Sex of Participants.* These factors can affect choice of educational aids as well as techniques. Leaders should be chosen, in part, so participants can identify with them and be more effective in the teaching-learning process.

C. *Professional and Social Backgrounds of Participants.* These give clues about the educational level, personal or work needs, and primary interests of the participants. Topic and goal selection are affected, as are all other components of the planning process.

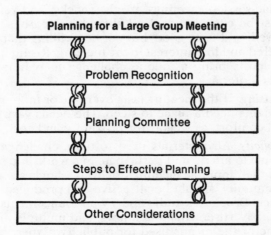

FIG. 6–1. Planning

D. *Sponsorship.* This refers to the groups, organizations, companies, or agencies that sponsor the meeting or will send the bulk or all of the participants. Interests and needs of sponsors necessarily affect the purpose, perhaps also the conduct, of the meeting. But, although visible involvement of sponsors can have productive results, too much visible involvement can also produce resistance in participants. Increasingly, large group meetings are co-sponsored by joint decision making organizations. Sometimes their support is only financial; others prefer to be directly involved in planning. This can multiply communications problems and cause complex planning procedures. It can also be very positive when each sponsor sends able and cooperative representatives to the planning meeting.

E. *Duration.* The length of meetings affects costs, meal planning, and housing. Consideration must be given to smaller, multiple meetings within larger ones. For example, two or three one-half day meetings, for participants who live nearby and can go home for the night, could be preferable to a continuous two-day meeting in residence with participants' expense increased for motel or hotel residence and extra on-site meals.

F. *Physical Environment.* Decor, size of meeting rooms, acoustics, visibility of leadership, seating, tables (if used), temperature and humidity—all affect the general atmosphere of the meeting and the efficiency of the teaching-learning process. A fine line must be drawn between providing comfort and letting participants become so comfortable that they get lost in drowsiness.

G. *Food.* If there is more than one session, and for many single-session meetings, meals, snacks, and refreshments must be considered. Food should be nearby, attractively served, and taste good, but not be so filling that people get stuffed and lose interest in the meeting. Rising food and labor costs bring a unique challenge to planners to meet these criteria.

H. *Housing.* If the meeting lasts over one or more nights, participants need a place to sleep. The needs vary for quality and comfort, as well as for proximity and cost.

I. *Publicity.* All materials used to urge, challenge, or entice people to attend and participate in a workshop or congress and their multiple meetings, or even a single session in your community, should be attractive and produced well in advance. Brochures, radio and TV announcements, news stories, advertisements, interviews, and multiple mailings are some of the means used for publicity. Expert and careful attention must be given here, or all the planning can go for naught. There is *no* meeting if participants do not attend!

J. *Transportation.* If participants travel from their homes to a
strange area, transportation must be planned for them. It
could be from the airport or train station to the site of the
meetings and a return trip at the conclusion. Should there
be multiple meeting sites, the planners must consider how
to get participants from one site to another. Group members without cars depend on either planned or public transportation.

K. *Schedule and Timing.* Every meeting should be carefully
scheduled. Detailed time outlines are necessary for some,
such as a banquet that includes the introduction of
"honored guests," speakers, or entertainment. For other
meetings merely a starting and ending time will suffice.

In the case of conventions or congresses with multiple
meetings over several days, integration of the many events
in the schedule is most important for the planners. Such
things as lag time for walking between meetings, time for
"breaks" and refreshments, meals, rest, recreation, sleep,
and entertainment as well as the general sessions and many
smaller meetings must be considered.

Also included in "timing" for the planners are dead-
lines for such things as selection of leadership, arrangement for housing and facilities, printing and mailing of
publicity materials, and receipts of registration fees and applications. Most large motels, hotels, and convention centers staff specialists who can assist in the planning. Involve
them.

L. *Leadership.* Some discussion has already been given to this
topic. The most capable leaders should be selected and
agreement made with them. "Well known" or "highly
placed" (the person with the "big" job or title) does not necessarily mean the most capable. Someone who can do the
job should be sought but only after it has been determined
exactly what the job is. If the leaders are not from the immediate area, arrangement for transportation, room and
board, and any fees or honoraria expected should be discussed openly and agreed on by all involved.

M. *Technique Selection.* When the topic, goals, timing, and
leadership are selected in the light of the population to participate in the meeting, the selection of techniques can take
place. Care and thought should go into this. Consider
leaders' skills, group size, physical surroundings, amount of
time, as well as what is to be accomplished. Your philosophy of the teaching-learning process will affect your
choices, also.

Maximizing participants' involvement should be a
goal. To that end, techniques that will help achieve maximum involvement should be selected. Subtechniques to

increase the involvement may be melded with other techniques. Educational aids, carefully prepared and presented, can also assist in meeting the goal of participant
involvement.

N. *Equipment Needed.* Careful advance planning will include
providing all necessary sound amplification systems;
movie, slide, opaque, or overhead projectors and screens;
extension cords; extra bulbs, in case of burnouts; and other
items that must be considered. Provision should also be
made for leadership and participant seating, adequate
lighting and ventilation, "breaks," and physical rearrange-
ment of the room if the various techniques necessitate
this.

O. *Public Relations and Courtesy Rooms.* In larger meetings
special needs nearly always arise; these can be met with a
courtesy room staff. Greeting arrivals and helping them get
registered and settled, answering questions about the facilities, site, and community, scheduling a "job mart" if it is
planned, and a message board will all be part of the public
relations. This can help make the atmosphere of the entire
meeting and cannot be emphasized too strongly. The importance of friendly, informed, courteous, and helpful
personnel on the public relations staff will facilitate the
success of the meeting.

P. *Evaluation.* Chapter Ten focuses on evaluation throughout
all areas of group functioning. It is sufficient here to say
that those who plan large group meetings should definitely
plan concrete evaluation and follow-up procedures as part
of their overall planning process. Failure in this area will
cause loss of information valuable to successive meetings.
Follow-up will include applying action decisions and evaluations to participants in this meeting as well as planning for
future meetings.

Q. *Budget and Financing.* Although this item was left till last
for emphasis, the other sixteen items would not work without it. Nearly every large group costs money; the larger the
meeting, the more important and involved is the budgetary
process.

How meetings are financed must be considered.
Much of the cost will come from funds left from previous
meetings, organization or agency budgets, or government
grants. The budget should allow for publicity, brochures,
newsletters, or other printed materials related to the meeting. Rental of films and equipment, honoraria or fees for
speakers or other leaders, and rental fees for the rooms and
meeting site are a few of the many items that must be considered in the budget. If the planning committee has travel
or meal expenses, these should also be included.

TECHNIQUES FOR LEARNING

The individual or committee responsible for planning structures the large group meeting. In the planning process decisions are made on how to combine the learners, their goals, the leadership, and the available resources with learning techniques to facilitate accomplishing the goals of the meeting.

The techniques described in this section are only suggestions. It is expected that planners and/or leaders will be creative in adapting, modifying, and combining techniques. The resulting meeting plan should be one that maximizes the learning opportunity for that group of learners in that situation. The following techniques are presented in alphabetical order with no intent to evaluate by priority.[4]

Colloquy—A highly flexible technique, the colloquy is composed of three units of participants—a panel of two to four outside resource persons, three or four representatives selected from the audience, and the audience itself. (See Fig. 6–2.) A moderator controls the interaction. The panel's credibility is greatly increased in the eyes of the audience, since some of "its own" are representing them. Audience representatives present a problem to the resource experts or ask questions that originated in the audience. Resource persons respond with information from their particular knowledge and interest in the subject. Audience members participate, under the guidance of the moderator, whenever feasible. This can be done either verbally or by sending questions to representatives on the panel.

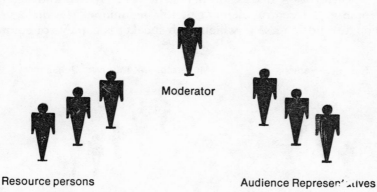

Moderator

Resource persons   Audience Represen'_.tives

Audience or learners

FIG. 6–2.   The Colloquy

The colloquy is effective in several situations: (a) when strong interest in a problem has been generated but the group is too large or feelings are too intense to have trust in the panel alone; (b) when interest in a problem is desirable but is low or nonexistent in a particular audience group; (c) when a follow-up technique of this nature is desirable after a panel, symposium, or speech.

Committee Hearing—The committee hearing is the questioning of one or two experts by a select group before an audience. (See Fig. 6–3.) This is a rather formal technique, used frequently by Congressional committees. Television has brought to our homes popular shows, such as "Meet the Press" and "Face the Nation," that use this technique. Less formally it can be used to obtain information from a consultant by a questioning committee. Television has done this in "What's My Line?"

While resembling the interview, the committee hearing permits the committee to control the situation and makes much greater use of variations in the questioners' and respondents' skills and knowledge. It allows deeper probing of resource experts or consultants, and is useful when a speech or symposium is not feasible because of certain circumstances—e.g., a knowledgable resource person who is a poor speaker. This technique also builds a psychological bridge between audience and platform leaders. In "touchy" or highly questionable situations, this "closeness," once developed, can facilitate learning better than a speech or interview.

Dialogue—A discussion before a group by two knowledgeable people is the central element of this technique. The dialogue is a thoughtful discourse in which each speaker is capable of communi-

Resource Persons   **Moderator (in center) and Questioners**

Audience

Fig. 6–3. The Committee Hearing

cating clearly his or her ideas and of listening and responding sensitively to the specific ideas of the other. Less formal than a lecture or a panel, the dialogue is conversational, quite informal, and allows shared responsibility and mutual support. Considerable interest can be developed among audience members, especially if the two engaged in the dialogue are articulate and/or witty. Visuals can supplement the spoken words and cues from audience reactions can be "read" to encourage validation, clarification, and probing deeper on points of questions. (See Fig. 6–4.)

The ease of planning and simplicity of physical arrangements make the dialogue a useful technique, perhaps not used enough in large groups. The two discussants should be given careful, clear instructions about the technique and its parameters and workings, as well as about the topic framework and time limits.

Demonstration—The demonstration is a presentation by an expert which *shows* how to follow a procedure or perform a skill or act. Appropriate oral and visual illustrations, questions, and explanations are included.

The major value of this technique is that the audience members first watch or listen to the expert's demonstration, and then they practice individually the skill or act. Examples would be cardiopulmonary resuscitation or the proper sequence of the leg kick and arm movements in the swimmer's breast stroke.

Planners or coordinators of this technique need to make certain that the demonstrator or his aide(s) can do three things well:

1. Personally accomplish the skill or art;
2. Vividly and clearly express the sequence of steps and key points of the skill;
3. Give expert guidance, corrections, and encouragement to audience members as they practice the act or skill they seek to learn.

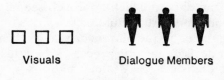

Visuals   **Dialogue Members**

Audience

FIG. 6–4. The Dialogue

Usually more effective with physical skills, the demonstration is the preferred technique when an expert instructor is available. On occasion, the expert may be more effective in describing the steps of the act or skill while a capable assistant performs the actual demonstration. Careful collecting of any necessary props is required. Evaluation of the size of the audience will guide determination of the number of skilled assistants needed to guide the practice efforts of the learners.

Experience-Based Simulation—Sometimes called simulation exercises or, incorrectly, the simulation game, audience involvement can be near its peak when this technique is used. The simulation should create for the spectators a real live situation that should ease them into the learning role. For this, the situation should not be too unfamiliar or unreal; it therefore needs to be thoroughly and carefully planned. The written materials and instructions must be specific, clear, and answer all foreseeable questions. Once the exercise has begun, there is no practical way to stop the action for further instructions, nor is it at all desirable. Persons usually become intensely involved in the exercise, and interruptions with additional instructions are distracting, even frustrating to the learning process.

The exercise should be some live situation or believable facsimile. Suppose, for example, you are attempting to sensitize a group to the problems and mechanics of enacting a bond issue. You might use the simulation approach. For all practical purposes, the group would go through the many steps involved in conceiving and implementing a bond election. It would need to develop necessary data about bond issues, plan its strategies for the election, and experience the consequences of its decisions. The simulation would provide the group with both psychological and intellectual involvement with the election process.

The simulation can be done with large audiences by dividing them into subgroups, each working on some aspect of simulation, or working independently as an autonomous body. Some reward or payoff can increase motivation to participate. The strategies developed by each autonomous group can be compared, and the audience or larger body can choose which approach seems to be the "best." Frequently, some money substitute or reward is included as an element of the simulation so the players can tangibly measure the effectiveness of their decision making process. When this element is introduced, involvement is generally intensified.

Each experienced-based simulation should be followed by guided, thoughtful appraisal of the exercise to focus the learning for the participants. Questions like "What did you do? . . . see? . . . sense? . . . what have we learned?" facilitate the learning and reinforce significant points of the learning process and content. Both process and content are critical elements in the simulation experience. In many ways, the simulation is a multi-faceted role play involving groups and decision making elements rather than individual roles and exercises in empathy.

Field Trip—This technique has the group going to visit a site or place of interest for first-hand study and observation. The trip should be led by a person or persons well-informed about the place being studied. The leadership should ask questions to stimulate the group's interest and associational learning and should point out characteristics of the site that group members might not notice.

This technique can take professionals to unusual or prototypical places like playgrounds, buildings, marinas, maintenance facilities, or parks. The major value is first-hand examination of something that by its nature cannot be brought to the original meeting site.

The field trip is increased in effectiveness if the learners are prepared before the trip with maps, brochures, or pictures. The trip should always be followed by careful interpretation analysis or discussion of the information obtained from the site visit. Small group discussion, speech forum, or panel forum are useful follow-up techniques.

Forum—The forum is an open discussion of a topic, directed by a skilled moderator, with each member of a larger group equally free to participate in the discussion. Time usually is from twenty to sixty minutes.

While the term "forum" is often applied to any large public educational meeting, in this chapter it refers more precisely to the large group-guided discussion. The forum can be a technique which stands alone. When the group is not over forty or fifty members, it is also of considerable value as a follow-up or additional technique after a panel, speech, symposium, dialogue, interview, or role play. (See Fig. 6–5.)

Interview—More formal than the dialogue and using fewer leaders than the committee hearing, the interview is accomplished with one resource expert being questioned by one interviewer. Usually the interviewer will be a member of the group, and the resource person or expert will have been enlisted from outside the group. Radio and television have used this technique extensively. Such interviewers as Mike Wallace, William F. Buckley, and Johnny Carson gained fame in using this process.

The interviewer builds an emotional bridge between the audience and the expert. If the expert is not skilled in public speaking, this

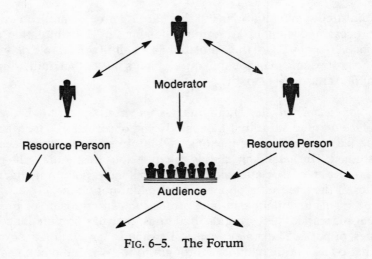

Fig. 6–5.   The Forum

technique can set the person at ease and bring a supporting style that enables him or her to share more readily the knowledge that caused the invitation to be extended for an interview before this particular group.

   Panel—The panel is characterized as a purposeful discussion by three to six persons on a preassigned topic. The number on the panel can be as many as twelve, but six or fewer is desirable. (See Fig. 6–6.) Their discussion is usually conversational and takes place before an audience. Time for discussion should be somewhere between twenty and forty-five minutes.

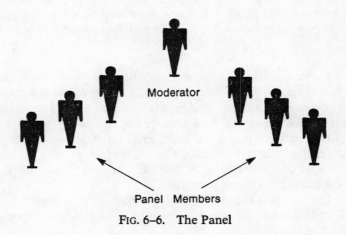

Fig. 6–6.   The Panel

The members of the panel should have interest and competent knowledge in the area of the topic and should be able to verbalize in a rational and reflective manner. Panel members need not be outstanding experts in the topic area, but should have experience and interest in the subject and skill of speaking before a group. They must stimulate interest in the topic and its issues and should *not* debate or be excessively dogmatic in their conversational style. A moderator guides the discussion and should be prepared with questions to raise significant issues, develop the discussion around the important facts, and keep the conversation flowing among panel members. The give-and-take among members of the panel should increase interest among audience members. Caught up in the give-and-take, panel members can lose an orderly or logical line of thought; the moderator should lead in a way that enables consistency in discussion on particular points of the topic.

Planners should be certain that panel members are seated so that they can see each other and be seen by the audience. Sound amplification, via microphones, or a place for notes or small visuals can indicate the need for seating panel members around a table. However, a table can be a physical and/or emotional barrier between the panel and audience.

The basic discussion question and facilitating questions from the moderator should be carefully planned and worded. Ernest Bormann suggests how these questions can be formed in four categories:[5]

1. *Questions of fact* that serve to inform the audience, such as, Has there been a five percent increase in the recreation budget? or Are there fifteen full-time professionals currently working on the recreation staff?

2. *Questions of value* that speak to an examination or reexamination of the audience's value system (e.g., Should girls be allowed to play Little League baseball? with boys?). While most questions for discussion, stated simply, will be understood by panel members and audience alike, instances might arise when a definition of terms will be needed to allow for more complete comprehension by all participants of the question.

3. *Questions of conjecture* that appear to be more suitable for exploring additional possibilities are placed before the audience for consideration. They are offered in a rhetorical manner and suggest further thinking such as: Should we legalize "pot"? or, If we legalize "pot" do you think recreation departments will have to allow its use on the grounds and in community buildings?

4. *Questions of policy* that ask for a direct answer to: "What should we do?" or "what should the policy be?" For example, "What should the policy be for temporary personnel in regard to holidays and sick leave?"

When selecting the question, keep in mind its relative importance to the audience; its interest is important to the program's success. Once it has been established and the discussion question has been simply and efficiently worded so that the audience retains it throughout the discussion, your program should progress with audience interest and comprehension of the ideas.

Securing a good discussion topic is only the first step in preparing the program. The second is to direct and keep the panel members and their individual contributions on the topic. It is advisable to have an outline that includes detailed information about the purpose, limits, and approximate time appropriated for each panelist. The purpose should state *why* the discussion is being held. Is it to direct the audience to consider new ideas or new approaches to some traditional way of thinking or acting? Is its intent to give information to the audience in the form of facts or figures? Is it to inspire audience involvement and therefore suggest more study? Or could there be a problem that needs attending to by the audience in hopes of warding off subsequent problems that may result if action is not taken? The audience must have a reason for coming beyond the opportunity for people to come together. A clear and concise statement of purpose assists in reducing doubt among the "well-intended."

The limits of the discussion should be carefully outlined to answer such questions as: Where should the emphasis be placed? What are the points of interest? What should be included and what is its relationship to the topic? How should the discussion be ordered? The panel members should be encouraged to focus on the discussion question itself and decide the best way to present their materials to ensure that all necessary information is communicated to the audience systematically and realistically. An example would be to discuss the pros and cons of a recreation bond election as a means of capital development. This topic would suggest a discussion along the lines of:

- The status of the current condition and use of the recreation resources (facts);
- The legal aspects of a capital improvement undertaking;
- The existing alternatives;
- The department's past experience;
- Anticipated results, etc.

In short, the limits of the discussion should specify and clarify the question: "What is our goal and how are we going to work toward it?" With the purpose grounded in the minds of the panel members, this phase of the outline can easily be made operative.

Determining how much time should be spent on each item is the final phase of preparation. From two to three minutes per item, relative to its depth and complexity, appears to be enough time for each speaker. Of course, some items may need more or less time than others. In addition to introducing the topic, the moderator is also responsible for monitoring time limits. While the discussion should flow without a rigid time schedule, the time available should be managed to allow maximum discussion by participants.

The outline then becomes very useful. It is intended as a reference guide for the panel members, to aid them in keeping the discussion "on the track," unified, and within the designated time frame. As well, the outline prepares the panel members, to some extent, to anticipate overlapping comments and diversions that might develop during the discussion. By carefully developing and thinking through the outline in advance, panel members are better prepared to handle these situations and move towards a resolution of the question.

Next, consideration should be given to the characteristics and responsibilities of those persons who make up the discussion group, namely the panel members and the chairperson and/or moderator. Although information relative to membership in the discussion group has been identified and discussed, the following may help in the selection of participants.

The Panel Members:

1. Should *be selected* on the basis of:

    —their familiarity with the topic under discussion;

    —their competence in public speaking, the ability to present ideas in a clear and concise manner;

    —their record of being open-minded and unbiased in listening to and accepting the contributions of other viewpoints;

    —their ability to demonstrate rational and reflective thinking.

2. Should *prepare* for the discussion ahead of time by:

    —making certain that the extent of the discussion topic is known and understood;

    —identifying the area(s) within the discussion topic that will be considered and making this known to other panel members so as to avoid duplication of efforts and overconcentration on a particular point or area of interest;

    —researching the topic and preparing an outline.

3. Should *actively participate* in the discussion by:

    —speaking within the realms of the discussion topic;

    —limiting remarks to short periods of time (2–3 minutes);

    —practicing good listening skills with the intent of challenging the views of other discussants as well as changing one's views as evidence is presented that invalidates or disproves a viewpoint;

    —allowing other discussants time to present their views by not dominating the discussion, and likewise drawing out discussants who may be silent, holding back, or in some way not actively participating.

The Moderator:

1. *Should be selected* on the basis of:

    —all the qualifications of being a good panel member;

    —the ability to coordinate and direct the course of the discussion;

    —his or her leadership style in inviting a balanced discussion, controlling the more talkative discussants, and encouraging interchange from the quiet discussants;

    —his or her ability to raise pertinent, clarifying questions without interjecting biases or (unsolicited) opinions.

2. Should *organize* for the discussion ahead of time by:

    —meeting with panel members and assuring that the topic under discussion is clearly understood;

    —assessing with the panel members the limitations of the topic and discern discussable areas with rough time limits for each phase of the discussion;

    —developing a working outline to identify the general direction and flow of the discussion;

    —determining the most conducive room and seating arrangements for participants.

3. Should actively *participate* in the discussion by:

    —introducing panel members and, through introductory statements, setting the stage for the discussion by explaining the format and procedures to be followed by all participants;

    —initially detailing the discussion topic, limiting the extent to which the panel members will explore the agreed upon subject area;

—beginning the discussion with a question or statement that will ignite the panel members to respond to the main point under discussion;

—maintaining a role of clarifier, summarizer, interpreter, and director of the discussion, never entering the discussion with opinions;

—stimulating panel members to work towards basic understanding by asking them, as a whole, reflective questions;

—presenting a final summary and closing the discussion if a chairperson is not used.

The Chairperson:

—More times than not the moderator doubles as chairperson and therefore incorporates his or her duties with those designated for a chairperson. The chairperson is viewed as an organizer, a person responsible for setting up the meeting, introducing the panel participants to the larger group, and then turning over all other responsibilities to the moderator. It is customary that the chairperson close the meeting after the moderator has given the final summary remarks.

Following the panel members' discussion it might be advantageous to break the audience into small discussion groups (buzz groups) so that all can discuss the topic and issues raised during the panel discussion. This can be termed an "Expanded Panel." In this technique the panel is the activating nucleus. The panel members should disperse among the audience so as not to maintain an "expert clique" that can cause the panel to turn into a question-and-answer period. (See Fig. 6–7.) The moderator should instruct (charge) the group with its responsibility as the transition occurs. A skilled moderator can assist both the panel and audience by arranging a warm-up period among panelists just before the meeting. Thus, special areas of knowledge, interest, or strong opinions can be pinpointed, and questions developed.

Time should be provided after the buzz period for the panel to reconvene as a panel and respond to questions or concerns that the various subgroups have developed.

Speech—The speech or lecture is an oral presentation by a qualified person to a group or audience. Careful preparation of the content of the speech is a necessity. It must be well organized and related to the interests and needs of the audience. Problems or issues of the topic area should be identified and clarified in the speech. The

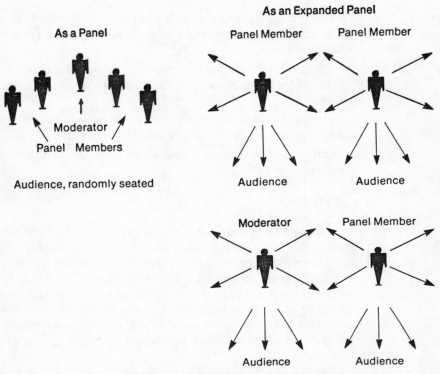

As a Panel

Moderator
Panel Members

Audience, randomly seated

As an Expanded Panel

Panel Member   Panel Member

Audience   Audience

Moderator   Panel Member

Audience   Audience

FIG. 6–7.   Discussion Groups

speaker should have a practical, stimulating delivery and should inspire action or further study of the topic. The speaker should be au-
thoritative without being authoritarian.

The speech can be risky. It is an "all-your-eggs-in-one-basket"
technique. A skilled, prepared, and challenging speaker will be a win-
ner, stimulating and generating ideas, questions, and reactions that
will keep subtechniques actively used for some time following. If the
lecturer is a poor speaker or not adequately prepared, the consequence can be disastrous. Either the audience will sit in silence
throughout the presentation, an embarrassed chairperson will mum-
ble "any questions?" and close the meeting quickly, or a frustrated
audience will show its resentment with an explosion of emotional
questions that attack the speaker or tax the skills of even an experienced moderator.

In the light of the potential of the speech, whoever selects this
technique should select the speaker with great care. The planner or
chairperson should prime the speaker with clear instructions and information and encourage careful preparation of content and deliv-

ery. Time, schedule, and fee or honorarium, if any, should be discussed and determined in advance.

For best results, the speech should be followed with some subtechnique(s) that capitalize on the content of the speech and involve the audience actively in discussing in the topic or issues. A question-and-answer period, audience-reaction teams, and/or buzz groups are among the more useful subtechniques.

Symposium—A series of speeches, lectures, or talks presented by two to five speakers on different phases of a subject or problem is a symposium. The speeches may vary in length from five to twenty minutes; the total time of the symposium should not exceed an hour.

The moderator introduces the topic, the speakers, and the general approach or subtopic of each speaker. He or she tells the speakers the rules of procedure and the sequence of speakers, and arranges for sharing some idea of the background and ideas of others speaking in the symposium. A brief warm-up period can accomplish all of these. If a buzz session or forum follows, this person should moderate that also.

The symposium is relatively formal and easily organized. Speakers and moderator can sit behind a straight table since they do not need to look at each other for discussion. They may also be seated more informally without a table, and each can move to the speaker's stand at the appropriate time. (See Fig. 6–8.) They can systematically and relatively completely present ideas without interruption. Complex subjects can be easily divided into logical components for the speakers to address. Thoughtful planning and instruction to the speakers and moderator allow considerable control over time allotments, topic duplication, and overall schedule, including use of any subtechniques. A large amount of information can generally be deliv-

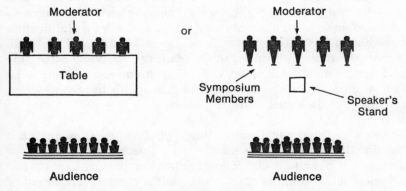

FIG. 6–8.   Two Ways to Arrange a Symposium

ered to an audience more palatably by several good speakers than by one long speech. Conflicting points of view can be addressed without debate.

Followed by an appropriate subtechnique that involves the audience, the symposium is an excellent choice for presenting information and for crystallizing decisions, opinions, or policies.

Modifications of Panel, Speech and Symposium Techniques

Following one cardinal rule of good learning, the audience should be involved as actively and as inclusively as possible. For several reasons audiences must often be led to participate. Audience members might resist or be confused by a mass of facts from the platform. They need to realize that other learners have similar misunderstandings or difficulties. They also learn better when they talk or think through ideas and the ramifications or applications of these to their own lives. Learning is concretized and reinforced by this more active participation.

For these reasons, considered planning for appropriate follow-up is desirable after a major technique, such as those named here, is used. Any of several subtechniques can be useful. To be most effective, each will require careful planning and preparation. Included would be any of the buzz group variations, audience reaction teams, reports from listening and observing groups, and the question-and-answer period. It is up to the planners and the moderator to select and plan for the use of one or more of these follow-up techniques.

Audience Reaction Teams. These are useful when topic or speaker(s) may be "over the heads" of the audience, or may cover material with which the audience is already familiar. Two to six members of the audience are selected to listen carefully, as representatives of the audience. Should points or subject matter as presented not be effectively communicated to the audience, a team member will stand and ask for clarification to reduce or eliminate confusion or lack of clarity. Members of the Audience Reaction Team are introduced to the platform personnel before the meeting. The latter must be familiar with this technique and willing to be interrupted when appropriate. It is most effective with the Symposium, Speech, Demonstration, Panel, or Interview.

Listening and Observing Teams. When platform personnel think it wise to "section the audience," this may be done. Specific topics, points, or question areas are given to each section (before the meeting begins). For example, "selection of summer staff" to the left section, "recruitment of summer staff" to the center audience section, and "pros and cons of using interns" to the right section. Persons in each section listen for ideas that need clarification or for points of disagreement. During the meeting comments can be written down and passed to a team leader who sorts and synthesizes them for presentation to platform leaders.

This subtechnique is especially valuable to encourage active listening and observing in large groups. Teams must be given specific instructions before the meeting (Speech, Panel, Role Play, Interview, etc.). Alternately, the audience can respond by directing questions to the platform, or each *section* can be divided into small discussion groups to focus on their assigned areas. In the latter, the small groups can conclude the technique, or ideas from their discussion can be fed back to the platform for comment.

Question-and-Answer Period.   After a speech or other platform presentation five to twenty minutes can be devoted to questions from the audience. These can be directed to the platform personnel in general to specific speakers. Questions can also be entertained during scheduled breaks in the platform presentation.

The chairperson or other platform leader should carefully explain to the audience the ground rules and plan for the use of question periods. Purpose, kinds of questions to be allowed, and time limits, if these are important, are included in this explanation. The audience can also obtain clarification or further information from questions written on cards distributed before the meeting. The cards are collected, sorted, and systematically responded to by the platform leaders following the Symposium, Panel, or other technique.

Screening Panel.   Two to four audience representatives reveal to a speaker or panel members information on the audience's nature or needs. The screening panel members meet beforehand to refine their information so that they can pass it on briefly but concretely to the platform leaders. The value here is that the speaker(s) is more likely to present only useful and relevant information or ideas, and the audience has visible proof that its needs and interests were considered carefully in the program design.

Educational Aids

The techniques and subtechniques described earlier involve people interacting verbally in group learning. Educational aids, by contrast, are impersonal resource materials that can be used at the meeting, at home, or in the office. They supplement the information shared in the techniques above and involve participants' other senses.

Printed Materials.   These are printed or multicopied materials distributed to audience members as they arrive or placed in their seats before they arrive. These handouts include outlines of subject areas, details of selected subject areas, annotated lists of supplemental reading, or sources of additional information. Case histories, information briefs, or even diagrams or pictorial presentations designed to supplement platform presentations can be helpful as printed materials.

Slides, Films, Overhead or Filmstrip Projections.   Today's variety of audiovisuals seems unlimited. Certainly visual presentation of outlines, still or moving pictures, diagrams, or quotations supplement verbal presentation. Combining music or other appropriate sound effects with these presentations adds another sensory dimension to the learning process. Skillful use of these aids assists the audience's interpretation and information integration. They also provide for the audience specific common experiences that might lead to discussion, questions, issues, or even further study following the meeting.

Videotapes.   Audio and videotapes recorded on reel-to-reel or cassettes can be played on a television (or on a screen with proper equipment). The videotape technique has an additional use, however. An immediate response to the audience can be presented by replaying the event, presentation, or exercise as part of the meeting. Immediate feedback increases learner involvement and learning efficiency.

Exhibits.   An attractive collection of materials related to the topic can aid learning. Cohesiveness of materials, good use of color, light, design, and lettering, and advantageous location increase the value of an exhibit. A carefully prepared exhibit will greatly increase the audience's learning, interest, and participation. Interpretation is a specialty taught to most recreation and park professionals, who will use the exhibit appropriately for large group meetings.

SUMMARY

Given the large variety and number of small and, especially, large group meetings in which professionals in recreation and parks participate, a good understanding of the teaching-learning process is desirable. Planning for these meetings will involve individuals and the planning committee in considering size, location, and time among many other variables that govern the selection of techniques, leadership, subtechniques, and educational aids. Judiciously combining all of these can maximize the effective use of time in large group meetings so that teaching and learning are optimum and predetermined goals are achieved through the meeting.

EXERCISES AND STUDY SUGGESTIONS

The following three exercises are designed to assist you in "testing out" the application of large group techniques. Each involves planning a meeting.

1. You are a first-year director of recreation in a small city (population 12,000). You have revised the policies for the Little League baseball teams, including the rules on age, weight, membership, playing time required, and role of officials, in order to accomplish better what you were told are the goals of the recreation commission. Many of the parents and coaches strongly resent the new rules; they have asked to meet with you. You have scheduled a meeting six days from now and anticipate at least 45 persons will attend. The meeting will probably last two hours. Given this information, plan for the meeting. Included in your plans should be (a) the goals of the meeting, (b) your time structure for the two hours, (c) room setting—size and arrangement, (d) leadership style to be used, (e) techniques, (f) subtechniques, and (g) educational aids that you will use during the meeting. You may also combine small group techniques with large group presentations but you should have no more than five people in your small groups. Approximately half of those attending will be parents; the other half will be officials.

2. You have been given the responsibility of planning the city/county recreation and parks awards and honors banquet. The banquet will be held seven weeks from now. Four leagues (eight teams in each league) of slow pitch adult softball are the basis for this banquet, sponsored by the department. A fee will be charged to cover the costs. You are chairperson of the planning committee for the awards banquet. In the past, approximately two-thirds of those who participated in the leagues attended the banquet. The director has asked you for a detailed outline of your banquet plan. You may use the same structure in planning for this as you did in planning for item #1.

3. Your state liaison officer has told you informally that your community will be awarded a grant from the Land and Water Conservation Fund for constructing a new swimming pool. As a part of the review process, you must conduct a public hearing which has been scheduled a month from now. The purpose of the public hearing will be to determine a location for the pool in your town of 17,000. You are aware that at least three groups have strong biases where the pool should be located; each represents a specific ethnic or socioeconomic group and wishes the pool to be in its own neighborhood. Each has strong political support and has asked for time at the meeting to present its view. You are responsible for planning and conducting the meeting. Using the structure offered in item #1, develop your plan for the meeting.

As you can see, each of the above exercises involves a specific situation. Each demands that you plan it as if you were the only individual involved. This is often the case, but good planners tend to sound out their plans with others. Consequently, we suggest you discuss each of your individual plans in a group setting. Divide the class into subgroups of six to eight and let one person in each group present the plan and offer justifications for the actions. Let the group discuss the plan's merits, giving constructive criticism where needed. If time permits, have each member of the subgroup, in turn, present one plan to the group for discussion.

For a learning group, structure one or more of your meetings along the lines of the large group techniques presented in this chapter. See if they work and what problems you encounter with each. Also, your group as a whole may wish to attend several meetings at which different large group techniques are employed. Observe the effectiveness of the technique. Would another technique have been more appropriate for the situation? In both instances—where you role play the techniques or observe someone else's use of them—discuss your observations and hypothesize what might have been the results if some other techniques had been employed.

Choose one of the following and develop a detailed plan for its implementation. Justify each element of your plan.

1. A park management and maintenance workshop. The theme of the workshop will be "Knowing and Meeting the Needs of the Public We Serve." Your state recreation-park society is sponsoring the workshop. It must be self-sufficient. You expect at least 35 registrants. The workshop is to last four days and will be held at one of the state parks. Participants will be from city, county, and state park systems. A proceedings of the workshop is to be published by the state recreation-park society.

2. A session at the annual state convention. You have been chosen as chairperson-elect of your state park and recreation society. As such, you will hold the post at the next year's annual conference and are expected at this year's conference to present your ideas to the planning committee, which is composed of 24 individuals representing the various districts, branches, and other populations within the society. You need their cooperation and support for your plan to be effectively implemented. They expect you, at your presentation, to state your philosophy of the educational responsibility of the conference, suggest goals for the meeting, comment on the techniques and subtechniques to be used, and offer guidelines for the various subcommittees charged with specific progam responsibilities. You will mimeograph your talk beforehand and distribute it to the committee after your address.

3. Meeting series. The local recreation and park commission plans a series of three meetings to deal with the general topic "Recreation for the Youth of Our City." Although the commission members will serve as moderators, the details of the series have been left to you. It has been suggested a different large group format be used for each meeting. A symposium, a panel discussion, and a forum seem appropriate. Each meeting should have its own subject content but must be consistent with the general theme of the series. Your responsibility is to help the commission organize itself for the series. You are not to assume the responsibility as moderator but should warn the commission of the moderator's responsibilities. At the next commission meeting you will be expected to present a plan for the series. In your plan you should consider the elements of time, subject matter content for each meeting, the techniques, subtechniques, and educational aids to be employed for each, etc.

Have the group watch one of the many educational or informational shows presented on either a commercial or a public television channel. Shows like "Face the Nation," and "Meet the Press" use some of the large group discussion techniques presented in this chapter. Have the class decide which show it will view. Each member should write a two-page report on the show, giving the assumed goals and philosophy underlying the program, the techniques and subtechniques employed, the leader's style and skill in carrying out the moderator's responsibilities, and assessing whether or not the show met its goals. The class may wish to discuss these observations by using one of the various large group techniques available, or the class may be divided into subgroups for small group discussions. Of course, you may wish to combine a large group and a small group approach with this exercise.

Panel Discussions

Try your hand at conducting and/or participating in a panel discussion. Choose a topic of general interest to the group. Some of the topics identified for the listening triad exercise might be appropriate. Divide the class into groups of five. Each small group will constitute a panel with four discussants and a moderator. Have the panel choose a topic and make its presentation (a discussion of seven to ten minutes) before the entire class. The group may wish to spend two to three minutes preparing its discussion. After the panel discussion presentation, have the class evaluate the effort—the moderator's and participants' effectiveness and their ability to listen and make meaningful comments, etc.

If you believe variety is the spice of life, this exercise can be spiced up. For some panels, assign the moderator; for other panels, have no moderator and let the group function as a small discussion group. For some panel groups, arrange the chairs in a straight row; for other sessions, arrange them in an inverted V (Λ) with the moderator at the apex; for other sessions, have the discussants in a row facing the moderator who is seated across from the discussants or perpendicular to them. Have the class discuss what effect the seating arrangement and/or the designating of a formal leader had on the discussion, as well as evaluate the group's effort.

ENDNOTES

1. For a more in-depth examination of education meetings in a retreat setting, *vide* John L. Stevenson, *A Comparative Study of Residential and Non-Residential Adult Religious Education Programs.* Unpublished doctoral dissertation, Indiana University, 1968.

2. George M. Beale, Joe M. Bohlen, and Neil Raudabaugh, *Leadership and Dynamic Group Action* (Ames, Iowa: The Iowa State University Press, 1962), pp. 271ff.

3. Adapted from Paul Bergevin, Dwight Morris, and Robert M. Smith, *Adult Education Procedures, A Handbook of Tested Patterns for Effective Participation* (Greenwich, Conn.: Seabury Press, 1963), pp. 10–28.

4. A variety of sources were examined before those in this chapter were selected. Among the most helpful sources were: Beale *et al., op. cit.;* Martha M. Leypoldt, *Forty Ways to Teach in Groups* (Valley Forge, Penn.: The Judson Press, 1967); John McKinley, *Creative Methods for Adult Classes* (St. Louis, Mo.: The Bethany Press, 1960); and David Potter and Martin P. Anderson, *Discussion in Small Groups, a Guide to Effective Practice,* 3rd edition (Belmont, Calif.: Wadsworth Publishing Company, 1976).

5. Ernest G. Bormann, *Discussion and Group Methods: Theory and Practice* (New York: Harper and Row, 1969), p. 44.

SUGGESTED READINGS

The Adult Education Association of the United States of America. *Conferences That Work.* Washington, D.C., 1956.

Leypoldt, Martha M. *Forty Ways to Teach.* Valley Forge, Penn.: Judson Press, 1977.

Warren, Virginia, ed. *A Treasury of Techniques for Teaching Adults.* Washington, D.C.: National Association for Public School Adult Education, 1964.

Zelko, Harold P. *Successful Conference and Discussion Techniques.* New York: McGraw-Hill, 1957. See Chapters 4 and 9.

Chapter Seven

GROUP PROBLEMS
(Issues of Interpersonal Relationships)

Situation.   You are the director of the city recreation department. For several years the recreation department has sponsored an annual spring carnival. The carnival idea and original planning came from one of the neighborhood groups. To facilitate the organization and operation of a carnival, the recreation department assigned one of its full-time staff members to work with the neighborhood recreation association. Initially, much of the work was done by the association and its volunteers, but recently an increasing amount of the details have been left to the recreation staff. Costs have risen and this year's attendance was down from the previous year. You recently received a report from your staff member on the project and a letter from the president of the local neighborhood association.

Memo from Staff Member.   My staff and I feel that although the attendance was down, this year's spring carnival was the best ever. We attribute the decreased attendance to weather conditions and the neighborhood recreation association's failure to carry out some of its responsibilities. According to their comments the participants seemed to have had a good time and would like to see us continue the carnival with more commercial rides and less attention to the craft exhibits and amateur performances.

I believe it is time for the recreation department to reevaluate its relationship with the neighborhood recreation association of this project. I think it should be sponsored totally by the department and moved to another location. More departmental staff should be assigned to the project. We have a first-class opportunity here to take a successful program and make it even more successful. With additional staff and some modifications, I believe we can make it produce revenue and will submit to you a formal proposal concerning this within the next two months.

Letter from the Neighborhood Association.   We have just completed our fifth year as sponsor of the spring carnival. We appreciate the recreation department's efforts in helping us, but we find it very difficult to work with your representative. He wants to do everything his way and we do not have time to argue with him. The carnival is no longer fun for us and we suggest it be discontinued. It was a good idea, but it has outlived its usefulness. The declining attendance for the past two years clearly reflects that. Also, many of our residents have complained about the damage done to their property by the carnival goers. We will not sponsor the carnival if it is held next year.

Having received these two letters, what do you do? What seems to be at the *heart* of the matter? There are two differing views of what has happened, and you are faced with an immediate decision and a long-range consequence. If you discontinue the carnival, groups and individuals who have supported and attended it will wonder why. Your staff member may feel his recommendation has been ignored. If you continue it, you will have to find a new location. In addition, there is the question of why the neighborhood recreation association wants to discontinue its support. Has the department alienated a neighborhood by its or its personnel's actions, or, has the neighborhood recreation association simply grown tired of the project?

As can be seen from the above illustration and set of questions, problem solving is not simple. It requires time, energy, and facts. When problems occur, and they do occur in any group situation, they must be dealt with effectively or else they may undermine the group's functioning. Through problem solving, groups frequently develop insight and strength. Some even approach problems as opportunities for growth. Group problems are generally of two types. They either evolve from interpersonal conflicts or stem from a disregard of the organizational and environmental factors affecting the group process.

INTERPERSONAL CONFLICT

Problems of this type may be related to external forces but more frequently relate directly to the personalities of the people involved. The development of cliques or the failure to deal with "ego needs" can disrupt the group tone and performance. For example, if one of the recreation staff feels left out, not getting "proper" recognition for her contribution, she may resort to complaining, special pleading, and blocking behavior. Her ego is bruised and demands compensation. Rather than seeing other staff as colleagues, she may see them as rivals who must be "put down" or embarrassed. Her energies are consumed by the conflict rather than channeled into productive activity. The same can happen on a team when a player feels he is not getting enough playing time, or among the professional staff when they think the volunteers are getting all the credit. Problems stemming from interpersonal relationships typically take the form of the negative role behavior discussed in Chapter Three.

Cliques can be equally destructive. It is natural for people to seek friends among those with whom they have the most in common. This is especially true in newly formed recreation groups or in general interest groups, such as teen clubs or a senior citizens' club. Without meaning to, these small subgroups become "in groups." All others are left out, particularly if a clique takes over the leadership positions. Clique members act in the interest of their subgroup rather than on behalf of the larger body. To counter this, other cliques develop, and instead of working for a unified effort, there is constant fighting for power and position.

Some group problems occur because of the failure of the group members to adhere to good group processes. Such problems do not result from personality factors but from inappropriate group action, poor communication patterns, and a disregard for the necessary details essential to group functioning. They are frequently characterized by apathetic participation, declining attendance, a high degree of anxiety and confusion, and misdirected energies and resources. Among the factors that most frequently contribute to creating these problems are:

1. A lack of attention to the levels of group functioning—proceeding to the next stage of group activity, such as producing, without first taking care of the antecedent stage (organizing);

2. Not getting the necessary information or facts before making the decision;

3. Failure to establish a mechanism for feedback and multidirectional communication—being insensitive to the messages being sent or failing to communicate clearly to the group what is needed and what is being done;

4. Not providing adequate time for planning and moving to a premature solution. Too often, groups mistake the issue at hand for the problem, rather than see it as a symptom of the problem, so they attack the wrong issue;

5. Selecting inappropriate techniques to deal with issues or handling group problems (remember that the means by which things are done are as critical as what is done);

6. Pressure by group members for conformity and agreement. Single-mindedness of purpose is desirable when carrying out the group's decisions but not when the group is debating what its decision should be. There, diversity of opinon is helpful.

When the group's problems are disregarded or when the group fails to take necessary constructive action to eliminate the condition, the group's health worsens. The group may be unable to come to decisions, move toward action, or have any sense of accomplishment or direction. Of course, when this happens to the group, it also happens to the individual members, and the quality of their group experience is diminished considerably. Disorganization and low morale are consequences of unresolved problems.

Conflict is natural and healthy. Properly handled, it aids in clarifying the issues, brings solutions into focus, and stimulates action. It is essential to creativity and production. Effective leaders actively use conflict as a dynamic to strengthen the group. They often seek persons of different views to be members of the same team or committee to ensure difference of opinion and conflict so *all* the issues and alternatives can be explored. Misused, however, conflict can be fatal to the group's life. To assist in conflict management, the following materials are offered.

Dealing with Conflict

In our society we often view conflict as undesirable. We try to avoid, subdue, suppress, control, or eliminate conflict. This reaction is probably based on the assumption that conflict leads to such unacceptable results as personal rejection, group immobilization, polarization, violence, or worse.

These assumptions ignore the *positive possibilities inherent in conflict.* In fact, conflict can lead to positive solutions to disagreements or problems, to a greater feeling of enthusiasm and adventure, to group cohesion, to a release of creative energy, to greater appreciation of differences, and to synergistic union of ideas and mutual commitment to the implementation of solutions developed together.

Conflict is a *given* in human interaction. It is simply inevitable when human beings deal with each other. Our values, interests, commitments, desires, and goals often clash. Conflict is closely related to our needs for affection, control, security, opportunity, goal achievement, recognition, and power. We depend on others to meet these needs. This interdependence exists at all levels of human interaction—intrapersonal, interpersonal, intragroup, and between groups.

If we can develop *belief* in the possibility of *constructive results* when conflict arises, the conflict is more likely to be accepted positively with an anticipatory attitude. The crucial task, therefore, is to find ways of dealing creatively with conflict. Large amounts of energy generated by the conflict, and so often expended in *suppressing* conflict in one manner or another, can then be freed for constructive resolution of the conflict. A major key to our crucial task is to view conflict with a positive attitude.

Styles and Strategies of Dealing with Conflict

Human beings deal with conflicts in a variety of styles and conscious or unconscious strategies. Some are self-defeating; others move toward positive resolution. Having an overview of the possible styles and strategies can be helpful. The suggestions in the following paragraphs based in part on conflict resolution ideas suggested by Virginia Satir can be useful when one is faced with conflict.[1]

I. Some styles of conflict resolution are more negative than positive in the long run, more destructive than constructive. Generally, though not always, these negative styles come from a "flight" rather than a "fight" posture. Often an individual's motivation is a wish to avoid dealing directly with the conflict or the issue causing it either by running away or by aggressive attack. Among the negative styles are:

a. *Blaming*—This style puts responsibility for your feelings on the group or another person. "If it weren't for you" in Eric Berne's game by the same name, is a style which denies the intention and feelings of the other involved person(s).[2] Sometimes blame is targeted on a third party: "If it weren't for him/them . . ."

b. *Placating*—"I'm sorry, it's all my fault." "Let's do it your way." "Whatever you say, chief, is okay with me." "I really didn't mean to upset you." These common placating styles ignore one's own feelings, deny the conscious or expressed levels of what is really going on inside ("I don't trust an honest expression of myself, my feelings"), and are a very difficult style to respond to. They often lead to the other person feeling frustrated or hostile.

c. *Avoidance* (sometimes called "denial")—This style masks one's feelings and does not allow you to deal with your feelings either. "No, your comment didn't hurt me." "Scared? Me, scared? Never. No way." "What makes you think I'm angry with you? Of course I'm not!" "Yes, that's what I said, but you know I'm not mad at you. I *never* get mad." Such comments are often said with a flushed face, trembling hands, or rising voice; the person is afraid to admit consciously to self or others the emotions so evident to others. Feelings are masked and not dealt with; neither is the issue. All are left unsatisfied in this style. As with placating, it is *sure to come back later*, one way or another, to haunt.

d. *Irrelevance*—This is the "nice weather we're having" approach to conflict. Question: "Did you mash the fender of the car?" Answer: "I saw a darling suit on sale today." or Answer: "Did you know Mary Quickly is in the hospital?" Question: "How long since the ball field has been lined? We have a game here in two hours." Answer: "Boss, I need two more volleyball poles and a net in the gym." This ignores the *content* of the issue and simply caps the explosion temporarily. Most people are thoroughly frustrated at an irrelevant response to a conflict initiating statement.

e. *Power (negative)*—Often this style is an appeal to "the right way," "the Bible says," or "I offer a substitute motion . . ." in parliamentary procedure or other sets of rules. Other negative power is, "As the President (your father, department chairman, etc.), I say it should be done this way." Any number of "shoulds" or "oughts" can be developed based on tradition, family or company policy, or community ways of doing things.

While not wrong in themselves, these conflict styles do not deal directly with feelings, yours or mine, nor do they deal with the forces/dynamics present in the situation or its context.

II. Other styles of conflict resolutions tend to be more *positive* in the long run. Feelings are usually dealt with externally as one tries to resolve the issue constructively. Inside, however, emotions often are anxiety, caution, fear or even anger, competitiveness, aggressiveness, or the joy of the interaction. Whatever the feeling, try to be authentic. Though this happens best in style "d" below, the earlier ones move in that direction.

a. *Power (positive)*—At times, survival is the only issue. A group (department, committee, agency, company) can come apart at the seams, become unprofitable, or completely stop production of its services unless positive action is taken. Under these circumstances, real or perceived,

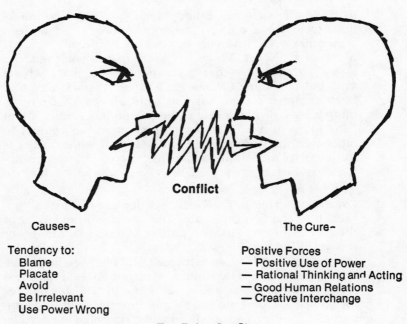

Conflict

Causes-	The Cure-
Tendency to:	Positive Forces
Blame	— Positive Use of Power
Placate	— Rational Thinking and Acting
Avoid	— Good Human Relations
Be Irrelevant	— Creative Interchange
Use Power Wrong	

FIG. 7–1. Conflict

such statements as "We are not going to adjourn this meeting until we come to a decision" must be made. Such statements compose a positive use of power and provide the climate and opportunity for dealing with personal feelings and issues. The use of power can also be positive when a polarization in a group or person immobilizes activity and some movement becomes necessary.

b. *Rational*—This approach to dealing with conflict deals only with the cognitive component of the issues. The "objective thinker" style is valued highly in many situations, such as traditional academia, and is the only acceptable style in some groups or organizations. The rational strategy can lead to power, avoidance, or blame. It denies or does not deal with personal feelings; it deals only with people's intellectual, cognitive realms.

c. *Human Relations*—This style is a combination of the rational with awareness of, and concern for, the feelings of persons involved. This style is more highly valued than the purely rational in that it deals with *both* the cognitive and the affective, both the rational and the emotional. Human relations as a style tends to deal with conflict on a basis of "I will consider your feelings here and now, as well as the intellectual part of the issue. However, I hope and expect to overcome the conflict because I have treated you well." Human relations strategy often works for some positive compromise suitable for all parties.

d. *Creative Interchange*—The most constructive, satisfactory way to deal with conflict falls under this term developed by Henry Nelson Weiman. This category allows for the release of creativity from all involved persons, resulting in growth and enrichment. The unique individuality of each person is discovered and expressed through:

1. *Interacting* (needs trusting, spontaneity, and honesty);
2. *Appreciating* (needs awareness, understanding, and accepting as effective conditions);
3. *Integrating* (needs openness, synergy, and actualization);
4. *Expanding* (needs interdependence, intimacy, and commitment).

It requires commitment, energy, and risk. The payoff is highest in a gestalt sense because—the whole of the resulting solution is greater than the sum of its parts, and more emotionally satisfying for all concerned. A word of caution: for the creative interchange strategy to work, all parties involved must be aware of this strategy and make an honest effort to use it.

In most conflicts, participants enter the disagreement with a feeling of "I don't like to lose. I like to win. I'll do whatever I can to win—or not to lose." This is a *win-lose* attitude, mostly found in the five negative strategies.

After the *win-lose* conflict resolution experience, the loser often says to himself or to his adversary, "I'll get you next time" or "You zapped me. I hate you and you'll pay for it." This *lose-lose* emotional response is all too common; it results in people hurting people, groups hurting groups. People lie awake plotting revenge. Creativity and energy are poured into strategies to "win next time!" A perpetual *win-lose* cycle needs to be broken.

The *win-win* attitude is most productive in resolving conflict. This approach seeks a way in which both parties can win and tries to ensure a *no-lose* approach to the conflict. It deals with emotions and ideas, people's affective and cognitive realms. The resulting feelings of satisfaction and progress release energy and creativity that all may use constructively. While the "positive power," "rational," and "human relations" approaches are useful, the most acceptable, effective, and productive conflict style is the *win-win* attitude which results from the "creative interchange" model.

Awareness and understanding of one's attitudes and beliefs are helpful in conflict resolution. An attitude is affective; a belief is more cognitive. Together they motivate much of our behavior. To achieve conflict resolution remember:

1. Believe that a solution mutually acceptable to all can be found;
2. Work toward a solution mutually acceptable to both persons groups;
3. Cooperation is more desirable than competition;
4. Each person involved is of high value, equal value;
5. The views stated by others are legitimate position statements;
6. Differences of opinion can be helpful in the resolution process;
7. Trustworthiness and openness of others involved in the conflict are necessary;
8. Sharing and working together can develop a *win-win* consensus solution for all concerned. Filley calls this "Integrative Decision-Making" or IDM.[3]

In some instances the persons in conflict are not listening to or really understanding each other even though they seem to be trying. One result is polarization; others are giving up, giving in to "a vote" or to some other nonfeeling resolution. At times like these or other unresolved or unsatisfactorily resolved conflict situations, a Change Agent who is mutually acceptable to all parties can be desirable. Examples are conflict consultants or organization development consultants, marriage counselors, or appointed arbitrators. Remember, the key is "mutually acceptable." Persons in the group or others from outside who are skilled at conflict resolution will begin to use their skills to help the group.

INTERPERSONAL AND HUMAN RELATIONS PROBLEMS

Like group dynamics, the term *human relations* has a variety of meanings and uses. Common to all of them is the art and science of maintaining and improving communications and understandings between various groups and subgroups. It is frequently applied to community race relations, but industries also use human relations experts, who resolve personnel conflicts and maintain morale with the principles and practices of group dynamics. From the experiences of these practitioners, some helpful suggestions for handling personal and organizational problems have evolved. Some of these problems have been discussed previously, but now we want to look at potential solutions for them.

Remember, there are many factors at work in the creation of group dynamics. The seating arrangement, the leader's orchestration of various roles, the arrangements of items on the agenda, and the amount of time available to discuss issues are among the many forces the leader can control and use in handling group problems. Take, for instance, the domineering individual who has difficulty letting others speak. If he or she is seated directly across the table from the leader or moderator, then every time the leader looks up, he cues the dominator into action. The moderator can avoid this by sitting next to the dominator, periodically reaching out and touching him to assure him that the moderator knows he is there. Reaching out can be accompanied with a slight squeeze, which might remind the dominator to "cool it." Of course, it also helps if while applying pressure, the leader acknowledges the dominator's point of view and asks, "Are there other viewpoints?"

When group members argue and block progress or disrupt the group's functioning, the situation can be handled with a smile and a summary. The leader needs to acknowledge both viewpoints with a smile as she summarizes the discussion saying, "We have heard from these two positions; are there other positions or points to be discussed?" By stroking those involved in the argument, while at the same time acknowledging other's need to be heard, the problem can be minimized. No one needs to be called down, only stroked.

When individuals become disinterested and appear to be tuning the group out, they can be brought back into the discussion without much fanfare. Simply call their name, ask a question, and let them respond. Do not embarrass them by asking the question before you call their name. That technique might be effective for shock purposes, but it has a negative tone effect and may waste time. If you are going to involve problem people, why not involve them meaningfully by letting them respond to a question or a summary?

In some discussions, silence can be threatening. Some leaders tend to avoid silence by talking constantly or pushing for decisions without allowing the group members time to reflect. Rather than act on the basis of one's own anxieties, why not use silence as a pressure builder? Rather than inject your own viewpoint about what's to be done, aid the group by briefly repeating viewpoints voiced previously. A leader who "primes the pump" too quickly and forces personal opinions into discussion tends to dominate and cues the group to listen, when he or she should be asking the group to involve itself. If the subject seems to be exhausted, the leader should move on to another point; there is no need to belabor the issue.

Quiet members can be brought into the group through a careful seating arrangement. If the quiet members are seated directly across from the moderator, the latter can cue them in with eye contact and ward off other would-be participants in the process. After all, some group members tend to speak on cue. The leader may also assist the quiet members by asking them either to assume leadership responsibilities, such as serving as secretary or process observer, or to provide feedback on its discussion. The leader might also ask them to gather information to report to the group; this encourages them to become involved verbally. One caution: a silent member is not necessarily a disinterested member. Look for other cues to determine what silence really means.

There are times when interpersonal conflict or negative role behavior are so severe that the tactics normally used to reduce tensions and handle these problems must be abandoned. They simply are too mild. However, before resorting to a more autocratic posture, two other strategies might be considered. One is to fall back on a very formal system of controls, such as *Robert's Rules of Order*. This limits discussion and systemizes presentations. The other is to be patient and hope the group will become incensed by the actions of the blocker or dominator and take its own actions to control. When this occurs, the leader does not have to show "fangs" but allows the group to assume authority and responsibility. When it does respond, it tends to develop a stronger sense of purpose and commitment.

Should the leader have to take control, it is best to call for a recess, then have a private conversation with the disrupting parties or individual, and not confront them directly in front of all the group members. This accomplishes two things—it saves the group from an embarrassing situation, and the disrupting parties get the message directly and firmly.

Cliques may be handled in various ways. If the seating can be altered, the leader might designate certain places for various people to sit, thereby physically breaking the clique. The leader may also handle the situation through subcommittee appointments, making sure that no more than one clique member is assigned to a specific subgroup. This creates new subgroups, interpersonal commitments, and alliances. Finally, the leader may have the group go through a training exercise, such as role play. By making sure one of the role plays involves cliques and their potentially negative effect on the group's functioning, the message gets across to all. Of course, role play can be used to deal with any interpersonal problem situation.

ORGANIZATIONAL PROBLEMS

Individual members perform more effectively within an organization when they know the organization's goals, understand the actions needed to accomplish these goals, know how the behavior of the various members or units of the organization can contribute to the whole, and know the criteria by which individual and group actions are evaluated. When these simple awarenesses are overlooked, various problems emerge. Generally, they manifest themselves as personnel dissatisfactions and inactivity. These conditions come into being most often when there exist poor personnel practices, inattention to the development and maintenance of staff morale, inappropriate lines of communication, inappropriate leadership style, and a failure to develop a proper system of rewards and recognition. Few things can create dissatisfaction in a group or an organization more quickly than these conditions.

Developing and maintaining good staff morale is an essential leadership responsibility. People like to feel they are needed and are making some contribution to the agency's goals. Financial rewards in many park and recreation agencies are not as great as they are in some other services; consequently a sense of accomplishment in what one is doing becomes more critical. Good personnel practices and organizational structure can help facilitate that feeling. The organizational structure—the grouping of employers into task groups—must make sense. Each unit of the organization must be seen as critical to the organization's total success. Although the director and the program specialists are the most visible members of a group, their success could not exist without the backup support of the custodial and maintenance personnel. Those units, too, need "stroking." An effective leader will ensure that all persons and groups receive appropriate, timely, and warranted strokes or feedback.

Rules and regulations should proceed from policy, and staff should have some input in forming policy. By being involved in decision making, employees are more likely to abide by the procedures established to facilitate the work of the organization. In all instances, form should follow function, rather than the reverse. To remain viable, rules and procedures must constantly be evaluated.

All employees should be treated equally when personnel policies and practices are enforced. Favoritism, unmerited promotions and salary increases, and special privileges for certain positions can tear an organization apart. Instead of working for the good of the group, individuals start doing those things to protect their own interest and advance their status. The results will include such behaviors as hostile intragroup fighting, absenteeism, sabotage of the services to be delivered, resignations, and/or apathy.

Communications

Communication is essential in the organizational structure. Recognizing the formal and informal networks that exist is paramount to successful functioning. Two conditions enhance communications: (1) getting the receiver's attention, and (2) sending a message worth receiving. Receivers tend to tune out endless memoranda and unending speeches, and when the communication system breaks down, feelings may be hurt, the program of the agency endangered, and group cohesiveness damaged.

In any communications network, there are sending and receiving stations. Each employee acts as both. And, as with a radio system, only those tuned in to a particular wavelength receive the message transmitted. But the analogy does not stop here. Some receivers are more sensitive than others; some senders are more powerful than others. Identifying which stations or units are sensitive and/or powerful is critical in creating effective communications. If you are trying to get a message across, you must be sure your more powerful senders are plugged in and fully operating. A leader must help both strong and weak senders in a group become aware of their styles and impact on each other. A leader should also help group participants to modify their sending style, should they desire it.

Communications experts tell us we are more likely to get the message when a multimedia presentation is used. In other words, our chances of being heard improve with the number of media we use to send our messages. They include body language, oral communications, and the written word. How we send our message may be as important as what we send (content). Our messages should be clearly stated and their source identified. If communications are personal, words like "I" and "my" should be used. If they are from the group, the pronoun "we" or the name of several group members should be used. The message must be complete and specific; verbal and nonverbal communications must be consistent. A leader should repeat the message, ask for feedback, and then follow up for assurance that those messages sent were indeed received and understood.

To get the receiver's attention, various techniques, such as color coding certain memoranda, can be used. For example, general informational statements may be sent on white paper while those requiring immediate attention may be place on pink. It is important, of course, that all of the receivers know the color coding system. You improve your chances of being heard by alerting the key sending stations (supervisors and informal communication leaders) to a forthcoming important statement or memo-

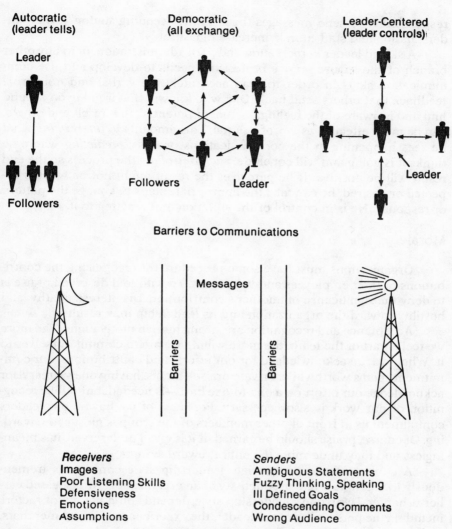

Autocratic
(leader tells)

Democratic
(all exchange)

Leader-Centered
(leader controls)

Leader

Followers

Followers   Leader

Leader

Barriers to Communications

Messages

Barriers

Barriers

Receivers
Images
Poor Listening Skills
Defensiveness
Emotions
Assumptions

Senders
Ambiguous Statements
Fuzzy Thinking, Speaking
Ill Defined Goals
Condescending Comments
Wrong Audience

FIG. 7–2. Types of Communication Networks

randum. They begin looking for the message and also alert others to its impending arrival.

The other half of good communications is developing sensitive listeners. By asking for and receiving feedback, you are able to determine if the message being sent is the message being heard. Various drills are available to increase sending and receiving skills. Some are included at the end of the chapter. The more open the communications system, the more successful the organization. If the receiver feels he or she has the right and responsibility to send messages (back to the "sending station"), then understanding and staff morale increase measurably.

A skilled leader in recreation and park administration, or in any other branch of the leisure service profession, needs to develop and use communication skills in order to read accurately the verbal and nonverbal feedback that others send back. One who knows what is going on around him and is aware of the feelings, actual or potential, in himself and others, can be more effective as a professional. This amounts to *interpreting* what he sees happening in the communications process, *predicting* where he thinks it is going and will conclude, and *controlling* the process so the end result will be positive. If he perceives the result might not be what is expected or desired, he can take the appropriate steps to change the pattern or response. He is in control of the situation, not reacting to it.

Morale

Organizations must have some procedure for recognizing the contributions of their employees and volunteers. To withhold deserved praise is to deny the significance of another's contribution. Disinterest, apathy, and hostility toward the organization and its leadership may result.

Acceptance and recognition are strong human motivations. The more we feel a part of the team, the more willing we are to commit ourselves to it. When we are acknowledged for our efforts and contributions, our commitment seems worthwhile. Private praise—that is, having one's supervisor acknowledge our effort on a one-to-one basis—is needed, but public recognition of our work is also necessary. For most of us, having our leaders compliment us in front of other members of the group is most ego rewarding. Of course, praise should be earned; if it is given undeserved, it is meaningless and may undermine the entire reward system.

A consistent and appropriate leadership style contributes tremendously to the morale and productivity of an organization. As discussed earlier (Chapter Two), one's leadership style depends on a variety of factors including the personality of the leader, the experiences of group members, and the situation. To minimize interpersonal conflicts, leaders should try to develop a group-centered leadership style, that is, a style that involves the group members in the decision making aspects of the organization. This style is variously termed "participative" or "democratic leadership."

Feelings of importance and contributions are enhanced when the organizational philosophy and approach to its personnel reflect a group-oriented leadership style. When possible, the democratic or participative leader will give those nearest to the problem the right and responsibility to make the decisions that bear upon that problem. After all, they are the ones most affected by the consequences of the decisions. Recognizing that every member of the organization is significant to the functioning and success of the organization adds to the dignity of work. To "pull rank" by asking for special privileges and behaviors negates this philosophy. It sets people apart and breaks the organization into first- and second-class workers. Any task critical to the functioning of the organization, regardless of the skills and training required, is worthy of human effort and recognition for all involved.

A leadership style that separates the decision makers from those who have to carry out the task creates an organizational structure with layers of bureaucracy. Leaders are isolated from workers, thereby compounding the potentials for interpersonal conflict and "poor" group morale. By their very nature, bureaucracies tend to set people apart according to levels of power and responsibility. They tend to centralize control, denying workers the opportunity for involvement in the planning and decision making process. It behooves recreators to work against those tendencies.

It is essential that the organizational structure of an agency is consistent with its philosophy of service and its view of mankind. If we believe people are important, we should transmit that in our approach to agency personnel and to their significance to the functioning of the organization. We should keep to a minimum those positions and tasks that tend to serve the organization rather than to assist it in expediting its responsibilities. Although bureaucracy may appear to improve the ability of the group to carry out its task, it may also work as a detriment to the group's morale and, therefore, in the long run, to the detriment of the group's functioning.

BOARD AND COMMISSION RELATIONSHIPS

Historically, most park and recreation departments have had either a policy board, an advisory board or a commission to assist them in their organizational functioning. Although these bodies are not a part of the line organization of employees, they do affect the recreation agency's programs and services and merit special consideration. Also, they are small groups in their own right and, since the recreation executive plays an essential leadership role in their actions, it is important for us to acknowledge and discuss their contribution. Finally, recreation boards and commissions are comprised of volunteers who frequently represent the power structure of the community and/or are influential in the decision making activities that determine the success of the recreative agency.

Rather than divide recreation boards and commissions into policy or advisory categories we will deal with them generically. All advisory/policy groups have a similar function—to influence the actions of the recreation agency. This is also true with neighborhood and special program advisory groups. They are advocates of the interest they represent. Because of their vested interest, they sometimes have difficulty in maintaining a broad perspective of the recreation agency's role and concerns. Consequently, they may unintentionally cross over the line of advising and assisting in policy formation and begin directing (or attempting to direct) the expediting of the agency's tasks by telling the executive how to function rather than assisting him or her in establishing the department's priorities.

Since these bodies are most often composed of influential members of the community, recreation professionals tend to give them more leeway, that is, not call their hand, than they might do with other groups. In doing so they may allow these bodies to usurp some of the recreation agency's responsibilities and rights. Legitimatizing this encroachment creates a difficult situation for the recreation agency when conflict arises between the two and the lines of responsibility and authority have to be redefined. Some conflict is inevitable since it is the function of the advisory and policy board to advocate or approve new programs, budgets, and management policies or changes in existing ones. It is, however, a most efficient mode of delivery.

Most problems associated with boards and commissions can be alleviated through the proper selection of group members, effective board training (including orientation sessions), and the development of an agenda of meaningful tasks and responsibilities within the purview of the board. By selecting board members who represent constituent groups and who have some influence in the direction of these groups, recreation departments can create a dynamic and valid advocacy force. This selection process will probably result in conflict, a necessary ingredient for productivity when properly used and directed. Differences of viewpoint allow groups to look broadly at the issues concerned and work toward a position in the best interest of all rather than "rubber stamping" the position of the agency or its select spokesperson (people who have been chosen because they represent the agency's view, not the view of the many neighborhood or interest groups in the community).

Board training is crucial. If board members are properly oriented toward their role and function, they are less likely to move from the position of policy formulation and advising to one of "interference" in program operations and execution. A sound grounding in agency policy and concerns; a realistic evaluation of agency accomplishment, resources, and capabilities; and some experiences to build the group's feelings and sensitivity can go a long way in developing effective boards and commission members. It is the recreation executive's responsibility to see that these experiences occur. Although the board will develop its own leadership and patterns of interaction, it is one unit of the total organization. As such, it is influenced by the same leadership processes and personalities that direct all other units.

Groups remain viable, and members committed, when the tasks they are asked to perform are realistic and significant. Recreation advisory boards and policy groups often have difficulty because they fail to develop a meaningful agenda. Occasionally, they get bogged down in details and nit-picking especially when their suggestions, which may be advisory, are disregarded by the professional staff. When this occurs, they tend to feel left out, seeing themselves as appendages to the "real action." Any group will quickly become disinterested and apathetic if repeatedly made to feel its actions are only window dressings and perfunctory.

In the medical setting, patient councils function very much like recreation advisory boards. They can be most helpful in assisting the professional recreation staff to develop meaningful programs and services. They can also be a therapeutic experience for the patients. They can be a laboratory for testing interpersonal skills, practicing leadership, and assessing personal strength and health. The comments made in previous paragraphs, addressed primarily to municipal advisory boards, apply to patient councils.

PROBLEM SOLVING

This chapter deals with group problems resulting from interpersonal and organizational activities and patterns. We have attempted to describe some of the conditions that breed these situations and offer suggestions on how they might be corrected or prevented. No discussion of group problems, however, would be complete without giving some attention to problem solving and its importance to good group functioning.

Problem solving is a process of arriving at solutions. It may be applied to a variety of group concerns. Among them are interpersonal and human relations problems, problems resulting from organizational structures and functioning, and the evaluation of programs and agency operations. It can be used effectively in supervisory and consulting conferences and meetings, is a good teaching technique, and is essential for maintaining group viability.

There is nothing unique about problem solving. We do it every day. When we have choices to make, we have problems to solve. Unfortunately, we frequently act without getting all of the facts, jump to premature conclusions, and ignore the potential consequences of our choice. In other words, our problem solving is haphazard and often ineffective. We are most aware of this when the situations are critical or have lasting consequences.

Theoretically, problem solving is a straightforward act involving observation and sensitivity. It requires that those seeking a solution become aware of the factors influencing the situation, be sensitive to the possible courses of action that may be taken, and be critical in evaluating what they should do in light of their goals and what the possible results of their action might be. Developing good analytical and observational skills is essential to its proper function.

There are five stages or sequences in problem solving: first, identifying and defining the problem; secondly, identifying or acknowledging the desired state or goal to be sought; thirdly, identifying and selecting the best means by which the problem can be resolved; fourth, implementing the plan; finally, evaluating whether the ideal state has been reached and, if not, why and what further action needs to be taken. Within each of these stages are various component parts and necessary action. (See Fig. 7–3.) Ignoring any one of them can negatively affect the problem solving process.

*Step One—Defining the Problem—*There is a tendency to look at problems as negative situations or conditions. Actually, problems may be of a positive or constructive nature. The desire to implement a new program requires problem solving as much as the need to reduce group tensions or improve communication patterns. We become aware of problems in a variety of ways: through evaluations, personal frustrations, or the presence of negative group roles. However, the condition or issue that brings us to this awareness may not be the underlying problem. It may be symptomatic of something else. The act of identifying and defining the problem requires a careful reading of what is at work before moving toward some solution.

Obtaining good data about the problem is essential. What are the facts? How did the problem develop? Who perceives it as a problem? The last point is critical. Some situations may be viewed as a problem by the agency but are not seen as a problem by the participant or the staff. The reverse situation may also exist. There must be an agreement among those involved in the situation that a problem exists before some program of change is implemented. The two necessary substeps in this process are: (1) determining the size and scope of the problem; and (2) obtaining agreement from those involved and affected by it, or its possible solution, that a problem exists.

*Step Two—The Ideal State—*If a group or an agency has clearly identified its goals or objectives, the requirements of this step are

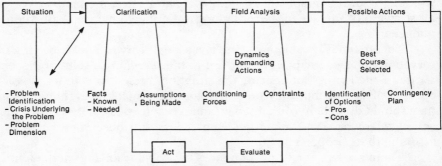

FIG. 7–3.   The Problem Solving Process

usually met. It is a matter of determining what the ideal is and how far the current situation is from that ideal. In other words, what do we want the group to act like or what will the program be? If goals or "ideals" have not been determined, then the people involved in solving the problem need to determine that state so they can measure the distance between the desired and the actual conditions. It is important that the group not jump to a premature conclusion about what are realistic goals or the ideal condition.

The substeps in this sequence are: (1) to identify the ideal or stated goal and objective; (2) to determine a reasonable level of achievement or state of being. To help facilitate identifying the problem, it is recommended that those involved in solving the problem write down what they consider the problem to be, what they consider the ideal situation to be, wht information they need before they move toward some course of action, and what they realistically see as an acceptable result.

*Step Three—Diagnosing the Problem—*Every problem or challenge is created by a variety of forces that bring it to the group's attention; to some extent, the solution to the problem is also determined by the same forces, some of which are in conflict. If there were no difficulty in finding a solution to the problem, there would be no problem. Problems exist because they are not readily corrected or because there is debate on what should be done. The success of the action depends on a proper reading of the problem's dimensions and the effectiveness of the potential solutions at hand.

It is essential to identify the forces or factors that contribute to both the problem and its possible solutions as well as those forces that serve as restraints. For example, the issue may be one of obtaining funds for the support of a youth baseball program. The obvious problem is to get the necessary funds, but the question is how? The funds might be obtained from the department's general budget; there might be a special fee assessed for teams or participants; teams could obtain sponsors who could underwrite their financial responsibilities; spectators could be charged an admission fee. Any number of techniques are available to raise funds. Which one or ones should be tried? Before choosing a solution, say having each team pay an entry fee, the facts of the situation need to be known. What is the public's opinion of entry or admission fees at the Little League contest? Do laws prohibit the use of one or more of these techniques? What are the implications for other programs if any one of these is selected as a source of funding? Will other programs also find that they must become self-supporting through the same approach?

You can see from the above questions and illustrations that the issue of providing support is not as simple as it might have appeared at first. You can see by the line of questioning that certain forces are being identified as contribution to the problem solution. Among them are the legal issues, the force of public opinion, tradition, and the policy and practices of the agency. Other forces might also be at work, such as population pressures, racial attitudes, and national trends, but appear not to be as important to this issue as they might be in another situation.

Many years ago Kurt Lewin concluded that in any problem situation there were a variety of forces working both for and against the situation.[4] He suggested that the nature and magnitude of each of these should be identified before action is taken. Once action is undertaken, a shift in these relationships occurs since the field is dynamic and always seeking a state of equilibrium. Students of problem solving have found this suggestion useful. It requires the identifying of both the helping and restraining forces. They might be organizational, social, psychological, or economic. In some instances, the same force may serve as both a positive and negative factor. For example, the traditions of the agency may restrain the use of a certain course of action while at the same time its traditions, such as the involving of the community in the decision making process, might hold the ultimate answer to what course of action should be taken.

It is helpful to list each of these forces according to their contribution—helping forces and restraining forces. Each should be ranked according to its importance and effect on the present situation and possible solution. In doing this, you can realistically assess the agency's resources to deal with the issue and the constraints that limit you to certain courses of action. From your assessment of these constraints and available resources, and the identification of the factors that created the situation, you should be in a position to select the best solution.

The ideal solution may not always be the best solution. By this we mean that what may be the most workable and satisfying course of action to follow may not be the ideal one, especially if the ideal involves more resources than the agency has to bring to bear on the situation. To assist in the choice of solutions, it is well to identify all courses of action available. For each course, identify the forces at work that support this course of action (the helping forces). Also, for each, list the factors that restrain the agency from pursuing this course. In other words, identify the pros and cons for each course of action and determine the "cost" for each.

To summarize this step we suggest: (1) identify all the forces affecting the creation and reduction of the problem; (2) rank them by their nature (help or restraining) and magnitude; (3) identify the possible courses of action, and for each course, list the forces involved;

and (4) for each course of action, identify the pros and cons and project the possible costs and consequence of action.

*Step Four—Action—*Having identified the various alternative ways to solve the problem, the group or leader can now act. The course of action should reflect the thinking of those who are going to be affected by it, as well as those responsible for implementing the necessary change. In all problem solving situations, the end result is change. We either alter the situation and thereby eliminate one problem, or we modify our attitudes about the situation so that it no longer is a problem. The leadership style used to facilitate the strategy of change (decision making) may have to be modified in the action stage. Execution may require a more autocratic posture than the planning or decision making stages. It certainly requires the assumption of responsibility and its concomitant accountability.

*Step Five—Evaluation—*The fifth and final step in the problem solving process is evaluating the action taken. Did it eliminate the problem or at least reduce it to an acceptable state? Also, were there any unexpected consequences that now need correcting to keep the situation in balance?

Evaluation really begins at the time of problem identification; it is a continuous process. All evaluations have to be in terms of the goals and objectives of the group or organization. In problem solving, the results have to be measured against the ideal condition to which the group subscribes. Both the results of the action taken as well as the process by which the group arrived at its desired course of action must be considered. Evaluation includes looking at both the process of change and the end product.

Not all evaluations prove positive. Sometimes the unexpected occurs or the chosen solution did not work. There are a variety of reasons that groups may fail in problem solving. Some of the more conventional ones are (1) failure to identify the real issue or issues involved; (2) failure to get all of the necessary facts needed for determining the size of the problem and the possible constraints; (3) failure to inform the people responsible for implementing a program of change about their role and responsibility; (4) failure to involve those who might be affected by the change of the nature and consequences of the course of action being contemplated; (5) premature testing of alternate courses of action or premature choice of action; (6) failure to anticipate the counter forces of change which negate the plan; and (7) failure to devote enough resources to fully implement the program within the necessary time limits.

Brainstorming and Other Group Thinking Techniques

We have not discussed the techniques by which groups or agencies may discuss problems or arrive at solutions. Since this is a text on group dynamics and much attention has been given to the necessity to involve groups in decision making and the techniques by which this can be accomplished, it was felt unnecessary to describe in this section the process by which groups arrive at decisions. This has already been done. However, we would recommend that you reread the sections on decision making and the small group discussion techniques (Chapter Five). Brainstorming and other small group discussion techniques are most appropriate to the problem solving process.

A Case Study

To illustrate the problem solving technique, the following case history is offered. Interpretations of the action considered are interspersed with the description of events.

Several years ago, the recreation department established a senior citizens club. For the past few years the club has functioned with its own group leadership, supplemented with departmental staff personnel. The club meets weekly and has had a history of "ups and downs." According to the attendance reports of the club, for the past several months it seems to be in a down period. At least, the attendance has declined to where only eight to twelve people normally attend the club's meeting.

Because of the declining attendance, the recreation director asked for an evaluation of the club to determine the problem. The staff member who had formerly worked with the club resigned from the department several weeks ago and no new staff person was immediately appointed to work with the group since the evaluation was forthcoming. Finally the director did assign a new staff member that responsibility and asked for an evaluation with recommendations.

When the staff person confronted the club members with the situation, she was told things were going very well. Yes, the group did feel its membership had dropped, but those who were attending were enjoying their meetings. They were not discouraged although they did ask the department for more support to help them with some projects they wanted to undertake.

The new staff person seems to have been given conflicting facts. The group is declining in membership yet the group appears to be healthy. There is minimum conflict among those who attend the meetings; they seem to be content with the situation. The department has a policy of assisting groups and allowing them independence, but some of the department's cost considerations suggest groups of fewer than fifteen members are too expensive to maintain. The senior citizens group wants to undertake some new programs and is asking the department for additional resources. Does the department disregard its policy on group size and spend more resources to stimulate this group, or does it discontinue its sponsorship of it?

Using good problem solving techniques, the recreation staff member first sought the director to clarify what she felt the situation was and what the department's policies concerning clubs and groups were. She then talked with the club members to get their assessment of the situation. Finally, she spoke with some of the former club members to determine if their perception of the situation differed from that of the department or active club participants. While undertaking the latter action, she also talked with other neighborhood residents, both young and old, to get their opinion of this golden age club—who attends and what they do. She discovered some interesting points of view.

According to her investigations, there were distinct differences in how people perceived this golden age club. The department saw the club as a program for all older persons—at least, one that should be available to all older people. The participants, however, felt the club was "theirs"; they had been together for several years and very much enjoyed the company of those who attended. Former members felt the problem was not one of finance or resources, but one of cliqueness; they stated the present participants had taken over all the leadership responsibilities several months ago and had discouraged others from participation. The former recreation staff person was willing to allow this group to assume total leadership for the group and did little to break down the clique's behavior. Other neighborhood residents thought it was a nice group of older people who got together weekly to have fun and were not too concerned about the group's size or goals.

Having developed these data, the staff person began the process of force field analysis. She looked at such factors as agency goals, group goals, past patterns of behavior, opinions of group members and former group members, the money being spent on the group, the amount of agency resources being devoted to it, the feelings of the community, satisfactions being derived by those who attended, etc. She concluded there were both positive and negative forces at work and set about to implement a solution.

Alternatives available to her were (1) to dissolve the club since it clearly violated the department's policy concerning support for clubs of less than fifteen members; (2) to conduct a membership drive and to discuss with the current club members the reasons former members gave for leaving the club and the opinions of the community about the club; (3) to go along with the club's current situation and allow it to exist as a small group that enjoys its own company, and in so doing recommend to the recreation department that it withdraw its staff support of the group but continue to support the group by providing it with facilities and some technical assistance; (4) to recommend to the recreation director that she assist the club with its project, which would probably result in publicity and additional members. Success would ensure the group's continued functioning.

After arriving at these alternatives, she discussed them with her colleagues, asking them to help her identify some of the potential consequences for each. She concluded course number two was the most appropriate solution. Discontinuing the group would result in ten people losing an opportunity to enjoy each other's company. Recommending support for the program without being open and honest to the group about the facts she had found in her investigation would be deceitful. The problem would not be resolved if the new members felt disfranchised from participation and were to leave. Recommending that the group be continued as it is, but without agency staff support, would set a precedent that might create other problems for the department with other groups wanting similar treatment. The second course of action seemed to be the most open and held the greatest potential for positive change.

The staff person presented the club with her findings and asked for its cooperation in resolving the situation. Believing that those most affected by change should be involved in the change process, she called upon the club to find a reasonable solution to the problem. She told the members of the study and of the department's policy. The group's initial reaction was as expected; it was somewhat resentful of her interference and denied the existence of the problem. It offered some justifications for its decline, such as death of some members and the moving away of others. She had anticipated this from her field analysis, having considered the possible reactions that her decision might elicit. She countered these charges by being understanding, giving the group ample time to look at the situation, and reaffirming the agency's policy and her findings. She did not force the group into a corner or offer them accusatory statements. She kept reaffirming her desire to help the club deal with the situation and asking them to develop solutions. Eventually, they admitted there was a problem and began honestly working toward a course of action that could attract new members. They, too, used a problem solving technique. High on their motivation for change was the fact they wanted to see the club continue its tradition of long service.

When the group began to work toward solving its problems, the staff person evaluated what she had done. She felt comfortable with the group's climate and direction. She would withhold her final evaluation of her decisions until after the club had had a chance to implement its solutions for attracting new members.

Through this illustration, the various stages of group problem solving are seen. Attention is given to both the activity of the staff person and the use of the problem solving technique that brought about the group's awareness that problems existed. The problem solving technique was then used by the group in dealing with the issues. We highly recommend this technique to you.

EXERCISES AND STUDY SUGGESTIONS

Problem solving exercises can be fun. There are so many interesting ones, each focusing on some specific aspect of problem solving such as decision making, consensus testing, the full utilization of data and logic, and the like. In addition, there are case studies which test one's problem solving ability when using the problem solving process discussed in this chapter. The following exercises are chosen as representative of the various facets of problem solving; with them, we hardly scratch the surface.

Consensus Seeking*

Goals: To test the group's ability to solve problems using consensus seeking as the mode of resolution.

Time Needed: Forty-five to sixty minutes

Setting: Divide the group into subgroups of five to seven discussants. Several groups may be directed simultaneously in the same room. It is desirable to have small groups seated around tables or to have the groups far enough apart that they do not disturb each other during individual phase of the exercise.

Process: Each member of the small group is asked to complete the following work sheet on "Characteristics of a Good Recreator" (see *situation*). The task is to rank the items according to the instructions on the work sheet. Participants are to work independently during this phase. This step should take no more than ten minutes. Once the individual phase is completed, subgroups of five to seven mem-

---

* Reprinted from: J. W. Pfeiffer and J. E. Jones (Eds.), *A Handbook of Structured Experiences for Human Relations Training*, Vol. IV. San Diego, CA: University Associates, 1973. Used with permission.

bers are formed and given the task of deriving a ranking of the items by consensus. There must be substantial agreement on the ranking of each item. There can be no averaging, majority rule, or "politicking" as the group moves toward its consensus.

Once the group has arrived at its ranking of the factors, it may share its ranking with the other groups. The entire group may wish to develop an order for the class. This phase is optional. Finally, each participant within each subgroup is asked to subtract his/her rank score given for each item from the score given that item by the ranking of the group. The totaling of these scores will give each participant the distance he/she is from the group's norm. The individual with the smallest score will be nearest to the group norm; the individual with the greatest score will be the one furthest from the group's norm. Have these two individuals talk about their feelings about the final ranking and their distance from the group norm.

Once the above is done, have the entire group discuss those behaviors that helped in achieving its consensus, those behaviors and actions that impeded its process, how it used its resources, who were the influential members, what pattern of decision making developed, and the value of this exercise.

Situation: Characteristics of a Good Recreator.

Instructions: Rank the items below, as you perceive their importance, from one to ten, one being the most important characteristic.

After each of you have made a ranking, you will then be asked to form a subgroup and discuss the items below until you arrive at a consensus about their importance as you see them.

WORK SHEET
Characteristics of a Good Recreator

Your ranking	Group ranking	Item
_____	_____	The recreator's office is usually well kept and highly organized.
_____	_____	The recreator may use various methods to keep in touch with how the participants feel about the recreation service, their own leisure patterns, and leisure interests.
_____	_____	The recreator sets high standards of program and maintenance performance and does not allow sloppy, careless work to get by.
_____	_____	The recreator admits his/her own program biases so all understand the position from which he/she comes.
_____	_____	The recreator allows participants freedom to enter into the activities of their choice, set their own rules and regulations of play, and structure their leisure experiences.
_____	_____	Other recreators report he/she is helpful, cooperative, and stimulating to work with.
_____	_____	Recreation board and commission members report that their conferences with him/her are valuable and enlightening.
_____	_____	The recreator keeps up-to-date on trends and techniques in recreation services.
_____	_____	Participants do not hesitate to discuss any facet of the recreation service system with the recreator. Respect is mutual.
_____	_____	The recreator places great emphasis on individual choice, freedom of expression, and the value of the recreation experience.

*Shoe Store: Group Problem Solving**

Goals: To observe communication patterns and the process em-
                 ployed in group problem solving.

Time Needed: Approximately 30 minutes

Setting: Divide the group into subgroups of four or five members.
                 Any reasonable number of small groups may be accom-
                 modated.

Procedure: Once the group is divided into its subgroups, explain to
                 the groups that they are to perform a group task in solving
                 a mathematical problem using the consensus testing tech-
                 nique. All members should be urged to observe the proc-
                 ess by which they find and agree upon the solution. When
                 they have reached a conclusion, they should raise their
                 hands. The facilitator will then meet with them to make
                 sure they have the correct solution and confirm that the
                 solution was reached through consensus testing, that is,
                 each person was in general agreement with the group's
                 answer. The process continues until all the groups have
                 arrived at the correct answer.

Situation: To begin the problem solving, the facilitator reads the fol-
                 lowing: "A man went into a shoe store to buy a $32.00 pair
                 of shoes. He handed the clerk two twenty-dollar bills. It
                 was early in the day and the clerk did not have any one-
                 dollar bills. He took one of the twenty-dollar bills to the
                 restaurant next door, where he exchanged it for twenty
                 one-dollar bills. He then gave the customer his change.
                 Later that morning the restaurant owner came to the clerk
                 and said, 'This is a counterfeit twenty-dollar bill.' The clerk
                 apologized profusely, and took back the phony bill and
                 gave the restaurant two good ten-dollar bills. Not counting
                 the cost of the shoes, how much money did the shoe store
                 lose?"

Discussion: When all the subgroups have arrived at a correct answer,
                 the facilitator should ask each group to discuss its process,
                 paying particular attention to their communication pat-
                 tern and the means by which they arrived at the solution.
                 Then, the facilitator should ask the entire group to discuss
                 the exercise: the comments and techniques that were
                 most helpful to them in problem solving, as well as those
                 factors that worked against the immediate solution of the
                 problem. He should enquire whether the phrase "mathe-
                 matical problem" caused any difficulty, were there block-

* Reprinted from: J. W. Pfeiffer and J. E. Jones (Eds.), *A Handbook of Structured Experiences
for Human Relations Training*, Vol. IV. San Diego, CA: University Associates, 1973. Used with
permission.

ers within the group, did anyone assume an "expert" role, and were any simulation aids (scraps of paper or real money) used? See if there were members who felt left out of the discussion, and have the group respond to their comments by offering suggestions on how these feelings of exclusion could have been prevented by the more active and/or more aggressive members.

(The solution to the problem is on page 204.)

Let's take a break from exercises and look at some other activities your group may wish to explore as it comes to understand the problem solving process better. One useful experience is to visit a recreation executive; the members may go in teams or alone. Discuss with the recreation executive her technique for problem solving: does she have a standard procedure, how did she develop the technique, what were some of the more recent problems confronting the group, were they able to resolve them, etc.? Report to the group the results of your discussion. Identify on the chalkboard those factors that the recreation directors had identified as most useful in bringing about a proper resolution of their more recent problems. Also, identify those factors that they felt tended to prevent problem solution. See if there are duplications in the list, that is, did the same force serve as both a negative and positive factor depending upon the situation?

Here are two more problem solving exercises. The first deals with information sharing; the second is an exercise in force field analysis.

The Northside Center: Information Sharing*

Goals: To explore the effects of collaboration and competition among groups in group problem solving and to observe how task-relevant information is shared within a work group as it develops its strategies and implements those strategies in a problem solving exercise.

Time Needed: Forty-five to sixty minutes

Setting: An unlimited number of groups of six in a room large enough to accommodate them without each influencing the others as they discuss the problem.

Process: Each group of six is given a complete set of *Northside Basic Information Cards*. One card is given to each member. Each member is asked to study the information on his or her card and not to show it to any of the other group mem-

* Reprinted from: J. W. Pfeiffer and J. E. Jones (Eds.), *A Handbook of Structured Experiences for Human Relations Training*, Vol. V. San Diego, CA: University Associates, 1975. Used with permission.

bers. Once each member has had a chance to review the facts on the information card, the problem solving phase begins. When the group has reached its solution, members should raise their hands so the facilitator can verify their process and solution.

Situation: The following are the basic information cards for the exercise. One should be given to each member of the group without any discussion of the assignment since the information needed to initiate the discussion is contained on one of the information cards.

You may tell your group what is on this card, but do not pass it around for others to read.

Information:

Eastside has Mr. Lee as an instructor for an arts and crafts class during the third day of the week.

Mr. Jones and Ms. Smith do not get along well, so they do not work together.

During the first day of the week, the instructor, whom Bill likes, conducts dance classes at the Southside Center.

You may tell your group what is on this card but do not pass it around for others to read.

Information:

All instructors teach at the same time but move from one center to the other each day. They are the mobile program unit.

Each instructor likes a different activity best. During the second day each instructor teaches at the center he or she likes best.

Each instructor teaches each activity during one of the first four days of the week.

You may tell your group what is on this card but do not pass it around for others to read.

Information:

The mobile program unit has two activity aides, four program instructors, and four designated program activities they are to instruct.

Ms. Martin is the leader for the mobile program unit.

Mr. Lee likes to work at the Westside Center.

Mr. Jones is at Eastside Center on the fourth day of the week but prefers Southside Center.

You may tell your group what is on this card but do not pass it around for others to read.

Information:

Your group members have all the information needed to find the answer to the following question: In what sequence are the instructors (by name) at the Northside Center during the first four days of the week?

Only one answer is correct and you can prove it.

Some of the information your group gives is irrelevant and will not help to solve this problem.

You may tell your group what is on this card but do not pass it around for others to read.

Information:

Ms. Smith and Mr. Jacobs disagree about how it would be best to program (teach classes at) the Southside Center, where there seems to be a history of disciplinary problems.

The mobile program leader has been with a mobile program unit for five years.

You may tell your group what is on this card but do not pass it around for others to read.

Information:

The mobile program unit leader is at the Eastside Center during the second day of the week.

Bill works at the Southside Center during the second day of the week.

Ms. Martin has been with the mobile program unit for the shortest period of time.

Discussion: When the group agrees that the solution has been reached, it should discuss how it solved the problem. Particular attention should be given to the strategies used and its methods for resolving conflict. When all the groups have offered a solution, the facilitator should announce the correct solution. He should post that on the board so all can see and discuss the means by which the missing information may be derived through deductive reasoning. The facilitator should then present a lecturette on the concept of shared information and shared leadership. The solution to this problem is on page 204.

The final exercises involve the use of the case study method.

1.   Given the facts below, have each individual state the position he or she would take on John's request for reinstatement. The individual is to use the problem solving method, which includes the identification of the problem, the identification of the factors influencing the decision (constraints and available resources), the alternatives available and the decision chosen. After everyone has had time to develop his or her solution for the problem, ask one or more individuals to present their solutions to the group. Have the group critique the solutions in terms of the process used and the potential consequence of the decisions rendered.

Case History*

John Jones has been with the recreation and park department for 22 years. For the past eight years he has worked as a greenskeeper at the municipal golf course. His general work performance is good, although he tends to be an "8 to 5" worker. He

* Joseph J. Bannon, *Problem Solving in Recreation and Parks,* © 1973, pp. 275–276. Adapted by permission of Prentice-Hall, Inc., Englewood Cliffs, New Jersey.

has not been active in any of the professional or labor organizations; many see him as a loner. He is within four years of retirement.

John is known to have a drinking problem. Five years ago he was reprimanded by his supervisor for drinking on the job. He was told if he was caught again violating that department regulation, he would be suspended or fired. Last Thursday morning John asked his supervisor if he could take two hours off during the morning for a doctor's appointment. He left at 9:00 a.m. and returned shortly before noon. Upon his return, it was noticed he was staggering and the smell of alcohol was quite prominent. His supervisor immediately suspended him and called the director to inform him of his action. John admitted he did not go to the doctor but had spent the time at a bar having a few drinks. Learning this, the director immediately fired him.

John felt the action taken by the director was severe. After all, he was not on the job at the time he was drinking, and this was the first incident of this type for over five years. Then, too, by being fired, he would lose some of his retirement benefits, and where would a man of John's age look for a job, especially when his past employer fired him for drinking? John requested that he be permitted to take his case to the personnel grievance committee of the Board of Aldermen. The director granted him permission; it was arranged for John to appear at the Board's next regular meeting.

At the meeting, John asked the Board for another chance. He stated that he had worked for the department 22 years and had given it good service. He reminded them of his age, the loss of retirement benefits, and his potential for employment elsewhere. He stated that his wife was unable to work and that his family depended entirely upon his income for support. He promised that if they would reinstate him, the situation would not happen again. He admitted he had a drinking problem but felt he could control it.

The Board of Aldermen's personnel committee felt that this was an administrative matter and that the decision should be left to the director of the parks and recreation department.

As park and recreation director, what would you do? Justify your decision by citing the process by which you came to it.

To guide you in your decision making, the following suggestions are given. First, identify the problem. What are the secondary problems, if any? Secondly, identify the facts involved. Are critical facts missing? If so, where would you go to get this information? Thirdly, list the forces present that bear directly on the problem resolution. Identify those that serve as constraints. Then, list those that can be used as resources in bringing about an effective solution. The fourth step is to identify the various options available to you in resolving this problem. For each option, list its strengths and weaknesses. Finally, choose the option that seems most appropriate. Justify your choice and predict what might be the consequence of the decision when implemented. Note any action you might take to negate some of the potential negative consequences of your decision. Have fun.

2. Ask small groups of five or six people to apply the problem solving model to the situation presented at the beginning of Chapter Seven. Each group should share with the larger group its solution and the process by which the group arrived at it.

ENDNOTES

1. Virginia Satir, *Peoplemaking* (Palo Alto, Calif.: Science and Behavior Books. 1972), pp. 59–79.
2. Eric Berne, *Games People Play, the Psychology of Human Relationships*, pp. 205–206.
3. Alan C. Filley, *Interpersonal Conflict Resolution* (Glenview, Ill.: Scott-Foresman and Company, 1975), pp. 60–71.
4. Kurt Lewin, *Field Theory in Social Science*, Dorwin Cartwright, ed. (New York, Harper and Brothers), 1951.

SUGGESTED READINGS

Bannon, Joseph. *Problem Solving in Recreation and Parks*, 2nd ed. Englewood Cliffs, N.J.: Prentice-Hall, Inc., 1980.

Filley, Alan C. *Interpersonal Conflict Resolution.* Glenview, Ill.: Scott-Foresman & Co., 1975.

Likert, Ransis, and Likert, Jane Gibson. *New Ways to Manage Conflict.* New York: McGraw-Hill Book Company, 1976.

Maier, Norman R. M. *Problem Solving Discussion and Conferences: Leadership Methods and Skills.* New York: McGraw-Hill, 1963.

Vroom, Victor, and Yetton, Phillip. *Leadership and Decision-Making.* Pittsburgh: Pittsburgh Press, 1973.

Walton, Richard E. *Interpersonal Peacemaking: Confrontations and Third Party Consultation.* Reading, Mass.: Addison-Wesley, 1968.

SOLUTIONS

1. Shoe Store problem (page 198). Answer: $8.00.
2. Northside Center problem (page 199) can be solved as follows:
   a. Make a blank chart similar to Fig. 7–4.

Days of the Week

Centers	Monday	Tuesday	Wednesday	Thursday
Westside	Jones	Lee	Martin	Jacobs
Eastside	Jacobs	Martin	Lee	Jones
Southside	Martin	Jones	Jacobs	Lee
Northside	Lee	Jacobs	Jones	Martin

FIG. 7–4

b. Using the information provided on the Northside basic infor-
    mation cards, fill in the names of the recreators who are
    known to be in certain buildings during certain days of the
    week. (This process is facilitated by using the clues to make
    one list of recreators and another list of volunteers in order to
    differentiate between the two.)

c. Use deductive reasoning to fill in the remaining blanks so that
    each recreator is in a different facility each day of the week.

Chapter Eight

LEADERSHIP DEVELOPMENT

Having good leadership is important. Any organization, be it American Telephone and Telegraph or a small city recreation department, exists and grows because it provides services and products that the groups it serves see as worthwhile. To become worthwhile, an organization must have employees who work efficiently. To a large extent the efficiency of the employees depends upon the leadership of the organization. Poor leadership can cause misuse of employee abilities and, as a result, low morale. Good leadership, however, can increase each employee's efficiency. It can bring about changes in behavior by providing learning experiences in which the employees acquire the specific knowledge, attitudes, or skills necessary to do a better job. Because good leadership can improve the efficiency of an organization, every recreation and park agency needs skills in developing its staff's leadership abilities. The end result of all learning is behavior change, and the objective of leadership development (leadership training and leadership development are synonymous) is a more efficient achievement of an organization's goals through the optimal effort of its employees.

Leadership development can be effected in several situations and settings. One major way is through the formal education programs of high schools, colleges, and universities. It may also be accomplished through various in-service and on-the-job training programs, such as continuing education, professional conferences, staff meetings, and individual study. This chapter will examine each of these areas.

It must be stated that leadership development is a continuous process. Jobs change, people change, new skills are developed, new equipment and new delivery systems are established—all demand that learning be continuous. Leadership development must be ongoing if we are to meet the emerging and often rapidly changing situations confronting park and recreation personnel.

Coupled with these continuous changes, leadership development must be continuous if people are to become their best selves. Developing skills in interpersonal relationships and communication, and in self-awareness and self-improvement, will aid the recreation and park professional in developing greater confidence, a more positive self-image, and consequently a more positive mental attitude to life, to problems, and to the job. The growing employee will very likely do a better job, become a better leader and be a happier, more responsible individual. These qualities increase productivity and add to the individual's eligibility for promotion to a more responsible leadership position.

Leadership development should be provided for every staff member in the recreation/park agency or organization. Funds should be allocated in the agency's budget to make it possible for each person on the staff to participate in continuing education. As employees become more competent, they become more valuable to the organization and will probably contribute more significantly to the department's leadership team. This means that everyone—administrators, supervisors, maintenance personnel, recreation leaders, center directors, seasonal personnel, secretaries, and volunteers—should be involved in the department's continuing educational program. All will do a better job and feel appreciated if they are viewed as contributing to the agency's goals in leadership roles.

PERSPECTIVES

Leadership development opportunities should meet the needs of the agency or organization as it perceives them. To accomplish this, each agency should develop a clear statement of its goals and objectives together with its plan for achieving these objectives on the way to achieving its goals. Included in the plan should be some provisions for leadership development to help reach the goals not presently attainable with the personnel currently employed. This plan will be more comprehensive if a large part, if not all, of the staff has input in its development. The agency's goal plan should receive regular evaluation of progress. It should also be revised and updated at least annually to keep pace with the agency's ongoing changes in both internal and external involvement. This whole process, developed from the perspective of the agency or the organization, can be called a "needs assessment." It also comes under the management process developed in 1964 by Peter Drucker and now properly known as "MBO" or Management by Objectives.[1] It is also referred to by some as "MOR" or Management by Objectives and Results.[2]

Goals and objectives, together with methods for achieving them, should be developed for each leadership training opportunity for each staff member. For example:

Goal: This agency will provide one or more leadership training opportunities for each staff member for one-day duration or longer during this year.

Objectives:

1. Financial support for this training will be provided in the department's budget as a line item on training.
2. Every employee will be notified before March 15, in writing, of at least three appropriate training opportunities during the year from which he or she may choose one.
3. Time off for compensatory time, in addition to financial support for travel, room, and board, all in accordance with agency policy, will be provided for each staff member for this training period.

A variety of organizational or agency needs can be met in leadership development programs or in training programs operated by a recreation and park agency. Programs can be created to meet other specific needs that develop in the job. Examples would include:

Skills and equipment operation
Time management
Budget process
Tournament planning
Law enforcement
New employee orientation
Agency policies and standing procedures
Telephone tips for good public relations
Writing and using goals and objectives
Problem solving skills
Employee supervision, and so on.

Besides agency and organization needs, a second perspective in planning for leadership development is that of staff and employee needs. Many professional organizations operate with reduced production and minimal effectiveness when they are not aware of, and working to recognize, specific needs of their employees and volunteer staff. To this end, regular surveys should be taken, evaluation and feedback techniques developed, and careful listening encouraged by administrators so that these needs can be determined and identified. Leadership training programs can be developed to meet them. Many employee needs will coincide with or be similar to those identified by the agency, while others will be more individualistically oriented. Illustrative of the latter are such training sessions as:

Training for Promotion
Interpersonal Relations Skills
Characteristics of the "Ideal Boss"

Planning for Retirement
Dealing with Difficult People
Personal Skill Development for My Job

NEEDED ELEMENTS FOR CONTINUOUS EDUCATION

Management Support Role

It is now axiomatic that a leisure service agency that desires maximum efficiency for its staff should provide for continuing educational experiences. Management should believe in this philosophy. The financial, practical, and emotional support of management for the in-service training and continuing education of staff is a must if its training programs are to be effective.

Management should emphasize to staff that all personnel are expected to update their skills by participating in the training program. A minimum number of hours per month or year may be suggested for each staff person depending upon position, responsibility, and previous patterns of activity. The recreation administrators should set an example by participating regularly in training programs.

The commitment to training, and the setting of objectives for individuals, and for the agency, should begin with the staff itself. It is a continuous activity. In fact, during the preemployment interview, it is well to mention to the prospective staff member that the agency expects its staff to be involved in continuing education. This expectation can be reinforced through staff meeting announcements and staff mailings. Furthermore, a line item in the budget should be designated "continuing education." Funds should be available for travel to training locations, tuition and fees, per diems, and other expenses incurred when participating in continuing education programs. These monies may be distributed among individuals within the department or to specific departmental units. The dollar amount or percentages available to each staff person should be clearly indicated.

We noted earlier that participation in state, district, or national meetings can be a form of leadership training and development. Nearly everyone knows that national congresses, state conventions, regional, and district meetings are a composite of programs and provide numerous social opportunities to meet people in a variety of ways. But sometimes the social and fraternal aspects of the meetings dominate the experience. Therefore, the continuing education leadership dollar is better spent on training programs that focus on specific areas of learning and that deal with the participants' individual growth needs or skill development. However, management might want to provide experiences of both kinds—the larger congresses and conventions and the smaller, specifically focused training events.

Management should be involved in its personnel's needs assessment. Through active listening, regular staff evaluations, surveys, evaluation reports, staff meetings, discussions, and other sources of data development, the needs of the agency and its individual personnel should surface. Identifying these needs is one of the two basic requisites for effective training programs. The other is management's identification of the training opportunities that exist within the community, state, region, or district. When a program promises to meet a need that management is aware of, specific staff members should be encouraged to attend and participate in those programs.

There are several other ways in which management can foster leadership training. Three come to mind immediately. First, paperwork should be kept untroublesome. Participants should be reminded of the need to keep expense vouchers, reimbursement forms, released or compensatory time forms, and other paperwork that verifies their involvement and accounts for their activity. Forms should be developed to facilitate these accounting procedures, and staff should be reminded to save their hotel/ motel receipts, travel expense records, and other such papers. If at all possible, the training expense should not come out of staff members' pockets. Advance support is suggested, but if these funds are unavailable, a rapid turnaround time for reimbursement of expenses incurred by staff is highly desirable. Staff members will feel more inclined to participate in training programs that do not take money from their everyday living.

A second way management can foster training for staff is by its attitude toward those who desire to participate in or become involved in leadership training programs. Participation in training should be a factor when staff members are reviewed for merit increases, promotion, and similar advancement increments. However stated, if management is even slightly opposed to or frustrated by the loss of time incurred while the staff participates in in-service training, the staff will become less interested in participation. It will perceive the department's attitude as one of "not really wanting in-service training." Since management has the power and authority to require in-service training, staff enthusiasm will be dampened unless management supports it totally. Whether staff interest in training wanes or grows depends on its perception of management's attitudes. The dividends derived from staff participation, in the form of increased productivity and morale, are enormous. Training is good for business, and it is the recreation agency's business to provide the best possible service and programs to its constituents.

A third way management can help in leadership development is to make someone on the staff responsible for leadership development. The title of a designatee might be "Director of Leadership Development" or "Training Director." The training director would be responsible for deter-

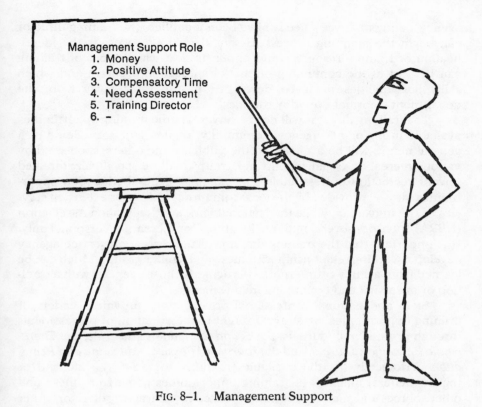

Management Support Role
1. Money
2. Positive Attitude
3. Compensatory Time
4. Need Assessment
5. Training Director
6. -

FIG. 8–1.   Management Support

mining the needs of the agency and staff members and for developing training programs consistent with the agency's goals and the needs assessment. Conceivably, the position would be full-time. In a smaller agency, the training director would have those responsibilities in addition to other program and staff responsibilities.

Needs and Resource Assessment

Having the recreation director's financial and emotional commitment and the policy support of the recreation commission or clinical director in the medical setting assures the proper foundation for an effective training program. Designating a staff person to assume responsibility for implementing and monitoring the program adds to that foundation. Its effectiveness, however, requires the development of meaningful programs and opportunities. The staff must view the program as useful and necessary, or else it has little chance of success. Conducting a needs assessment survey is the first step in establishing the program's validity.

Once the needs assessment has been conducted, and both the

agency's and employee's needs have been identified, the training director can begin the planning process. Essential to this process is the identification of training resources and opportunities: which types of training can be part of the continuing on-the-job education program and which skills and abilities must be developed in programs away from the department's normal everyday routines.

The training director will need to inventory the training opportunities available in his or her agency, community, region, and area. Some of a general nature will be available to the public, while others, sponsored by various recreation organizations and groups, will be specifically directed toward recreation professionals. For example, general education opportunities may be provided by the local community college or extension services of the university, while the National Park and Recreation Association (NPRA) sponsors several national institutes for recreation personnel only. It is important that the training director of the recreation service agency develop a working relationship with these and similar groups. Much can be learned from agency counterparts, particularly those agencies with a tradition of in-service and continuing involvements.

State and national professional organizations provide a variety of training opportunities. Most are brought to the attention of professionals through professional journals. *Parks and Recreation Magazine*, the *Therapeutic Recreation Journal*, and the *Journal of Physical Education and Recreation* periodically list the available training programs by state and/or region. General mailings of training opportunities come from these and other sources and should be routinely routed to the training director. Other sources of information include the offices of the mayor, city manager, hospital administrator, regional park director, etc. The training directors should make sure the recreation agency is on the mailing list of those agencies and groups that sponsor leadership development opportunities and programs of continuing education.

In the second half of this century, new systems for information storage and retrieval have been developed. Since the "half-life" of most professional's information lasts between five and ten years after college, unless continuing education is a part of their careers, the information they rely on quickly becomes dated. In light of this, training directors themselves will have to read regularly and search diligently to develop the best possible information sources and lists of training opportunities available. In fact, their own skills will rapidly wane over the years without a strong effort to stay current.

One can keep up'with changes in the profession several ways. Among them are book reviews and abstracts of professional journals, working bibliographies, and the abstract catalogues like *Current Index to Journals in Education, Research in Education*, and *Education Index.*. Their reports are sent to various clearinghouses, such as The Educational Retrieval Information Center, where the data are processed and stored. Most colleges have access to the ERIC information retrieval system. The Educational Retrieval Information Center (ERIC) publishes the *Research in Education, Current Index to Journals in Education,* and other useful documents. Among those nonrecreation journals that would be most useful to recreation training directors are:

- *International Journal of Continuing Education and Training,* Baywood Publishing Co., Inc., 43 Central Drive, Farmingdale, NY 11735;
- *Journal of Extension,* 807 Extension Building, 832 North Lake Street, Madison, WI 53706;
- *Personnel Journal,* 100 Park Ave., Swarthmore, PA 19081;
- *Training and Development Journal,* P.O. Box 5307, Madison, WI 53705; and
- *Training,* 731 Hennepin Ave., Minneapolis, MN 55403.

Finally, general information on training can be obtained directly from the American Society for Training and Development (ASTD), P.O. Box 5307, Madison, WI 53705. Of considerable use is their latest edition of *Training and Development Handbook,*[3] a broad general source with scores of articles covering a variety of subjects directly related to training and the job of the training director.

THE TRAINING PLAN

With these sources at hand, training directors can take specific actions to further their departments' training effort. First, they can develop a written list of training opportunities that can be circulated to the staff. From this list staff members can select, and supervisors can suggest, programs that will most likely help meet individual and/or agency needs. Secondly, the training directors can select a program that will assist in developing their own skills as directors. They should participate in some ASTD or other recognized training organization's programs that are designed specifically to upgrade their skills and information about training.

Finally, training directors can begin developing their programs and collecting training packages available for purchase or on a rental basis. Especially valuable will be the improvement of the staff's general administrative and public relations, motivating the staff to participate in programs that will improve their abilities, and updating recreation and park content information. Even highly motivated staff members can be turned off by a bad program, poor timing, poor planning, and inadequate organization and leadership. The training director who stays on top of the training program and constantly works to improve personal skills will be better able to "weed out" the poor programs and leaders. He or she will be better able to recommend selected programs and leaders who will be most beneficial in accomplishing the agency's goals and meeting the staff's needs.

The training director will want to be aware of the variety of people within the agency so that programs of benefit to each can be made available. A program designed for the maintenance staff may be of little assistance to center directors, the office and support staff, or the administrators; orientation programs for volunteers and part-time personnel are "target population specific." Perhaps in the routine listing of training programs, certain ones can be highlighted (recommended) for each target population within the agency.

With the increasing demand for accountability of financial expenditures, the training director may find it economically advantageous to join with other agencies in planning and sponsoring leadership training events. "Other agencies" can mean other recreation and park departments in the area that might wish to co-sponsor training efforts, as well as those community social service organizations, such as the YMCA, Human Service Departments, or youth authorities, that use similar approaches and methods in providing their service to the public. Not only does co-sponsoring add potential financial benefits to all concerned, it can also foster interagency cooperation as community groups get to know and trust each other enough to plan and work together in future ventures. It is wise for the recreation training director to be directly involved in planning these co-sponsored programs. By doing so, the recreation department will be more involved in the public relations and publicity, the selection of trainers and training sites, and the content of the program.

The quality sought in the co-sponsored training programs should be no less than what the department would expect if it alone were responsible for it. Involving staff members in planning those efforts that are for their department only also improves the "learning" potential of the training effort. It may be advantageous for the training director to involve others as a committee (a staff-development committee) to aid in selecting and planning the department's overall training programs. Whether working alone, with a small committee within the agency, or with representatives of co-sponsoring organizations, the training director should remember that a training program contains several components: methods, techniques, subtechniques, and educational aids. Each is specific in function and form. The following are definitions for each.

Method—A method is a systematic arrangement of performing some large act or operation. It usually implies the way an organization or institution responsible for educating participants arranges the overall teaching-learning opportunity. Examples would be a two- or three-day conference, a two- or four-year academic curriculum at a university or college, a correspondence course, or a community development program meeting six consecutive Tuesdays.

Technique—The way planners or educators arrange the relationship between resources and learners to facilities (the teaching-learning experience) is referred to as technique. One or several techniques may be used in an educational method. For example, a semester course in the study of Group Dynamics (part of a method) might employ several techniques including group discussions, role plays, lectures, and reports. Although the terms technique and method are occasionally used interchangeably, each has a specific, distinct meaning.

Subtechnique—These are techniques that are used to facilitate learning-teaching situations and would not ordinarily stand by themselves. Examples would include a buzz discussion after a lecture or a question and answer period following a panel discussion.

Educational Aid—Educational aids are resources which supplement or assist the learning process for the participant but do not involve the participant in the actual presentation. Examples are books, pamphlets, exhibits, audiovisuals, and case studies.

A PHILOSOPHY OF TRAINING

Training does not happen in a vacuum. It is an extension of the agency's philosophy and its administration's commitment. It is important that the training directors and planning committee (if one is used) articulate their philosophy of teaching and learning. We subscribe to the following and offer it for your consideration.

In a meeting each participant is open to some kind of personal change. No matter how small, he or she can expect at least the possibility of change in one or more of the following areas: attitudes, intellectual knowledge, values, interest, opinions, mechanical or physical skills, and general understanding. This does not mean that change is definitely going to take place. However, since a widely accepted basic definition of education is "changed behavior," it follows that if any education takes place at a meeting or group gathering, then some change also takes place. As a planner or leader you do not force or manipulate a change; you merely make it possible for a person to grow, learn, or change by some educational experience. The most appropriate techniques, subtechniques, educational aids, leadership, and other resources available to the participants further the possibility for growth, learning, or change.

There are some basic precepts which the authors hold in the teaching-learning process. They are based upon a considerable body of knowledge on learning theories, philosophies of education, or educational psychology; we offer them to you for your use.

1. Learning sometimes involves changing comfortable and established attitudes, beliefs, opinions, or skills. People often resist those changes. Planners and leaders must respect the people in-

volved and their individual rights of choice. The challenge is to motivate learning in spite of this natural resistance.

2. Learning is an internal, personal process.

3. Learning is most possible when related to the experience and knowledge of the learner.

4. Therefore, in the same experience it is likely that different participants will learn different things at differing rates of speed. This is true since each will relate components of the learning experience to his or her own unique combination of values, experiences, beliefs, and interests.

5. Learning involves using the mind; learning, therefore, should challenge and involve the learners in the learning process.

6. Learning will be better if the learner's involvement is based on personal needs and interests.

7. Learning is often more effective when learners relate or associate what is being taught to something they already know or can apply to their lives.

8. What is understood, applied, and synthesized with the learner's prior knowledge or skills will be retained longer than what is merely memorized.

9. Repetition is desirable to reenforce learning and can be applied to the learning process.

10. Successful and/or pleasant experiences facilitate and reenforce learning.

11. Learning is more effective if the learners experience the situation and are personally and physically or emotionally involved in the experiential learning process.

DEVELOPING LEADERSHIP SKILLS

There are two primary methods for developing leadership skills in programs of structured training: formal academic training in a degree-oriented program, and in-service training or continuing education. Ideally, both should embrace the concept of learning based on experience. Also known as laboratory learning, this approach stresses "learning by doing" and the continuous evaluation by the learner of what is being learned. To learn is to change and develop. Doing and experiencing, then reflecting on what has been experienced, is an excellent way to learn.

Active participation in the learning process is necessary in experience-based learning. Experience-based learning encompasses both verbal and reflective written participation. It involves sharing experiences with others and the systematic evaluation of what one has learned. It is dynamic in contrast to so much of our formal educational experiences which require the learner to be a passive listener. To facilitate the learning process in either of the two formal training situations, we suggest the use of the Experience-Identify-Analyze-Generalize (EIAG) model of learning.

EIAG MODEL

Experience—(do)—The first phase of learning results from people talking and thinking together about something of common concern. It can be facilitated by having a planned participation experience, usually in a small group, which serves as a basis for interaction.

Identify—(look)—The next step is to isolate a specific portion of the experience and focus the group's attention on that behavior so that analysis and reflection are furthered. Some questions that may help participants in this stage are:

1. On what behavior shall we work?
2. Would someone recall this exactly for us?
3. Let us explore the effects of this on each of us.
4. What did each of us say?
5. What did each of us feel?
6. What did each of us hear?
7. What nonverbal behavior did we see?

Occasionally, it may be helpful to have each learner write his or her response to these questions before discussing them in the group. In this way, the learner is encouraged to generate personal observations rather than react to the observations of others.

Analyze—(think)—The third stage is to move beyond the generation of these data and deepen the group's understanding of its chosen interest. Several questions may help this process; among them are:

1. What sense do you make of all of this?
2. How would you interpret these data?
3. What are the cause and effect relationships within these data? For example: When X happened, did A, B, C result?

Generalize—(learn)—Having identified and reflected on the occurrence, and having developed some insight into causative factors, the fourth stage asks the individual learners (and the group) to go beyond their immediate experience. It forces them to look at the generalized learning that is occurring. Questions that may help this process are:

1. What did you learn for yourself?
2. What was reinforced that you knew before?
3. By what were you surprised?
4. What conclusions can you draw?
5. Can you state a principle that will help you in a similar situation?
6. How might this be tested in the future?
7. For example, when X is present, then will Y follow?

Though quite productive as a model for learning, the EIAG model is not the only effective method of leadership training. In fact, EIAG is more effective when supplemented with the traditional models of library study or other outside reading, written assignments, and lectures. Preferable to the more traditional extended lectures are ten- to fifteen-minute "lecturettes" of material closely related to the EIAG experiences. Outside reading and individual thinking (written assignments) aid the learning group because each learner generates more facts and insights that can further the group's understanding and development.

With the EIAG model in mind, let us look at the entire learning process, which includes models, methods, and techniques. The leadership trainer or planner must select or have a planning group select the method for the training program (workshop, retreat, clinic), must choose the leader(s) who will conduct the program, must select the technique(s) to be used in conducting the program, and must determine the location and duration of the training experience. The demands on the participants' time and the budgetary limitation must be clearly acknowledged and understood during the planning process. They are practical and determining factors.

Before the training program is developed, the planner should review the materials covered in Chapter Six (Techniques for Large Groups). Notes on available methods, common problems of large group meetings, and the critical areas of consideration, which were discussed in that chapter, must be understood. A simple formula for the planner to remember is good planning plus the right technique plus the best leadership available equal a successful training program. GP + RT + BLA = SUCCESS.

Perhaps most important to all is the leadership selection and the charge or assignment given the leaders selected. The right leadership can go a long way toward making the leadership training program effective.

Poorly selected or uninstructed leadership can destroy planning that was otherwise excellent. For example, a large municipal recreation and parks department engaged a professional trainer for a two-day training workshop. While making arrangements for the training session, the recreation administrator told him, "Please involve our staff in the learning process." So an experience-based workshop was carefully planned with two staff consultants. On the appointed days the trainer met with about 55 glum, resistant, and even hostile faces. The staff's presence had been required; most of them were there against their will. Considerable energy was necessary to overcome the hostility; but by break time, nearly all 55 were becoming rather enthusiastically involved in the EIAG process. During the break, the three primary leaders chatted with the staff and asked why the resistance was so strong at first. It certainly had not been anticipated in the planning process and, without careful and effective leadership, it would have negated the learning experience.

It seemed, according to the participants, the park and recreation department had been awarded a training grant by a state agency the previous year. Without realizing the possible disastrous consequences of poor planning, two professors from two different campuses had been invited to lead a training program and received no instructions other than the time limits for the training and the numbers of people to be involved, all of whom were required to be present. The setting was inappropriate (55 chairs were arranged in straight rows) as was the chosen training method (lecture). Each professor stood before the assembled staff and, in turn, read modifications of his college classroom lectures to these playground and community center workers for $3\frac{1}{2}$ hours, with only a luncheon and two brief refreshment breaks. After two consecutive, seven-hour days of that, the entire group of 55 was turned off to leadership training of any sort. Now they were again being asked to participate. No wonder the trainer and his colleagues had met such resistance and hostility. The situation was perfect, however, to lead beneficially into an informal, experience-based learning program. The response to and evaluation of the EIAG approach used was highly supportive. Leadership style and training can make a tremendous difference. So can the methods of techniques used. They must be consistent with the maturity of the group, its experiences and expectations, and the nature of the subject matter.

Summary

Obviously, in any leisure service agency, the individual responsible for leadership development and training has a big job. In this chapter, we have described some of the sources for assistance and have suggested how one might carry out training responsibilities. The amount of materials on this subject is enormous; we have identified some of the more critical ones for you and have suggested the application of the EIAG model. Good planning, good leadership, and the financial and emotional support of the agency are essential to the training process. Adequate time to do the job is a must if it is to be done well. Creativity on the part of the training director is essential. Once the leadership development process has begun, it has a way of fueling itself. No leisure service agency can expect success without good and systematic leadership growth.

EXERCISES AND STUDY SUGGESTIONS

To assist in your understanding of the process by which leaders are developed, the following exercises are suggested. The first is a technique we highly recommend for your personal use in any leadership development experience. By its very structure, it forces one to be reflective.

The Journal of Awareness.   It is recommended that all individuals in a leadership training program keep a journal of their experiences. As something highly personal, the journal should be shared only with the trainer (instructor). The purposes of this journal are (1) to help you crystallize some of the theories, models, experiences, readings, and other learnings from your leadership experience; (2) to increase your awareness of your personal style and your feelings as you relate to others; (3) to increase your awareness of other persons and their feelings and behaviors; (4) to become more aware of those conditions that separate individuals and often contribute to feelings of loneliness and isolation; and (5) to help you become more skilled in observing persons (including yourself) and reporting your observations.

The journal should have two parts. Part one requires some writing at least twice a week, depending on the intensity of the leadership development experience. A paragraph or more per page is suggested for each entry. The date and day of the week for each entry should be included. Number each page. Typical entries might include various insights into yourself. The entry may describe why you or others behave the way you do, what this course or current experiences are teaching you about leadership, education, groups of people and group processes, etc. An entry may describe an experience or idea, but wherever possible, each entry should be related to your readings, group discussions, and formal learning assignments.

You also may want to include or copy what others have written (poems, quotations, words to some songs) or pictures that communicate a basic or deep feeling for you or with which you identify. You could write or select the words of others that express such feelings as loneliness, hurt, joy, happiness, concern for persons, reaching out, embarrassment, fear, enthusiasm, self-confidence or inadequacies, or any number of other emotional expressions. When using the thoughts of others, make sure you cite the source (title and publication source, if known).

Of *special* importance in this part of your journal are awarenesses or changes in your insights, feelings, growth, and personal values. Emphasize "I learned," "I realized," and "I was surprised that," kind of statements related to *your* growth. Seventy-five percent of the journal's value is here in part one.

Part two requires written observations about some groups or individuals. Select one person and one group and carefully observe them for at least five training sessions. (If you are doing this as a part of a course on leadership development or group dynamics, make these observations over a five-week period.) Note your observations—how each expresses happiness or frustration, how they deal with stress, how they express their values, what you like or admire about them, *etc.* From your notes write a profile of these individuals or the group *and* what you learned from carrying out these observations. Do not tell the people you are observing about this part of your journal. Put all of these observations at the end of your journal in a separate section; treat each individual or group separately, keeping all your observations on that individual together as a unit. Begin each profile with a general statement about the individual's or group's background. (E.g., Group A is comprised of three women and four men of the same age, who meet each day at noon for lunch; individual A is a twenty-two-year-old college student from an eastern community of 15,000.)

Note: This journal is personal. Enjoy it and let it become a way of expressing your own awareness of self and others. It will be yours to keep. Should your instructor desire copies of any of the pages or items, he or she will so indicate when the journal is returned to you.

Feelings.   Another technique to help develop insights and understanding is to write a one-word feeling on each of eight pieces of paper (3" × 5" index cards). Examples can be *fear, loneliness, love, rejection, anger, embarrassed, success, appreciated,* etc. Ask for eight volunteers to meet with you, say in a corner of the room, where each will select one card. No one but the person selecting the card knows the emotion involved. Ask each to think of a personal situation in which that feeling was intense. When the volunteers return to the group, let each one, in no particular order, name the feeling and then spend up to two minutes describing the experience in which the feeling was heightened.

When all eight volunteers have shared their experiences, ask the group to identify other feelings that might have been discussed. Have a volunteer write on the board the various feelings identified. This can be done in a modified brainstorming approach. Set a time limit of ten minutes for this phase of the exercise.

To reinforce the group's awareness of the nature and importance of feelings in motivating behavior, have the instructor give a mini-lecture dealing with the actions we take to avoid unpleasant experiences or to seek those settings or situations that evoke positive and desired feelings.

Feedback.   Toward the end of a training experience, it is helpful for groups to provide each member with feedback from peers. It is suggested the training group be divided into subgroups of three or four persons; where possible, groups are to be composed of people who did not know each other well at the beginning of the training experience. For three or four minutes, each member of the group is evaluated by the other members. The person being evaluated must not respond or make comments. Evaluations should include how the group members perceived the person being evaluated at the beginning of the course, how that person has changed during the experience, and how he or she appears now to the others. This is done until all members of the subgroup have been evaluated. Then, each person can ask the other members of the subgroup what he or she had done to cause those perceptions. Emphasis should be on observed, specific behavior, not opinions or wishes.

Three cautions with this exercise: It is to be constructive, not a "dog pack" in which the others jump on one and chew for awhile, or a "witch hunt" in which the subgroup persecutes the one being evaluated. Evaluations must be made objectively, without judgment, and be based on facts. The second caution is that candid and caring honesty is the rule. Dependable, accurate information to reinforce a desired style or modify an undesirable behavior is the purpose of the exercise. The third caution is "don't shuck." It is too easy to drift into small talk about sports, last night's events, what one's plans are when this is over, and other forms of escape. Stay with the assignment; present honest comments. Otherwise you discount and devalue the other person by not caring enough to give good constructive feedback. Have all members of the subgroup reinforce the learning by noting their reactions in their journal of awareness.

Other Methods for Developing Leadership.   It would be well to visit a recreation/park agency and discuss training with the director or whoever is responsible for in-service education. Explore the adequacy of programs that prepare recreation personnel. Do graduates come well prepared? What are the most glaring deficiencies of current programs? What are the obvious strengths of these programs, etc.? Report your findings to your training group or class. You may wish to break into subgroups to discuss your observations. Again, it is suggested that one member of the subgroup provide feedback on the working group's performance and your participation as a leader or follower.

Finally, have each member of the group assume responsibility for planning and conducting a 30- to 45-minute training session involving all the group members. In addition to actually conducting the exercise, the student trainer should determine the goals of the session, the methods and techniques to be used (exercises), the leadership style he or she needs to assume, the amount of time necessary for reflection, and an evaluation. At the end, the group should critique the student leader's effectiveness.

ENDNOTES

1. Peter Drucker, *Managing for Results* (New York: Harper and Row, 1964).
2. George L. Morrisey, *Management by Objectives and Results in the Public Sector* (Reading, Mass.: Addison-Wesley Publishing Company), 1976.
3. The above source and other sources useful to the training director can be found in the latest edition of *Training and Development Handbook, A Guide to Human Resource Development*, 2nd ed., Robert L. Craig (New York: McGraw-Hill Book Co., 1976).

SUGGESTED READINGS

Craig, Robert L., ed. *Training and Development Handbook, A Guide to Human Resource Development*, 2nd ed. New York: McGraw-Hill Book Co., 1976.

Luft, Joseph. *Of Human Interaction*. Palo Alto, Calif.: The National Press, 1969.

Tubbs, Stewart L. *A Systems Approach to Small Group Interaction*. Reading, Mass.: Addison-Wesley Publishing Co., 1978.

Wood, John. *How Do You Feel? A Guide to Your Emotions*. Englewood Cliffs, Prentice-Hall, Inc., 1974.

Chapter Nine

SUPERVISION AND CONSULTATION

Supervision and consultation affect every recreation agency. They are part of the helping process, related, but distinctively different. They overlap in the area of technique and intent; they differ in authority and responsibility.

Any organization or group that needs various levels of authority for its functioning must concern itself with supervision. Supervision is related to the internal control or directing of the personnel responsible for carrying out the agency's activities. It is a function of the *line, that vertical array of leadership and skills needed to get the job done.*

For an organization or agency to do its job, it must create a series of work groups. Each of these work groups requires some overall coordination and direction. The group leader is responsible for each task group, and in some instances the task group may be subdivided, and subleaders are assigned a certain amount of authority and responsibility. The ultimate responsibility and authority are vested in the individual or individuals who have the final say. This pattern of organization is pyramidal, that is, the largest number of groups, with the least authority and responsibility, is at the base of the pyramid. Such organizational structures are absolutely necessary for the efficient functioning of an agency. A good system is one in which all workers know for what and to whom they are responsible, and in which decisions can be traced from those who make them to those who carry them out. It is a method for dividing the work to be done and encouraging the delegation of authority to accomplish an assignment commensurate with responsibility inherent in the assignment.

In a typical recreation agency, the *line* is comprised of those positions necessary for providing activities and services of a recreational nature. At the first level of responsibility is 'the Superintendent of Parks and Recreation or the Recreation Director. Working closely with the superintendent are the section chiefs who are second in line. (See Fig. 9–1.) The specific organizational structure of the agency will vary according to the type of

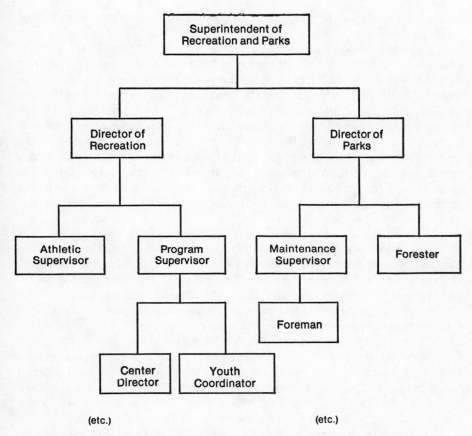

FIG. 9–1.   A Typical Organization Pattern of a Recreation and Park Agency

clients served or the parent structure of which the recreation department is a part. For example, in a hospital the recreation service may be one of several departments within either the division of adjunct therapy or the nursing services. In a municipality it may be a major unit, a department of recreation and parks, or a department of parks with a subdivision of recreation, and so on.

The third level or set of *line* responsibilities is made up of those supervisors who are responsible for specific program areas. For example, in the recreation division of a municipal department, the service may be further subdivided into athletics, community centers, services for special populations, etc. Generally each of these is on the same level but may have a further subdivision. In the final analysis, the recreation participant often relates only to the activity leaders on the playground or in the community building, not with the administrators who are "up the line" and rarely see participants. Yet the participants' activities are influenced by the planning and the leadership style people near the top of the hierarchical structure of the organization.

Closely related to the concept of line is *span of control*, which holds that one person can effectively supervise only a limited number of persons or positions. The nature of the task, the place where the job is done, the experience of the supervisor, and the tradition of the organization dictate, to some extent, the numbers a person can direct. In committee work, for example, the chairperson may divide the group into a variety of subcommittees, but if that number becomes too great to supervise, he or she may create some vice-chair positions. To each vice-chairperson are assigned a certain number of subcommittees. The chairperson of each subcommittee then reports to the vice-chair. In this way, the chair's span of control is achieved through good organizational structure. Bureaucracies are the natural result of such structures.

There are both advantages and disadvantages of the bureaucratic approach to services and actions. As stated earlier, in an organizational structure, group members know their roles and assume specific responsibilities. Organization facilitates communication between members and enables group leaders to coordinate and direct the group's activity. It "fixes" authority and responsibility. But in that "fixing" activity lies the danger of bureaucracies. The communication distance between those responsible for carrying out decisions and those making the decisions may be too great. Consequently, the decision makers might ask their workers to carry out a seemingly necessary but unrealistic task. Their request might be unrelated to the realities of the workers' everyday responsibilities. The decisions are divorced from the personnel's activities; they are influenced more by the needs of the organization than by the needs of those served.

This can be demonstrated in a variety of ways. Take, for example, the recreation department that operates on a centralized authority concept. The superintendent, with the advice of departmental heads, may ask the recreation workers to collect information on the background of all the participants in the program. This seems like a reasonable request since information of this type would be helpful in the department's planning decisions. However, the additional task of the program leader to get information from the participants while simultaneously trying to organize and provide services for them may be unrealistic. First of all, the participant does not have to give the program leader that information. Secondly, the time taken to complete the forms on each participant is time taken away from other required activities. Also, the program leader may feel "put upon" by such a request. Poor morale and hostility toward the agency might result. (See Chapter Seven, "Conflict Resolution.")

One technique employed to prevent the emergence of "red tape" is to minimize standing committees and decentralize authority. For example, rather than have a standing committee on publicity, a teenage club may organize a publicity committee only when it needs to publicize its activity or a specific event. Once the event is over, the *ad hoc* committee can be disbanded. If it is needed again, a new committee, composed of those more interested in the project, can be chosen. Likewise, decentralizing responsibility and authority in an organizational structure can promote relevance. By allowing each playground supervisor to develop a training program for her summer employees, rather than having all summer employees go through the same departmental program may accomplish several things. It gives that playground leader a sense of importance, ensures a more relevant orientation program based on the needs of the participants at that location, and minimizes the need to employ more staff persons to carry out the activities of the central office. In this manner, gathering information, considering possible optional solutions to problems, making selections and setting strategy for the solutions, and putting it into effect are done by those persons closest to the problem. The decentralizing of authority and responsibility is basic to the maintenance of good group morale.

Most organizations use the terms *staff* and *personnel* interchangeably. Typically, when we speak of the recreation staff, we are talking about the professionals who work with the recreation agency. Yet, technically, most personnel are involved in a *line* relationship. They are the ones responsible for carrying out the mission of a department, the deliverers of the recreation service. *Staff* personnel are those specialists who facilitate the organization's internal functioning; they are concerned with administrative tasks, such as budget, personnel, planning, and liability. Being involved in planning, advising, and assisting others, they support the personnel. Execution is a responsibility of the *line* personnel; *staff* assists the line in that execution.

Inasmuch as *staff* employees have no direct authority in carrying out responsibilities, they function somewhat as consultants. The consultation process believes that those offering direction and technical advice are not a part of the line. Consultation may come from staff personnel or from persons not employed by the agency in a line relationship. Whereas supervision is a process within the line, consultation is a staff function. Consultants only advise; supervisors carry out responsibility. For example, when the recreation department needs advice on lighting—the type and amount of illumination required for an athletic field—it may seek out technical assistance. It might go to a lighting firm where it gets consultation. When a program specialist in the line needs assistance in recruiting part-time staff, he goes to the personnel officer of the department or agency. The personnel officer offers assistance by identifying candidates and maintaining the department's personnel records. The program specialist may have the final say on the selection of the specific individuals to fill the jobs; the personnel officer (a staff position) determines whether or not those individuals meet the necessary qualifications and can be hired.

Staff positions may also have a supervisory responsibility. Within a large agency, the personnel director may have several assistants for whom she is responsible. The personnel office becomes the subhierarchy with its own line. (See Fig. 9–2.) However, personnel selection and management for the entire department remains a staff function. The supervision of personnel is a line function. Staff members, like outside consultants, function best when they aid the line in the most efficient expediting of the department's responsibilities.

SUPERVISION

Supervision is the art of shared leadership. Traditionally, it was viewed as "overseeing." Supervisors were middle management personnel, assigned the responsibility of seeing that the work was done; they supervised the "workers." In practice, all personnel have supervisory responsibilities. Supervision, in its purest form, occurs at all levels of the organization. For example, the Director of Recreation and Parks in a local municipality is responsible for all its personnel and is the immediate supervisor of his assistants. In turn, they are responsible for specific divisional personnel and supervise their immediate aides.

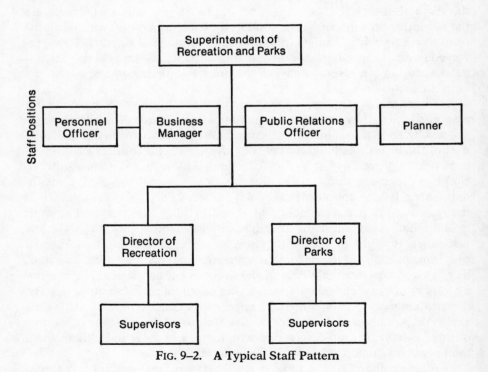

FIG. 9–2.   A Typical Staff Pattern

In most organizations, there is a level of line functioning known as the supervisory level. Those persons functioning at this level carry the title of supervisor. For them, supervision is an everyday reality since their total job is involved with the supervisory process. As intermediaries between the administration, they plan the means by which the job is to be done and determine the leaders who actually provide direct services. To supervise effectively, the supervisor has three basic types of responsibility: technical, educational, and behavioral.

Technical Responsibilities.   The supervisor should know the technical aspects of the jobs for which he or she is responsible. The aquatics director needs to have experience and training in pool management, pool operations, and aquatics programming. Without them, she is handicapped in assisting the pool managers to carry out their responsibilities or in evaluating the effectiveness of their work. It does not hold, however, that the supervisor has to be an expert in every facet of those jobs for which he or she is responsible. The aquatics director *need not* be an expert in the repair of the pool filtration equipment or, for that matter, an expert swimmer. What are important are her knowledge of the overall responsibility of those who work in her area and her competence as a supervisor. It is important that she be technically competent in the supervisory process.

Educational Responsibilities.   Supervising requires the development of good observational skills, a sound understanding of the agency goals and objectives, a knowledge of available resources, and the ability to evaluate. In other words, supervisors are practitioners of the group process. They must understand the principles of group dynamics. Since their major responsibility is to develop and assist those for whom they are responsible, they must be effective teachers. They must understand the policies and procedure of the agency, be sensitive to the needs and abilities of their subordinates, and effectively "teach" these policies and procedures.

Behavioral Responsibilities.   Probably the most effective means of teaching is to set the proper example and create a climate of cooperation and mutual respect. Being an effective student of human relations is a must. Supervisors are the key to good staff morale. They are the primary motivators who influence others by their approach to supervision, their understanding of their responsibility, and their ability to instruct and assist subordinates.

Supervisory Process

Since supervision is the process of shared leadership, it requires the development of an open communication system based upon trust and respect. The following are some suggestions that may aid in that process:

1. Establish the reasons and necessity for the action you desire from your subordinates. By involving the workers in determining what needs to be done, an understanding of and greater commitment to the necessity of the work are assured.

2. Make sure the action is fair and reasonable and applies to everyone alike. If the community center is to be open in the evening, it is important that the supervisor come by occasionally during the evening hours. If the workers see the supervisor functioning only on an "8-to-5" basis, they wonder why they should not do the same. They see their evening work as less desirable since the supervisor does not work those hours. It is also difficult, if not impossible, to enforce a "one-hour-for-lunch" regulation if the supervisor does not adhere to it. Consistency and fairness are absolute necessities.

3. Be immediate and consistent in enforcing policies, rules, and regulations. Ignoring poor work habits only encourages their continuation. In areas of safety and liability, rigorous enforcement of "proper practices" is absolutely necessary.

4. Develop effective instructional procedures. This can be accomplished by:
   a. Having a good job description;
   b. Carefully selecting the best person for the job;
   c. Setting goals for each part of the job;
   d. Having a timetable and training plan (know how much skill you expect the worker to develop, and how soon);
   e. Breaking the job down into its essential steps;
   f. Having everything ready, including equipment and facilities;
   g. Providing immediate feedback and evalution.

Teaching is an art, and awareness of good teaching practices makes it possible for all of us to become better artists in supervision. To facilitate the art, the supervisors should let workers know what is expected of them and how they are performing. They should give public credit when credit is due and recognize workers for their extra or unusual performance. Likewise, supervisors should give the worker constructive criticism in private when the performance is not up to par. Negative criticism is destructive unless it is accompanied by positive comments; that is, the supervisor should demonstrate or inform the worker of what should have been done and how it could have been accomplished. The employee should be told in advance about any changes which will affect her, why they are necessary, and what kind of new behaviors are expected. Make the best use of each employee's ability. Encourage the development of unusual skills and reward (by praise, money, and increased responsibility) healthy and positive behavior.

The Supervisory Visit

Although reports and records assist the supervisor in assessing the worker's performance, direct observation of those for whom he or she is responsible is critical to the supervisory process. The supervisor needs to see the workers in action. The observation accomplishes two things: first, it provides the supervisor with first-hand information about what is going on; secondly, it solidifies the supervisor/subordinate relationship. Then, both worker and supervisor are experiencing the same thing; they are functioning as a team with a common concern.

When the supervisor is planning an observational visit, she should alert her subordinates of her coming. True, there are occasions when the supervisor may drop by, but these should be unintentional visits—not a surprise "stopping-by-to-catch" the worker doing something wrong. Nothing will destroy the shared leadership relationship more quickly than the workers' feeling that the supervisor is a "snoopervisor." If the supervisor has established proper climate, the worker will see the supervisor as a friend, not as someone who only scolds or punishes.

Ideally, the relationship between supervisor and subordinates should be so positive that the subordinate will ask the supervisor to come by and observe situations that the subordinate feels need a "third-party" view. For example, if the center director is having problems with a group, e.g., a neighborhood social club, she might invite the supervisor by for an observation. The visit should occur at a time when the center director is working with the group. The supervisor can observe what is happening and the two can talk about the observation later. This enables them to develop jointly a strategy for program development. The supervisor can assess the techniques being employed by the center director and assist in evaluating the effectiveness of the strategy and implementation. By working together to solve the problem jointly, the supervisor and subordinates develop a spirit of cooperation.

The routine scheduling of supervisory visits is helpful from the supervisor's view, but may not provide all of the data necessary for the supervisor and personnel to solve problems jointly. Then, too, the observation is only one facet of the supervisory process. It is of little value unless planned ahead and followed with a supervisory conference.

Before the observation visit, the supervisor needs to confer with the subordinate about what issues might develop and what will be the purpose of the visit. If the supervisor is expected to assist the subordinate in solving some of the problems, it would be helpful for the supervisor to review past notes and reports. Thus informed, the supervisor comes to the situation with a more critical eye. She or he is better able to make critical observations. The goals of the visit can be established and the evaluation facilitated.

Whether the observation visit be a part of a general assessment of the worker's performance or in response to some problem affecting the worker or his program, a supervisory conference is needed. Sharing observations and discussing needed actions form the basis of the supervisory conference. (See Fig. 9–3.)

Supervisory Conference

The supervisory conference is a one-to-one relationship. It should be held in private and should not be interrupted. Some supervisory conferences are routinely scheduled while others result from specific observations. They are the time for sharing information, resolving problems, and developing future plans and strategies.

As stated previously, some planning should precede the supervisory observation and conference. Both the supervisor and the subordinate must attend to the nature of the conference before it begins. Subordinates can facilitate the conference by noting some impressions they wish discussed and problems observed; supervisors should refer to their notes and reports as a basis for the formulation of the conference schedule. Essentially, the conference is an *interview* and follows the general plan of an interview: the development of rapport, the sharing of pertinent observations and facts, the raising of problems and concerns, and the recording of critical comments, which become a part of the employee's record.

When the supervisory conference results from an evaluation of the worker's performance, such as when a merit evaluation or job analysis is being done, supervisors have an additional responsibility. They need to

FIG. 9–3. The Supervisor Conference—"A Private Affair"

state clearly to the employee the reasons for certain criticisms of the employee's performance and share these observations with the employee. By doing so, the two can jointly develop a plan for further personal development and can begin active work on eliminating any negative qualities, while maximizing the employee's special skills and abilties. Promotions, shifts in responsibility and/or position, and salary increases generally follow these merit evaluation conferences.

Essentially, the supervisory conference is a feedback mechanism. How else are subordinates going to grow and develop unless their supervisors share with them and help them mature in the profession? If these conferences are honest and open, positive working relationships will develop. However, if they are nothing more than social get-togethers, little critical thinking will occur. This is more toward the 1.9 leadership style in terms of The Managerial Grid (see Chapter Two). The focus will be on "being liked" rather than on being helpful.

There are two problems that arise when the supervisor fails to develop the proper relationship with the employee. One involves "acting"; the other pertains to employee records. If the subordinate distrusts the supervisor, he may "stack the deck" when he knows the supervisor is coming. In other words, he creates a special environment so the supervisor can see him and his program in the best light. If the employee has problems, this "acting" will certainly not aid him in dealing with those issues. Through reports and other feedback, it is likely the supervisor will become aware of this situation and then try to "catch" the employee by dropping by at an unexpected time. A cat-and-mouse game results, and the program suffers. Both the supervisor and subordinate subvert the goals of the agency and the supervisory process as they engage in "one-upmanship."

The other problem relates to the employee's personnel records. If the supervisor and subordinates have been honest, then each knows what is in the employee's record. Employees have a right to know what is in their record. They should be able to see the supervisor's evaluation since this may be the basis for promotions and merit increases. If the supervisor has been dishonest in criticizing the employee and has graded the employee lower in particular qualities than she suggested she had, and if the employee discovers that his evaluation ratings are different from those the supervisor has told him he has received, then the employee certainly will not trust the supervisor. Likewise, if the supervisor knows the employee has access to the employee's records, the supervisor is more likely to be objective in recordng her observations. Her entries will be systematically made rather than result from impulse or whimsical reactions.

Supervision is a basic element of every job involving interpersonal relationships and should not be taken lightly. The use of interview schedules, rating forms, and other observational/recording devices aid in carrying out this responsibility.

CONSULTATION

Supervision was defined as shared leadership. Consultation is the helping relationship. It involves sharing expertise in the development of a commitment on the part of the client to do something about the situation that caused the need for consultation. In its purest form, consultation is the giving of advice, and, as with all advice, there is no requirement that what is suggested must be followed.

There are two types of consultants: those who provide technical information expertise and those who work toward a more effective process. Both are similar in intent, that is, to assist in solving some problems that affect the agency or the worker's performance. This is accomplished through providing data and technical information or by assisting the client in analyzing the situation and in developing a strategy to deal with that situation. Our concern in this chapter is for the latter.

To get the most out of consultation, both the consultant and the client should know the consultation process. The more the two can help each other with their respective roles, the greater the likelihood of success. Problem solving requires good data, asking the right questions, and being honest with the response. Consultation is problem solving; knowledge of the problem solving process will assist both client and consultant in doing their respective jobs. It begins with a clarification of the client's expectations and goals.

Expectation of Client

Why do clients request a consultant? Do they want someone to reinforce some ideas already developed, or do they want someone to aid them in developing ideas? Are they buying a name or a set of credentials, or are they looking for someone to help them solve a problem? Are they truly receptive to suggestions and ideas, or have they already made a decision and only need the consultant to serve as window dressing? Do they expect specific answers, or do they want general directions and assistance in sorting out alternatives? All of these are important considerations for both the client and the consultant. It is the consultant's responsibility to uncover the client's expectations early in the consultation. The consultant should accept the contract or assignment only if he or she agrees with the client and has client support from the top on down.

The Process

Once the consultant and client have clearly identified the goals and understand one another, the consultant can get to work. Through questioning and reviewing the records and reports, the consultant can get some idea of the problem and the client's feelings toward it. Why have these personnel matters become issues? Are they related to the reward system? If so, what has been the department's promotion policy in the past and how many personnel have been promoted from within? What are the employees' feelings about the promotion policy? The answer to these questions should come from both the client (director) and those affected (personnel). When a consultant is developing data, he needs information both from those who may be responsible for implementing any recommendations as well as from those who will be affected by them.

Having gotten some insights into parameters of the problem and feelings for the depth of the problem, the consultant can begin exploring the client's ideas about what can be done. It is the client who has the responsibility for carrying out the plan, not the consultant. It is essential, therefore, that the plan be one to which the client is committed. Commitment comes through involvement; people tend to follow those ideas they believe to be their own.

To return to the illustration, having received information from the director and the staff about promotion policies, the consultant needs to discuss with the director his investigative findings and explore possible ways of dealing with the problem. The data may suggest certain courses of action, such as a written policy on promotions and the establishment of a personnel grievance committee. These may be suggested for consideration, but the final decision of implementing these, or any other action, is that of the director. The consultant can only recommend and suggest, not require. He facilitates the client's process of developing his own solutions and plans by guiding, inspiring, and providing information.

The best tack the consultant can take is to have the client critically explore various alternatives. The consultant may have a favorite solution but must guard against imposing ideas on the client if he detects that the client resists or hesitates to use that alternative. Mutual trust is developed as the two parties approach an agreement on what needs to be done. (See Fig. 9–4.) Once the specific course of action is determined, then a timetable for implementing it can be made. The timetable gets at the anticipated results and enables the two to measure their action against the desired result(s). In other words, the consultant should help the client move toward change, if that is indicated, anticipate the effects of change, and get a feeling for how long it will take to implement those changes.

The concluding phase of the consultation process is the evaluation phase. Both parties should recognize the importance of it and make it a part of their initial agreement. The client should expect the consultant to assist in the evaluation; the consultant should expect to be involved in it. After all, he, too, needs to look at the effectiveness of the process. In what ways did he most help the client? In what areas was he least helpful? Why was change accepted? Rejected? Remember that the client is more interested in problem solving than in the effectiveness of the consulting

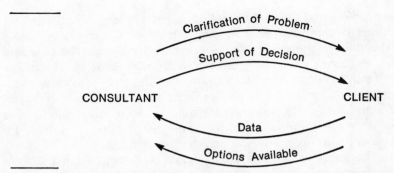

FIG. 9–4. The Helping Process—"The Decision Is the Client's"

process. If the desired results and outcomes occur, then the client is satisfied; the consultant did the job for which he was hired.

Consultation does not have to be a formal arrangement, nor does it always require employing a consultant. It simply recognizes that when someone outside the chain of command is asked to assist those within the line to resolve a problem, the consulting process is in effect. If a community center director calls on the arts and crafts supervisor for help in developing a craft program, then the arts and crafts specialist becomes a consultant. The program the two agree upon will be implemented by the community center director, not the crafts specialist. If the crafts specialist, as self-styled consultant, tries to impose on the center director some suggestions which the director does not wish to implement, or if the program is inappropriate for the neighborhood, the results could be negative. The community center director may question the credibility of the arts and crafts supervisor, may not include art in her program for the future, and might even resist that area of programming.

To carry this one step further, if the agency director requires the community center director to implement an arts and crafts program supervised by the arts and crafts specialist, then the *supervisory* relationship, not the relationship of consultant, is in effect. The arts and crafts specialist becomes responsible for implementing the program. Consultation exists only when those offering aid and direction have no authority for implementing their ideas. It is a recommended role for those counseling others.

The theory of the helping process holds that those with the problem are the ones who also have the answers for resolving that problem. The good consultant helps the client understand what the problem really is and sort out the available alternatives. Since it is the client who will resolve it, the final determination of what can and should be done is that of a client, not a consultant.

Today many consultants, though not all, focus on assisting clients with personnel problems which may be with one or several individuals.

The problems may also deal with more general malfunctions throughout the system of the organization. Consultants in these areas often apply the tools of the behavioral sciences. These consultants are considered to specialize in organization development.

ORGANIZATIONAL CHANGE

In a society as fluid as ours, change is inevitable. It results from new technologies, new directions and agency goals, new leaders and leadership styles. New data, theories, and practice in leading and enabling more efficiency in organizations and agencies continue to point to the need for change in future-oriented organizations. All those involved in the organization, as well as those served by the group or agency, are affected by change. The consequences of change should be thoroughly understood by those who are responsible for it and who assume leadership roles.

Recreation services are provided by recreation organizations. Some aspects of organizational theory and functioning have been covered previously. Basically, an organization is a collection of people following specialized task and work procedures structured in such a manner that the lines of authority and responsibility are clearly defined. It is a system of interdependent relationships, all necessary for the achievement of the corporate body's goals and objectives. In other words, organizations consist of specialists (positions) working together through some coordinated means (hierarchy) toward the achievement of some specified goal(s) (purpose). Recreation organizations exist to provide meaningful opportunities for recreative expression by the population they serve and are affected by changes both within and outside the recreation system. How those working in them respond to change is the concern of this section.

The Nature of Change

Recreation organizations are undergoing a variety of changes because of new technology. The use of the computer has affected program planning and accounting procedures. When computer systems are employed by recreation departments, immediate decisions, based on up-to-date information, can be made. Consequently, changes seem more frequent and more manageable. Technology has also affected the recreation patterns of a participant. Lightweight materials have made camping and backpacking more popular. Technology has given us the CB radio and the CB hobbyist. It has made us more mobile and more knowledgeable. Some technological changes have even resulted in a shift in the role and responsibility of recreation agencies.

The role of the recreation professional is changing. In part, these changes are a function of increased professionalism, but also they come in response to changes in public expectation and leisure behavior. These changes require shifts in the mission or direction of recreation and park departments; new interest groups must be served; new delivery systems must be implemented; new facilities must be designed, constructed, and maintained; new program priorities must be established; and new "types" of recreation professionals employed.

Some changes in the direction recreation services are taking are due to legislative changes. When the federal and/or state governments enacted legislation making public buildings barrier-free to the handicapped, recreation departments necessarily underwent change. The rights of the physically handicapped had to be protected, and that meant changes in the design and structure of recreation areas and facilities. Legislative mandates to provide recreation services for specific minority and disabled groups have required modifications in staffing patterns. Recreation departments have employed those who could work with these special populations and some of these employees have come from these disadvantaged groups. New program units have been established and that has meant modifications of the organizational structure and agency priorities.

Finally, changes in recreation organizations occur with changes in leadership and leadership styles. The employment of a new city manager or the election of a new mayor may radically affect the municipal recreation service system. This is especially true when the new authority wishes to reorganize government and recreation happens to be one of those departments to be "reorganized." Imagine the consequences of dividing parks and recreation into two separate agencies or of merging recreation and parks with some social service unit, such as libraries or schools.

Supervisors and consultants play an important role in planning for, and acceptance of, change. They may instigate it or lead reaction to it. *All recreation personnel with supervisory responsibility, regardless of position, should view themselves as change agents.* They, more than anyone else, are able to control the tensions brought on by change. These tensions are normal and are a part of our tendency to resist the unfamiliar.

Transitions in change can best be accomplished when change is planned and its results anticipated. In the following illustration we discuss some of the elements of change and offer a strategy for dealing with it. This strategy is applicable to both the consulting and supervising process.

The Happy Valley Recreation Department is interested in expanding its services to certain populations in the community. To do this, it must employ additional staff and seek additional funding. To date, its basic source of support has been local community sources. Those resources are limited; consequently, the new program will be supported with funds from a federal grant.

To meet the requirements of the federal granting agency, the

Happy Valley Recreation Department had to create an advisory board, establish a new program unit (which was being funded by a federal grant), and adhere to certain federal reporting regulations.

The department was successful in obtaining the grant, and the community would now have an active program for many of its disadvantaged citizens. From all outward appearances, this shift in program focus and mission seemed highly desirable. All agreed that the objective of providing meaningful recreation opportunities for all the citizens of Happy Valley was closer to being fulfilled than it had been before.

But with the advent of the federal monies and the establishment of a new programming unit within the department, a variety of changes occurred. Some were anticipated; others were not. In both instances, no strategy had been developed for coping with the changes. Among the more serious ones were:

1. *Community Expectations.* With the receiving of a federal grant and the implementation of the program for special populations, two community reactions arose. First, the community wondered why the recreation department had not relied more in the past on federal funding. Could additional monies be obtained from other federal sources? If so, wouldn't this lower the recreation tax? Secondly, a new set of citizens were being given an opportunity to participate in the recreation program. Would there be other demands for services and if so, would the recreation department shift its priorities to serving the disadvantaged and minority populations, or would it continue to serve, as its primary group, its former constituents?

2. *Formulation of Advisory Bodies.* The traditional approach in Happy Valley had been for the recreation director to establish departmental policy and procedures. There had been no advisory body, but with the federal program came the regulation requiring the establishment of an advisory body for this special program. How was the director to cope with an advisory group? Would other advisory bodies be established? If the lay people were going to be involved as advisors to the executive, why not involve the staff more in the decision making process? Could the director really develop a more group-centered leadership style, and if not, would his autocratic style conflict with the advisory body and federal regulations?

3. *New Personnel.* In order to implement the program, the recreation department employed two new staff specialists. Their training was in the area of recreation for special populations. They were more process-oriented than the other staff members and more inclined to use management by objectives and evaluation procedures. These were the first people from outside Happy Valley to be appointed to the recreation staff in years. How would they fit in? Would they be viewed as outsiders? Would their philosophy be compatible with the

other staff and director? Would their loyalties be to the people they serve or to the department? Would their pay, being on a federal grant, be greater than that paid to other staff at comparable levels of responsibility?

4. *Organizational Structure.* With this new unit in the organization, the organizational dynamics of the department were altered. The special populations program was assigned to the supervisor of special activities. This act made the special activities division the largest unit of the department. It now exceeded athletics. Athletics traditionally had been the most prestigious organizational unit in the department. Would the special activities division's new status and size change that relationship? Would the supervisor of special activities become the "informal" organizational leader? Does this signify decline in the significance of the athletic program in Happy Valley? What internal dynamics could result in staff meetings? Between staff on the job?

5. *External Relationships.* Traditionally, the disadvantaged and special populations had been served in Happy Valley by private associations and the community's department of social services. Suddenly, the recreation department was in the picture. Would it take clients away from the private agency or interfere with the social service program? Should recreation be involved in serving the disadvantaged, or is that a responsibility of social welfare? In the future, would the recreation department ask for municipal support in continuing this program, assuming the federal grant were discontinued? Would this take funds away from the social service budget? Will the community begin to expect the recreation department to provide these services and no longer contribute to United Fund's drive for the support of the private agencies?

6. *Accounting Procedures.* The federal agency awarding the grant to the Happy Valley Recreation Department had some very stringent accounting regulations. The paperwork associated with the grant was greater than that associated with other programs of the Happy Valley Recreation Department. How would the accounting department help the city respond to the federal regulations? Would additional staff be needed to monitor the federal grant? Would new forms and procedures be implemented? How would these be financed?

In all, instituting this program for special populations at Happy Valley brought many changes to the recreation department. Some resulted in new services to the public, new ideas and approaches to the department, and a greater vitality. In other instances, it caused more paperwork, organizational frustration, and a blurring of lines of responsibility. Tensions were increased both in and outside the department.

Fortunately, the department was able to deal with these and

make the best of the new opportunity. Such is not always the case in those instances where there is failure to plan for change.

Strategy of Change

Since Happy Valley had anticipated some of the consequences of change, it should have begun to develop a strategy for change. That strategy should have included:

1. Remembering that a change in any part of the system results in changes in every other part of the system. Examine how the establishment of this special populations program affected the accounting department, the prior relationships within the units of the department, and the department's relationships to the private recreation agencies in the community.

2. Remembering that the planning for change should ordinarily start with the policymaking unit of the agency. When the director gave the green light to the supervisor of special activities to prepare the federal grant application, he was giving birth to change. At that point, he should have asked the question: "If we get this grant, what effects will it have on our department and the relationship of our department to other services in the community?" Had he made contact with the private recreation agencies and told them of his plans and asked for their input, he might have avoided one area of tension.

3. Remembering that both the formal and informal organizations must be considered when planning for change. It was obvious to the director that the awarding of the grant would alter his organizational pattern. A new program unit would be established. By involving key informal leaders in the planning of the new program, making them feel it was they who were submitting the grant, he would have avoided any "outsider" feelings.

4. Remembering that the success of planned change is often directly related to the degree to which the people affected by the change have been involved in the planning process. Were the opinions and support of the disabled and disadvantaged in the community solicited? Fortunately they were, therefore the citizens were eager for the department to develop the new program and wanted to be involved. Had the department not chosen specialists who were responsive to this expectation, there could have been program failure from the outset resulting from their insensitiveness to the community's view.

SUMMARY

The degree and effects of change can be determined through a good evaluation procedure. That procedure should include a review of plans for change as well as the effects of change. It requires an analysis of the forces that promote and support change as well as those that change. It requires an assessment of the relationship of each element of the system to every other element.

Supervision and consultation are important processes. They require an understanding and knowledge of problem solving techniques and group dynamics. Change is often the outcome of these processes. Those changes can be most effectively dealt with when supervisors and consultants understand their role as change agents and prepare their subordinates or clients for change. Both processes are founded in the belief that people want to be involved in the decisions that affect their lives, and when given an opportunity to aid in the planning for change, they welcome and support it rather than resist it.

EXERCISES AND STUDY SUGGESTIONS

The exercises in this chapter allow us to continue to develop our skills in problem solving and role playing as we increase our understanding of the supervisory and consulting process. Effective supervisors and consultants rely heavily on the problem solving method and have developed considerable skill in listening and in asking the "right" questions. Keep these qualities in mind as you enter these exercises.

Exercise on Giving and Receiving Help

Goal: To develop skill and understanding in giving and receiving help.

Time Needed: Forty-five minutes

Setting: A room large enough to accommodate four-member groups. Several groups can perform the exercise simultaneously.

Procedure: Divide the training group into four-member groups. Members are designated as O (Observer), P (Person with problem for discussion), Q (Person giving help according to briefing suggestions), and R (Person giving help according to briefing suggestions). P presents the problem; R first tries to help; Q then tries to help; Observer (O) reacts and gives feedback. At the end all four discuss the experience. The role should be distributed privately to each participant. Each participant should be instructed not to discuss his or her role with anyone else until the exercise is over.

Roles: Observer; Person with problem; Questioner; Recommender.

Instructions to O (Observer)

1.   Listen thoughtfully to problem as presented.

2. Observe, without comment, discussion between P
    and R. Note:
    a. What do you think were the unspoken feelings of
        each?
    b. How were proposals from R given and received?
    c. What seemed to be helpful? Why? What did not
        seem helpful? Why?
3. Observe, without comment, discussion between P
    and Q. Note:
    a. What do you think were the unspoken feelings of
        each?
    b. How does Q's behavior differ from R's and with
        what effect on P?
    c. What did Q do that seemed helpful? What did not
        seem productive?
4. Act as timekeeper following this approximate sched-
    ule:
    a. A brief period—2–3 minutes—for P to organize his
        or her thoughts while Q and R read their briefings
        separately. Ask them not to disclose them to one
        another or to P.
    b. 10 minutes for P to explain the problem. Suggest
        that he or she take the full time.
    c. 10 minutes for R to discuss problem with P and
        try to give help.
    d. 10 minutes for Q to discuss problem with P and
        try to give help.
    e. 5 minutes for P to tell how he or she felt as R and
        Q gave help.
    f. 5 minutes for O to share his or her observations
        as suggested above.

Instructions to P (Person presenting Problem)

Choose a problem on which you would like help—perhaps
some aspect of problem you have written up. It should be
important in your type of work and something you want
to do something about. However, it should not be too
large to be realistically discussed in a brief time. You will
have about 10 minutes to tell about it and about 20 minutes to discuss it, 10 minutes each with two helpers.

Present problem during first period, then discuss freely
with R, later with Q. Try to get help from each. Test out
their suggestions and explore their ideas. Try to give them
real understanding of your problem. Ignore Observer and
Trainer.

Note whether your feelings change during the discussions.
Try to connect any changes with what R and Q say and do.

After the discussion you will have about five minutes to tell the small group how you felt and what ideas you found helpful.

Instructions to Q (Questioner) (Do not disclose briefing.)

1. Listen thoughtfully to problem as presented.
2. Your task is, by raising questions, to help P diagnose his or her own difficulty. Refrain from giving any advice, making suggestions, or citing any experience of your own or of others. Keep probing to help P bring out new aspects of the problem. Keep responsibility for the answers on P. You will have succeeded if you enable her to redefine her problem, see new or different dimensions, see problem more clearly, recognize different factors from those she first presented.

Remember: Make no suggestions.

Instructions to R (Recommender) (Do not disclose briefings.)

1. Listen thoughtfully to problem as presented.
2. Respond with any of the following types of help.
   a. Recall and describe similar experiences you or someone you know had to deal with. Tell what you or that person did to solve problem. If P doesn't seem to hear or to accept and you still see it as a good solution, try to explain further more clearly. Try to help by explaining relevant experiences.
   b. Recommend, in order, steps you would take if you were in P's situation. If P doesn't accept these, make other proposals until you hit on something she finds helpful.

Discussion: After all have completed the exercise and each subgroup of four has completed its discussion and evaluation of the exercise, the facilitator may wish to reconvene the entire group and have it evaluate the exercise in terms of: (a) those aspects and procedures that were most helpful in the resolving of the problem; (b) those aspects and procedures that were least useful to solving the problem; (c) the usefulness of this procedure in supervisory conferences; (d) the usefulness of this procedure in consulting situations; and (e) the general "learnings" from this exercise.

A Supervisory Role Play

Goal: To develop skills in giving critical feedback to subordinates.

Situation: The Morrisville Recreation Department has an active program of services for senior citizens. It relies heavily upon
volunteers for this service. It is the department procedure
to evaluate volunteers every six months and to use these
evaluations in the continuation or termination of individual volunteers. You have just completed your evaluation
of those volunteers for whom you are responsible. As their
supervisor, you are expected to talk with each one individually about his/her performance, based upon your evaluation. This role play begins with the supervisor conducting
a supervisory conference with Mrs. Smith who has been a
volunteer with the department for a year and who is the
wife of a prominent physician in the community.

Roles: *Supervisor.* You are the supervisor for the senior citizens
program. You recently evaluated each of the volunteers
for whom you are responsible. One of those volunteers is
Mrs. Smith. You have asked her to meet with you in your
office for an evaluation conference. You must determine
at the end of the conference what course of action you will
take and tell Mrs. Smith of that action. Mrs. Smith has not
seen her evaluation. You have her evaluation form in front
of you (Fig. 9–5). For some reason, there was no six-month
evaluation on Mrs. Smith, so this is the first time she has
had a supervisory evaluation conference. Her basic responsibilities to the department are to aid in transporting

Six-Month Evaluation
Mrs. John Smith

Item	Rating			
	Excellent	Good	Average	Poor
Promptness		X		
Attitude				X
Cooperativeness				X
Thoroughness			X	
Needed Skills	X			
Potential for Continued Service				X

Date: _March 6, 1981_   Supervisor: _Mary Jones_

FIG. 9–5.   Evaluation Form

senior citizens to and from various program locations and to assist in any way she can at those destinations. She works one day a week.

Mrs. Smith. You have been volunteering services to the Morrisville Recreation Department for a year. This is your first formal evaluation session with your supervisor. Your basic responsibility to the department is to work one day a week assisting in the transportation of senior citizens to and from the program destination. You also understand you are to aid in conducting activities at those destinations. You have become somewhat disenchanted with the recreation program provided senior citizens. You think the programs are "childish," not befitting the dignity of "aging." You have discussed this with your husband because you are deeply concerned about services to the aging population. You have a strong social conscience. You have not seen the completed evaluation form on your performance.

Questions: Once the role play is completed, ask the participants to share their feelings about their roles and the supervisory consequence experience. Ask the observers to evaluate the supervisor's performance—did he/she do what a good supervisor should do? Ask them also to evaluate the performance of the volunteer—did she effectively contribute to the supervisory conference? Ask the observers to identify other strategies that the supervisor could have assumed in performing his/her role. Conclude the discussion by asking observers and learn what they thought the purpose of the role play was.

William Smith: A Case Study

Bill Smith reported to work at 8:00 a.m. and was assigned to a small repair job on the backstop at Meyer's Park, a job that should take about two hours to complete. After carrying his tools to the job and obtaining the necessary materials, he was told by his supervisor to move to another job at about 9:15 a.m. Before he could complete the second job, he was told by his supervisor to start another job of more importance at Umstead Field. It seems some city councilmen were coming by at noon for an inspection of the facilities. He refused to start the third job and after some argument was finally allowed to complete the job he was doing.

All of this maneuvering was caused by the fact that the general foreman had made several changes in the priorities of the three jobs and could not decide which was most important, although he was aware of all three of the jobs one day before the situation occurred. Bill Smith has worked for the department for twelve years and has an excellent reputation as a good worker. The situation has been brought to your attention and as Director of Parks and Recreation you must act.

Using the above case data, divide the group into subgroups of five to seven participants and have them discuss the situation. Let the following questions serve as a guide:

1. Should Bill Smith be disciplined for refusing to do the third job?
2. Was Bill Smith's supervisor at fault in this case?
3. Could the General Foreman have prevented the situation by establishing a priority for each job sufficiently in advance to permit the assignment of repairmen?
4. Had the General Foreman failed to evaluate the situation adequately?
5. Did Bill Smith show little respect for his supervisor when he refused to do the job?
6. Does this type of supervision show a lack of cost consciousness and result in wasted time, material and disgruntled employees?
7. Is there evidence of poor planning in this case?
8. What action will you take in dealing with Bill Smith, his supervisor, and the General Foreman?

A Field Exercise

Have each of the class members individually, or in teams, interview a recreation professional who has supervisory responsibilities. The team should probe to determine the supervisor's philosophy of supervision, techniques and motivation, uses of job descriptions and job evaluations in carrying out supervisory responsibilities, on-the-job training strategies, and the sources of data used in planning and evaluating workers' performance, etc. Having developed the information along these lines, have the interview teams ask the supervisor for her impressions of the supervision she receives from her "superiors." You may wish to ask the same questions as before but in terms of what the supervisor perceives to be the job done by her boss, as her supervisor.

Using the information gathered from the interview, discuss the results of the interview. Is there a discrepancy between the supervisor's philosophy of supervision and her perception of her boss's philosophy? What is your rating of the supervisor in terms of good supervisory techniques and supervisory practices? Would you want to work for this supervisor? This department? Why? Reports back to the instruction group can be in writing or oral, depending on group needs and instructions by trainer or leader.

Here are a couple of exercises that get at the problems of consultation. The first touches upon some organizational concepts while the second has more bearing on training strategies. In both instances, you, the learner, should assume the role of consultant.

Case Study: Vacationland

Although Vacationland, a commercial amusement park, is small compared to some of the larger theme parks located in the same region, it is a viable enterprise. John French is proud of his ability to judge local demand and offer programs and entertainment through a variety of promotional efforts. Over the years, he has probably used every promotional technique known in the entertainment field. He has been in business for twelve years and has seen the park develop to the point where it now has an assistant director and three program managers, each of whom is responsible for coordinating a major element of enterprise— live entertainment, concessions and novelties, and "rides."

Mr. French considers himself semi-retired and no longer spends more than forty hours per week at the park. In fact, he would like to cut down the hours he spends at work even more but has concluded it is impossible. For one thing, the assistant manager, who happens to be his wife's nephew, makes no decisions without first consulting, and so French finds that if he is not there, decisions affecting the overall operations of the park are not made. The department managers tend to operate more independently but even here, French finds it necessary to move them into good management practices that they seem otherwise to ignore. If he had more time to review the department manager's activities, French is sure he could further improve their performance and the profit of the park. However, since he is approaching his sixty-fifth birthday and feels that he has earned the right to slow down, he would really prefer to reduce the number of hours he spends managing the business without jeopardizing its continued success.

As a consultant what action would you take in assisting Mr. French? What do you think would happen if Mr. French simply stopped coming to the park? Are his fears realistic? To what extent has the concept of decentralization been applied? How might it be extended? How might a fuller development of his subordinate managers be achieved? Can Vacationland, as Mr. French knows it, really survive without his active management? What types of information do you need in order to assist Mr. French in making his decision?

To benefit fully from this exercise, it would be well to have each student analyze the case study, answer the questions posed, and prepare a consulting brief or consulting prospectus. When this is done, the group might be organized into subgroups of five to seven discussants in which one or more members would be invited to offer their plan. The group would evaluate and critique the prospectus. A general group discussion could then follow.

The Consultant Role Play

Goal:
To develop insight into the consulting process and practice the skills necessary to function effectively as a consultant.

Situation:
Recreation and Park Administration 173, the Application of Group Dynamic Concepts to Recreation/Park Services, requires each student seeking an *A* to assist the instructor in critiquing the course. The student becomes a consultant; the instructor has the problem of evaluating the group's performance, his training plan, and his role as facilitator. All those seeking an *A* in the course have to arrange a thirty-minute consulting visit. This role play begins with the student entering the instructor's office. Remember, the student enters as a consultant; the instructor becomes the client.

Roles:
Consultant. You are a student in group dynamics and are working for an *A*. You understand that to qualify for the *A*, you must demonstrate your ability to function as a consultant. You are not totally aware of the instructor's problem, other than that it deals with some aspect of the group's performance and his effectiveness as a teacher. You have reviewed your notes on the consulting process and feel comfortable in your ability to carry out a meaningful initial consultation conference. You initiate the process.

Client. You are the instructor for Recreation 173. You have used this exercise in the past and have found it helpful in evaluating your course and your own performance. You have made changes in your approach to the course based upon these conferences. You know that most of the students who enter this role play do enter it seriously; after all, they are the better students (they are seeking an *A*). You thank the student for coming by as a consultant and then leave it up to him or her to initiate the consulting process. The specific problem under review is your desire to have the student assist you in your assessment of the course. Remember, you are a helpful client but not the expert—that role is assumed by the student.

Discussion
and Questions:
This role play may be performed in front of others or done privately between the instructor and the student. Regardless of the setting, the student and instructor should discuss the role play upon its completion. How did the student feel in the role of the consultant? How effective was he or she in that role? Were there helpful suggestions and understandings? Was the instructor helpful as a client? Did he become defensive when the student probed on

matters of strategy and style? Did the consultant have a good beginning and ending of the conference? What might have been done to improve the entire learning experience?

SUGGESTED READINGS

Kazmier, Leonard J. *Principles of Management,* 2nd ed. New York: McGraw-Hill Book Co., 1969.

Lucio, William H., and McNeil, John D. *Supervision,* 2nd ed. New York: McGraw-Hill Book Co., 1969.

Schein, Edgar H. *Process Consultation: Its Role in Organization Development.* Reading, Mass.: Addison-Wesley Publishing Co., 1969.

Sterle, David E., and Duncan, Mary R. *Supervision of Leisure Services.* San Diego, Calif.: San Diego University Press, 1973.

Chapter Ten

EVALUATION

Evaluation is a continuous process. It is fundamental to growth and begins the moment the group becomes aware of what it is doing and asks the question: "Why are we doing this?" or "Are we accomplishing anything?" Unfortunately, evaluation has a bad reputation. This is due, in part, to a feeling that evaluation implies judgment or criticism. This is a misunderstanding often fostered by persons too insecure to risk the growth which often results from evaluations. It is also too often seen as the last activity a group does and therefore something of a lesser priority. In addition since it is done after-the-fact, it may be seen as "anticlimactic."

Even in this book, we have placed the section on evaluation at the end of the text. *But* throughout the book we have stressed the need for evaluation, that it is an ongoing process. We have accented the elements that influence group performance and therefore are critical to the evaluation process. We have also spoken of the value of setting realistic goals or objectives so that a realistic evaluation could occur. The first step in the evaluation process is identifying objectives. Evaluation is measurement against those objectives.

We learn through evaluation. It might be a simple act—reflection on what happened—or it might be a highly structured, formal process with observers and survey data. In either instance, it is an exploration of what occurred, why it occurred, and the results of the occurrence. In other words, it is an assessment of the way the group acted (means) and the degree to which it reached its goals (ends).

The benefits of evaluation are numerous. Evaluations give directions and therefore are a part of the planning process. Using the data developed, groups can determine if they are achieving their goals, plot future courses of action, and determine which modes of operation best fit their style and needs. Evaluation enables group leaders to make decisions, allocate resources, and set priorities. It is critical to accountability, a measure of performance and productivity.

DIMENSIONS OF EVALUATION

Evaluation, as a process, is constantly occurring in the form of "feedback." However, as a formal act, evaluation generally occurs at the end of a session or at the completion of a project. When the recreation director is conducting a staff meeting, the body language of the staff, the questions they raise, give him immediate feedback. He has some appreciation of the group's feelings, the degree to which he is communicating, and their response to the ideas presented. Likewise, in recreation settings, the comments of the participants—complaints as well as compliments—provide direction for the recreation professional. Programs are often continued or adjusted on the basis of these comments and observations. Take, for example, the impact of "This is one of the greatest programs we've ever had" or "He's a great entertainer." Hearing that, would you want to schedule that program again and use that person in more activities? On the other hand, think what "This was sure a waste of time" would have on your future program plans for that activity.

In this chapter, we are going to describe the basic steps of evaluation, determine its dimensions, and suggest some techniques that can be used to facilitate evaluations. We realize we run the risk of making evaluation appear a formal act—a quasi-research activity. It *is* that; but it is also an art. Evaluation implies becoming aware of what is being done, how it is being done, and what results. Like sensitivity, it is something one feels. Feeling is basic to evaluation, but so is interpretation.

Evaluation begins with the establishment of objectives. The more specific the objective, the more precise the evaluation. Suppose, for example, the objective is to involve 60 percent of the residents in nursing homes in the evening recreation program. That is an easy objective to measure against. We simply look at the numbers that participate against those that might have participated. On the other hand, if we set "providing satisfying experiences" as our objective, we have a more difficult evaluation task. What is meant by satisfying, and how do we measure it?

Measurement is the second step in evaluation. The objective statement directs the measurement activity. Measurement is the obtaining of information, the development of data. To facilitate measurement, we use a variety of techniques and instruments. For example, we take attendance as a measure of participation. We develop interaction charts to measure the degree of interpersonal relations and types of responses. We "read" facial expressions and body language as a measure of receptiveness and acceptance. Remember, however, the means by which we measure are as important as what we measure. Your information is no better than the means used to solicit it or the questions asked to generate it.

Having developed information, the third step in the evaluation process is to assess its value. It is the act of data analysis. It involves organizing information in a useful manner and interpreting its significance. Information taken out of context is of little value. Suppose you know that thirty people attended a recreation program. What conclusions can you draw? If the objective was to fill the room to capacity and the room holds sixty people, then the information takes on one set of significance. On the other hand, if you knew it was snowing and that attendance is normally cut in half on evenings of bad weather, then the attendance data take on a different meaning. Essential to the analysis phase of evaluation is identification of those factors that influence the experience and the degree to which each factor plays a role.

Finally, having set the objectives, collected the information, placed the data in a meaningful context, the final act of evaluation occurs—giving it *meaning*. This involves judgment and skepticism. Were the results as planned or were there some unexpected "happenings"? Were there deviations from the normal pattern of action; did someone act differently and if so why? These are a few questions one asks when assessing the meaning of evaluative data. The results of the assessment become the directions for future activity and the basis for comparisons. (See Fig. 10–1.)

THE EVALUATION PROCESS

Having stated that evaluation is a continuous process, the prime question is, Who evaluates? The answer: ALL OF US. Consciously or unconsciously, all participants in any group experience make judgments about the experience. Was it worthwhile? What happened and why? Would you do it again? Each answers according to personal expectations—goals, objectives, and feelings. In the organized recreation setting, those evaluating are the professionals, participants, and the citizenry at large. Within the recreation agency or during a specific group activity, evaluations are basically made by the leader and followers (i.e., those involved). Problems generally occur in the evaluation process when the leader ig-

---

Steps in Evaluation

1. **Develop Objectives**
2. **Select Measurement Instruments and Techniques**
3. **Collect Data**
4. **Analyze and Assess Data**
5. **Interpret Results**

FIG. 10–1.   Steps in Evaluation

nores the group's feedback or opinions or relies too heavily upon personal judgment or that of a biased segment of the participants. The more people are involved in the evaluation process, the more realistic the evaluation.

In most recreation situations, three or more levels of goal expectations are present—the goals of the agency, the goals and objectives of the leader, the goals and objectives of the participants, and the goals or objectives of the community. They are not necessarily the same, although they may overlap. Take, for example, conducting a teenage club. The community may see it as a means of reducing delinquency; the agency, as a professional responsibility; the leader, as "his job"; and the teenagers, as a place to have fun. Since the program exists, the community and agency may feel its needs are being met, but what about those of the teenagers and/or the leader? Why does the club attract only three percent of the community's teenagers, and are those participants "having fun"? Is the leader doing his job? To answer these questions, an evaluation is needed, one that takes into consideration the views of the agency, the leader, the participants, and those teenagers not participating. Of all, the most important considerations are those of the participants and the leadership. Those involved are best qualified to determine the satisfactions they are receiving from the experience.

The process used to evaluate group performance is no different from that used to evaluate the recreation program of any agency or institutional effort. It is the measuring of performance against objectives, actions against expectations. In reference to group dynamics, it is the assessment of group performance and group feelings in relation to group goals. As stated previously, it is a continuous process that is most frequently emphasized and conducted at the end of an exercise as a part of the group experience, yet it is occurring throughout the experience.

Although all aspects of group activity require evaluation, the basic considerations are the goals and performance, the techniques and process used by the group to attain its goals, and the styles and skills of its leadership. The following concerns and discussions may serve as a guideline for evaluation. They touch most of the dynamics that critically affect group functioning.

A. *Goals and Objectives*
   Concerns:

1. The degree to which goals and objectives are clearly understood by group members;
2. The degree to which group goals are realistically stated;
3. The degree to which group goals may be realistically achieved;
4. The compatibility of group goals with those of the community, the recreation agency, and the recreation profession.

In determining the degree to which the group achieves its objectives, whether it be the training of staff in new leadership techniques or the involvement of participants in program planning, goals must be realistically stated, achievable, and reflect the desires of the participants and the values of the community. If the expectations are unrealistic, a negative evaluation may result, even though the group did as well as it could and might have even achieved its goals (had they been realistically stated). Because of their wording, failure or moderate success was all the evaluation would show. (You may want at this point to review pages 96–97, which discuss writing style and content for well written group goals.)

A second problem related to objective setting and group success is telling participants what they can expect. If from the outset the participants are aware of the possible outcomes and objectives of the activity, they are in a better position to evaluate the experience. All group research supports this contention.

B. *Group Process and Techniques*
    Concerns:

1. The effects of the general social climate (atmosphere) of the meeting;
2. The effects of seating and other physical aspects of the setting;
3. The role of time;
4. The emotional level of the subjects discussed;
5. The involvement of various members of the group and the interaction among them, and between them and the leader;
6. The background of the group, its previous experiences and expectations;
7. The group's standards and the members' awareness of those standards;
8. The presence and effects of group maintenance efforts; and
9. The techniques employed by various group members to facilitate group performance.

These are but a few of the elements that affect group process and functioning. (Review Chapter Four, "Forces Affecting Group Functioning.") They deal with the means by which groups get things done and the factors that influence performance. If the group is formal and its members are relatively unfamiliar with each other, the group may proceed rather quickly in disposing of its business. It may show little emotional commitment to its decisions, since they, for the most part, are reached mechanically. If the group members know each other and are to work together over a period of time, then time should be spent in developing a good social tone; the group functioning is much different. It is dynamic, with a strong sense of accomplishment.

C. *Leadership Styles and Techniques*
   Concerns:

1. The appropriateness of the leadership style to the situation and group;
2. The appropriateness of the styles and techniques employed to the forces affecting group functioning;
3. The compatibility of the styles and techniques employed to the stated objectives; and
4. The effectiveness of the leadership with its various uses and styles.

A wide range of leadership styles and techniques may be used to help the group obtain its goals. In fact, some groups are effective even when the leadership appears to have used the wrong techniques or styles! Then, too, in some situations the appropriate style may appear to produce unfavorable results. The lasting consequences of one's leadership style must be considered in addition to its relevance for immediate goal achievement. For example, if the recreation director is autocratic, the department may be very effective in its use of the staff meeting and its implementation of staff decisions. The director gets things done. So the staff models after the director and uses the same style in developing leadership programs. When this happens, they may find that participants reject both the ideas and the approach. After all, no one is required to participate in a recreation program; unfortunately, the staff may be unaware that this style of leadership, so effective in one setting, is inappropriate in another. It may actually prevent participants from carrying out the department's ultimate objective—the development of meaningful recreational opportunities for the participants.

PROBLEMS OF EVALUATION

At best the evaluation process is subjective. It deals with people, their feelings and behavior, and their interactions with each other and with their environment. So many things are involved in any group experience that it is difficult to determine which factors are affecting what behavior, when, and to what degree. Even so, some measures of the dynamics and their consequences are possible. They relate to (1) making and recording observations; and (2) analyzing them. Among the major problems associated with the evaluation process are the complexity of the evaluation process, the tendency to "use one's own experiences and feelings" as a basis for interpreting one's observations; the fear of an unfavorable evaluation; and the appropriateness of the methods employed in attaining useful feedback.

Complexity.   A multitude of forces are at work in each group experience; many are from human interaction and are intertwined. Was it the emotionality of the topic, the leadership style, the interaction between the group members, and/or the timing that caused the group to leave the meeting feeling elated, with a sense of accomplishment? Or was it the personalities involved, the chemistry of the people sharing the experience? Chances are it was all of these plus some factors previously mentioned. In the evaluation process it is important to identify the more important ones so that replications of the process can be made. If the group reacted negatively to the program, why? Was it the leader's style, the setting, the people who were there? The answers to these questions become important, especially when planning future programs. By developing charts and techniques to aid in recording and analyzing one's observations, some of the problems and complexities of evaluation can be reduced. We recommend a single dimension analysis first—that is, to look at each factor (temperature, lights, etc.) and its effects independent of the others. Then, we suggest a multiple factor analysis—to look at the relationship between two or more factors (light, setting and roles played) simultaneously at work. The evaluation of both the leader and the group should be then made (assuming the two have been done independently) to see how their perception of the experience affected their view of what occurred and why.

The Halo Effect.   One problem to guard against when evaluating any group experience is the general feeling about the meeting or group that results from some single, specific action that occurred during the meeting. There is the tendency to "halo," that is, to generalize from one specific experience and feeling. For example, if one of the topics under discussion at the recreation advisory committee created negative reactions, the group might feel the entire meeting was negative when, in fact, most of the group's time was spent in a very positive, constructive manner. The negative feelings of the specific experience would tend to override all other feelings and therefore the "halo" effect. The same effect may apply when a group rates itself high in performance because it felt good about the actions it took on one item while ignoring its lack of action or poor decisions on other items.

The "halo" effect is especially a problem when group members have a predetermined expectation. If they believe the group experience will be a positive one, they may rate it so (a self-fulfilling prophecy) regardless of its real outcome. If you like someone, or your particular point is well-received by the group, there is a tendency to "halo." (See Fig. 10–2.) Stereotyping and prejudices are similar to the halo effect. All are generalizations from some specific event, preconceived notion, or accepted myth. Objectivity is a difficult state to achieve.

The tendency to "halo" can be limited in a variety of ways, the sim-

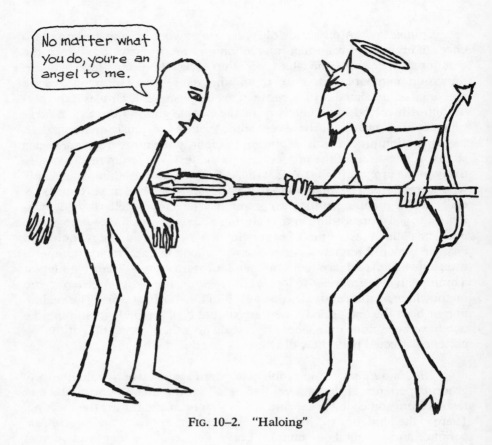

FIG. 10–2. "Haloing"

plest of which is to be conscious of the halo effect. By recognizing it, one can guard against it. Secondly, two separate evaluations can be made: one during or immediately after the meeting; the other, sometime later when the emotionality of the experience has diminished. For example, the immediate impressions of the interview may override the "realities" of it. You may be so pleased with the presentation and appearance of the interviewee that you forget to look at the substance of the interview—what did the interviewee really say and what skills does a person really possess. The latter points are more important than the candidate's general appearance, although that, too, may play a role. The third technique is to use some standardized forms or evaluation schedules which force the evaluator to consider all aspects of factors affecting the meeting rather than allowing the observer to rely on his or her feelings and memory about what transpired.

Fear. For some reason the evaluation process has a negative connotation. It is like criticism; we expect it to focus on the things that were negative or "what went wrong" rather than accepting it as a statement of what occurred and why. All group situations should be evaluated, not just those with negative outcomes. It is well to know what went right, what positively influenced the group, as well as what went wrong. When one accepts evaluation as a useful and necessary tool, then the negative feelings about the evaluative process are diminished.

One sign of maturity is being able to give and accept constructive criticism. Honesty is essential. If the group leader allows the discussion to get out of hand, then the evaluation process should aid her in understanding why that occurred. She is probably aware of it happening, so why not talk about it and develop coping strategies if a similar situation occurs in the future? It is critical that the evaluation process focus on the factors that influence group action and not dwell on personality behaviors or personal beliefs.

Personal and group growth is enhanced through the evaluation process. Take, for example, the recreation director who encouraged his staff to evaluate the effectiveness of staff meetings. At first, staff members rated the meetings positively when, in fact, they felt the director had "talked too much," "not listened to them" and called the meeting at a time inconvenient to many. In other words, they felt the director had not been sensitive to their feelings. There was some grumbling after the meeting and many negative feelings. When one of the more secure staff members told the director what had occurred, the latter felt uncomfortable. Why had they given the meeting a good rating when they had so many ill feelings about what happened? Didn't they trust him? When the group met for the next staff meeting, the director expressed his concern and assured them they were in this enterprise together. The staff took his word to heart and had an open and fruitful discussion. From that point on, staff meetings were lively, two-way discussions. New programs and procedures were developed; the group felt like a team and the community benefited from their effort. Imagine what might have occurred in this department had the director not been sensitive to the comments of one of his staff. Even more so, imagine what would have occurred had one of the staff members not had the courage to bring this concern to the director. Fear is an inhibiting and destructive force.

Methods Employed. Finally, the methods and techniques used to evaluate affect the quality of the evaluation. Many evaluation techniques have been developed; some have been faulty and all have been misused. There is a time and place for the suggestion box, the questionnaire, the process observer, and others. Each technique has its strengths and weaknesses. Human error can affect interpretation, as can a reliance on the data as if it were infallible because it was developed through evaluation methods. Evaluations are as biased as the opinions of those who participate in the evaluative process. Casual evaluations tend to be subjective, superficial, and nonbeneficial. In fact, they may be destructive and result in faulty planning and inappropriate decision making.

By knowing the advantages and disadvantages of the various techniques available, this problem can be controlled. It is important to have systematic and structured evaluations, to evaluate periodically the evaluation methods used, and to remember that evaluations are means to an end, never ends in themselves. Groups need training in evaluation as they do in all other aspects of group functioning. We must learn both to give and receive constructive criticism. Likewise, we must learn when to evaluate, what to evaluate, and how to use what we have learned through evaluation. No one is born with these understandings and skills; they are developed through practice and experience.

TECHNIQUES AND METHODS

A wide range of evaluative methods and techniques are available to the students of group dynamics. All have one thing in common; they are based on observation. Evaluations are behaviorally oriented, that is, they are statements of what happened and a measure of the factors that might have caused the "happening." Observations can be highly structured with well researched and highly developed recording methodology, or they may be informal and impressionistic. They range from depth interviews and surveys to suggestion boxes and personal notations of one's observations. We recommend you be aware of the variety of available methods, the advantage and disadvantage of each, and the appropriate situation for using these methods. We have included a number of illustrations and sample evaluation forms for your guidance.

Informal Techniques

Among the informal techniques available are the suggestion box, the end-of-the-meeting comments and suggestions, and the appointing of a feedback committee of observers. All provide useful information and are of a qualitative nature. They seek out feelings of satisfaction/dissatisfaction, estimates of worth, suggestions for directions, and impressions.

Suggestion Box.   The suggestion box is an old idea. It allows people to make comments anonymously. For those who might be somewhat fearful of reprisal or rejection, the suggestion box offers protection. On the other hand, it denies the group the opportunity for further developing an idea when presented; also, the idea may be misunderstood or misinterpreted by the person to whom the suggestion was given. A modification of the suggestion box technique is to have the group write its impressions or suggestions on slips of paper at the end of the meeting. These slips may be unstructured thereby allowing any comment to be made, or they may contain a series of open-ended questions that solicit specific kinds of information. (See Fig. 10–3.)

End-of-Meeting Behavior.   By listening to the comments of people leaving a meeting, you can learn much about their response to the meeting. If they are talking about what just transpired or if they tend to remain in small groups to continue the discussion when the meeting ends, the meeting was probably successful. If they leave very quickly or if their conversation as they exit is about something totally unrelated to what transpired, then the meeting may have been less than successful. If their side comments about the meeting are negative, then you have some indication of what they have felt. By reading body language and behaviors and by being attentive to side comments, general impressions are facilitated. It should be remembered, however, that these are only impressions and should be used as such.

Closely related to the end-of-the-meeting comments are the questions the leader is privately asked at the end of the meeting. If individuals ask for clarification of points made, then possibly the leader failed to clarify them during the presentation. If questions or comments encourage the leader to

---

<u>Suggestions</u>

Your ideas are appreciated.

1. Your overall impression of this meeting? (please check)

Positive _____ Negative _____ Indifferent _____

2. How can we improve our meetings? _____

_____

_____

3. Suggested topics for future meetings. _____

_____

_____

4. Other Comments _____

_____

_____

Thank you

FIG. 10–3.   End-of-Meeting Suggestion Slip

have more programs of this type, then some explorations of the validity of these should be made. One should not plan the future on the basis of these side comments or those comments that result from "haloing," but we certainly suggest attention be given to these concerns.

Appointed Observers. Finally, individuals known to be sensitive to the group process may be asked to "observe" what goes on. After the meeting, the leaders may request these individuals' impressions and ask for suggestions (feedback). It is good to have people on whose honest and forthright evaluations you can depend. These observers can provide useful information. Ideally, they should represent the various interests of the group so that subgroup biases may be minimized. For example, when working with a group of senior citizens, it is well to ask three or four in different sections of the room or from different subgroups for their opinions about the group's meetings, the arrangements, and invite them to "observe" for you. They are probably doing this anyway, so why not benefit from their observations and formalize the relationship?

Formal Techniques

The formal techniques of evaluation are an extension of the informal ones. They demand the evaluator be better trained and involve the development of valid instruments—observational schedules and questionnaires—and a more critical analysis of the data developed. Some of the major methods and techniques are: the process observer and/or expert, observational scales and rating forms, and surveys (questionnaires and interviews). They may be used individually or in combinations. Like the informal techniques, they deal with both the end product of the group's activity and the means by which the group interacted. The factors influencing group behavior, too, are the concern of those conducting formal evaluations.

Process Observers and Experts. It is difficult for those involved in the group experience, whether they be recreation participants or staff members conducting the activity, to evaluate what is going on at the time the experience is in process. Participants and leaders get caught up in the "doing" and therefore are unable to analyze what is happening objectively. It is almost impossible for them to overcome the halo effect, to measure group productivity accurately, and chart the group's process. By having an observer who is not a part of the group—an expert in group process analysis—observe the group in action, a more accurate evaluation can be provided.

Evaluation specialists rely heavily on observational schedules that have been developed to assist in recording observations. They also devote much attention to a reading of the dynamics that influence group productivity (Chapter Four). The observer may work alone or involve other experts in the observation process. Even a skilled analyst has difficulty recording and measuring the infinitesimal number of dynamics and interactions at work: who is speaking, when, in what tone, for what length of time, in what sequence, and in response to whom?

Some of the more basic questions directing the observer's analysis are:

1. What proportion of the group's time was spent on the matters related to the problem or discussion?
2. Which group members were responsible for its leadership? Which ones played what roles and when? Which ones negatively affected its performance?
3. What was the leader's style(s) and what was the group's response to it?
4. How effective was the group in its problem solving? What was its sequence of action (process)?
5. Did the group adequately explore all the alternatives available to it? Was it aware of its resources? How did it use them?
6. How much time was spent on each item and on each stage or phase of group action (stroking, organizing, producing)? What was the group's tone, and what contributed most significantly to it?
7. What was the communication pattern, and how effective was it?
8. Were the members pleased with their experience?

In preparing an evaluation of a group experience, the observer should include both a quantitative analysis of observation as well as impressions about what was involved and how the group might either maintain its positive tone or correct the problems it is experiencing.

Observational Skills and Charts. To assist observers in recording their observations, a variety of skills and recording forms have been developed. They are primarily concerned with four major facets: the role and effectiveness of the leader, the roles and contributions of individual group members and their process, the external factors that influenced the group's and leader's performance, and the interaction dynamics of all three.

One charting technique has the observer note the position of each member in the group, assigning a number to each position. When the individual speaks, his or her number is noted as is the number of the individual to whom he or she speaks. For example, John may be seated in position 3 and speaks to Jill in position 4; the notation is 3-4. If John happens to speak to the group at large, the notation is 3-G. A running chart of comments can be plotted, showing the number of times each individual spoke and to whom. (See Fig. 10–4.)

Frequently used in tandem with this charting technique is a schedule that identifies the major tasks and group maintenance roles, generally on the left-hand side of the chart. At the top of the page in column form, the names of the individuals participating in the group are identified. The process observer then notes which speaker played which role. This information can be most helpful to the group's leadership to see where problems exist, which members function best in what capacity, etc.; in other words, where the group's strength and potential resources lie, as well as those who contribute negatively or may be potential problems. (See Chapter Three, Exercises and Study Suggestions.)

Another useful charting technique is to state the various factors expected to influence the group and to identify, qualitatively, the degree to which they were present. This can be done in the form of a scale (see Fig. 10–5). Of course, the schedule can be used to assist in the overall evalua-

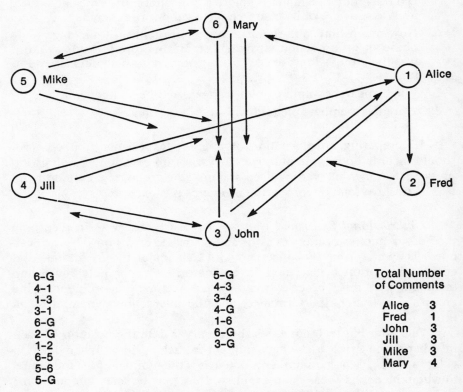

		Total Number of Comments
6–G	5–G	
4–1	4–3	Alice 3
1–3	3–4	Fred 1
3–1	4–G	John 3
6–G	1–6	Jill 3
2–G	6–G	Mike 3
1–2	3–G	Mary 4
6–5		
5–6		
5–G		

FIG. 10–4.   A Simple Charting of Member Responses

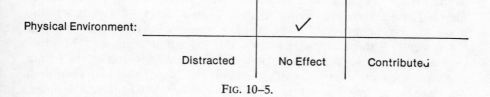

Physical Environment: ✓

Distracted | No Effect | Contributed

FIG. 10–5.

tion of the experience, or it might be kept for each specific topic or for a specific time period, such as a ten- or fifteen-minute interval.

Rating scales are available to facilitate one's evaluation of the leader. They, too, can rate the leader's overall performance or on his performance for specific time periods, e.g., fifteen-minute intervals. The scale typically identified the leader's characteristics in rows, with the performance ratings identified from greater to lesser magnitude, column by column. (See Fig. 10–6.) Beal, Bohlen, and Raudabaugh offer an excellent section on evaluation with a variety of charts and evaluative forms. We recommend this section to you.[1]

There are some built-in problems with the use of observers and observation forms. Observers rely on their observation of what is happening

Leadership Function	Rating			
	Done Well	Average Performance	Done Poorly	Not Observed
– Defined Goal(s)				
– Organized the group for action				
– Created proper social tone				
– Handled conflicts				
– Used all group members				
– Summarized				
– et cetera (list whatever functions needed/ appropriate for the situation				

FIG. 10–6.   Leader Performance Chart

in the group; they may not be aware of the actual feelings of individual members since they are cueing off the external factors—facial expression, body language, comments, and tone of comments. Secondly, they are unable to read all the factors that are occurring simultaneously. Therefore, they are selective in their observations and recording. Finally, their notations and the forms that are being developed to assist them with their notations are subjective. The forms ask for the rating of the presence or effects of a given factor. This is asking for subjective judgment.

On the other hand, properly trained observers can note more accurately the factors at work in a group experience than can the participants. The observer is not caught up in emotionality and therefore is better able to reconstruct and analyze the experience. He is in a position to observe the interaction between the follower and the leader, and the leader and the followers, item by item. Through the use of rating skills, qualitative measures can be developed to provide useful data for the group and its leadership. The more the individual scale is tailored for the specific group and its activity, the more useful are its data.

Questionnaires and Interviews.   In order to get the feelings of the leader and the group members about the experience, some type of survey methodology may be required. The members need to be asked about their feelings and observations of what has occurred. This can be done through evaluation forms (questionnaires), by conducting a group evaluation discussion, and/or by interviewing individual group members. Normally, the last is done by an outsider (process observer or consultant) while the first two may be done either by the group's leadership (leader) or by a consultant or process observer.

Two fundamental principles must be adhered to in the survey process. The first is to have a valid sample of respondents; the second is to ask appropriate and meaningful questions. The data developed are no better than the questions asked from the people who respond. Ideally, all of those who have been involved in the group's activity should be polled for their opinion about the effectiveness of the group, its leadership, the problems confronting it, and other reactions. If this is not feasible, then a representative sample should be selected. If the observer or group leader (whoever is evaluating) asks only those who are available or who volunteered to give their opinions, biases in the response can enter in. It is well to get the opinion of those who do not participate in the group but who are aware of its activities (possibly former group members) as well as those who do participate.

Surveying is the art of asking questions. The questions posed should pertain to the activities of the group, the factors that might have influenced its performance, the feelings of its leaders and participants. The questions asked may solicit an open-ended response or may suggest a particular response, i.e., agree, disagree, no opinion. The briefer the questionnaire, the more likelihood of it's being answered. Generally, brief questionnaires are open-ended. When the interview or questionnaire is more structured with expected patterns of response, more specific questions can be asked. Structuring the questionnaire with fixed responses facilitates the analysis process—that is, the tabulating of data—but typically discourages extemporaneous comments.

Open-Ended Question
1. What might we do to increase the significance and impact of our staff meetings?

Fixed Response Question
1. What might we do to increase the significance and impact of our staff meetings? (Check all answers that apply.)
    ____ Meet at another time
    ____ Meet at another location
    ____ Have various staff members responsible for presenting specific items
    ____ Establish a mandatory time limit
    ____ Other items: please specify _____
    _____
    _____

One of the advantages of using a questionnaire or participant evaluation form is that everyone can evaluate simultaneously at the end of the meeting, or can complete the form and return it at some later date. It is a less time-consuming technique than the interview. On the other hand, it does not allow for the exploration of opinions and responses in the same manner as the interview process. The questionnaire is a pencil-and-paper approach to evaluation, while the interview relies on vocal exchanges and the interaction of the evaluator and participant.

For those interested in the research aspect of the evaluation, several publications are available. Among them are works of Weiss[2] and Suchman.[3] Both deal with the evaluative research process as it relates to the human service system, but neither deals directly with evaluative research in recreation and parks. Evaluative research is action research and follows the same basic format of conceptualization and implementation as does all scientific research. It differs from other research forms in that it is problem-oriented and the research findings are immediately implemented.

With our discussion of evaluation we have come full circle. Evaluations are critical forms of feedback, and feedback is necessary for goal orientation. We need to know where we are, where we are going, and at what rate we are progressing. Setting objectives aids groups in determining their direction; feedback and evaluation provide them with an understanding of how well and how fast they are moving toward the goal achievement. Good process leaders are sensitive to the need for evaluation; they do not allow it to be an after-the-fact matter.

We sincerely hope this text will be helpful as you develop and use your skills as a group member. We have attempted through the exercises and information provided to aid in your understanding of your role as a group member and the importance of good group function in providing more meaningful recreation opportunities and organizational structure.

EXERCISES AND STUDY SUGGESTIONS

Throughout the text, we have stressed the importance of evaluation. Many of the exercises suggested at the end of each chapter asked you to evaluate the exercise and to give feedback to the instructor and to group members about their performance; they served to stimulate personal reflections on your role and learnings. We have encouraged the use of process observer with those responsibilities. In Chapter Eight we suggested a specific feedback exercise to be used in conjunction with personal development training. In this chapter, rather than suggest an additional series of evaluation and feedback experiences, we offer you (1) a grouping of instruments that may be used in determining the success of a meeting and your effectiveness in conducting conferences and discussion groups; (2) forms for charting group interactions; and (3) a closure activity. We hope you find these useful and adaptable to many group learning and performance situations.

End of the Meeting Evaluations

A variety of forms are available to assist you in evaluating a group meeting. They are easy to develop. They require the identification of the critical factors that might influence the meeting, as well as a statement of the goals you wish to achieve. The form shown in Fig. 10–7 can be distributed at the beginning of the meeting; the instructor only needs to inform the group that he or she is interested in having each participant complete the form at the end of the meeting and place it in the suggestion box upon leaving. The rest is up to the group.

If you need a more detailed assessment of the meeting, a more complicated form will be required. The questions included on it should reflect the goals and objectives of the meeting as well as solicit the kind of infor-

---

End of Meeting Evaluation

Please indicate your overall rating for each of the following items. Check the column that you feel best describes the item's contribution to the meeting.

	Very Poor	Poor	Average	Good	Very Good
1. Physical Arrangement and Comfort					
2. Orientation to Goals and Objectives					
3. Group Atmosphere					
4. Interest and Motivation of Pastimes					
5. Productiveness					
6. Leadership					

Please answer the following:

1. What is your overall assessment of this meeting? _____

_____

2. What were its strong points? _____

_____

3. What were its weak points? _____

_____

4. What might we do to improve the meeting? _____

_____

Thank you.

FIG. 10–7.

mation the leadership feels it needs in order to improve its performance. The following questionnaire may be used in conjunction with one of the large group of techniques or as the end-of-the-meeting questionnaire for a training conference.

EVALUATION SHEET

Conference leader _____
Topic or session _____
Date _____

Place a check (✔) in the blank space opposite each point at which you feel there was a definite lack or which revealed weakness. While more than one weakness may be indicated in a statement, the presence of any one is reason enough for checking that statement.

_____Inadequate introducton to topic; group did not understand the purpose of the meeting or the subject under discussion.

_____The leader was nervous, ill at ease, erratic.

_____The leader referred too frequently to notes or written materials.

_____The leader apparently was ignorant of the topic; unprepared; had done little planning.

_____The leader lacked zest, enthusiasm, and humor.

_____The leader was slow to grasp and develop pertinent points offered by the participants.

_____The leader was too talkative and tended to dominate the discussion.

_____The discussion was monopolized by a few participants.

_____The discussion failed to arouse and/or sustain interest in the topic.

_____There were too many irrelevant comments and sidetracking discussions.

_____The topics and arguments were underdeveloped and/or personally offensive.

_____There were too many lags in the discussion.

_____Numerous questions were left unanswered.

_____Questions asked were poorly structured and not designed for meaningful answers.

_____The time allotted for discussion was inadequate.

_____There was a failure to draw conclusions or summarize the points made.

_____The visual aids used were inappropriate, or there were no visual aids when there should have been.

_____The seating arrangement was inappropriate.

_____The meeting began late.

_____The meeting lasted too long.

_____The physical environment was inadequate—poor lighting/too hot/too noisy.

_____The conference failed to meet its goal or stated objectives.

Please suggest actions which we might take to improve future conferences.

_____
_____
_____

Please identify topics you feel need to be discussed and would be appropriate for future conferences._____

_____

_____

Thank you.

For those more interested in the internal dynamics of group functioning and the effectiveness of the group in using those dynamics to achieve its goals, a type of end-of-meeting evaluation schedule in Fig. 10–8 is suggested.

Evaluation Schedule: Effective Use of Internal Dynamics.
Please check the appropriate column.

Internal Dynamics	Effectively used	Marginally used	Inappropriately used
1. Orientation of goals & objectives			
2. Atmosphere and social climate			
3. Communications			
4. Participation			
5. Group composition			
6. Programs & techniques			
7. Leadership			
8. Group size			
9. Group standards			
10. Group evaluations.			

Please comment on how you feel we could more effectively use the internal dynamics of our group._____

_____

_____

Thank you.

FIG. 10–8.

A similar approach could be used to determine the degree to which external dynamics influence group behavior and the group's effective use of those external dynamics.

Bales Interaction Schedule

In the early 1950s Robert F. Bales, at Harvard University, did a series of classic studies on group interaction. From his data, he developed twelve categories of behavior which he felt were present in every small group situation. They dealt with task and social-emotional behaviors. Three of the categories dealt with positive emotions; three constituted the negative emotions. Six categories dealt with task performance.

Bales' research reported that the positive emotional responses were twice as frequent as the negative emotional responses. Both the negative and positive responses constituted approximately fifty percent of the total interaction. The remaining percent, about fifty percent of interactions, dealt with getting the group's task achieved (task behaviors). Using his category of twelve responses as a basis for evaluation and analysis, the observational schedule in Fig. 10–9 is offered.

The Bales observational schedule may be used by both the process observer or leader when evaluating individual actions and reactions within a specific group setting. Simply identify the individual members by name in the appropriate column and record their behavioral responses according to the category that best fits their responses. The Bales interaction schedule can be used independently or in conjunction with other observational schedules. One of the more favorite combinations is to use the Bales interactional schedule with a sociometric charting (as shown in the graphic at top of Fig. 10–4) of the group's interaction.

Key terms:
  Social-emotional area (positive)
  1. *Shows solidarity*, raises other's status, gives help, rewards.
  2. *Shows tension release*, jokes, laughs, shows satisfaction.
  3. *Agrees*, shows passive acceptance, understands, concurs, complies.

Task areas
  4. *Gives suggestions*, directions, implies autonomy for others.
  5. *Gives opinions*, evaluates, analyzes, expresses feelings and wishes.
  6. *Gives orientation*, information, repeats, clarifies, confirms.
  7. *Asks for orientation*, information, repetition, confirmations.
  8. *Asks for opinions*, evaluation, analysis, expression of feelings.
  9. *Asks for suggestions*, directions, possible ways of action.

Date_____Group_____

Observer_____

Time :_____to_____

Individual Member Names

											T O T A L S

POSITIVE EMOTIONS

Individual Behavior

Shows Solidarity

Shows Tension Release

Agrees

Gives Suggestions

Gives Opinions

Gives Orientation

Asks for Orientation

Asks for Opinions

Asks for Suggestions

Disagrees

Shows Tension

Shows Antagonism

TASK

NEGATIVE EMOTIONS

TOTALS

FIG. 10–9.   Bales Interaction Schedule (From Johnson/Johnson, *Joining Together: Group Theory and Group Skills,* c1975, pp. 50–51. Adapted by permission of Prentice-Hall, Inc., Englewood Cliffs, New Jersey.

Social-emotional area (negative)

   10. *Disagrees,* shows passive rejection, formality, withholds help.
   11. *Shows tension,* asks for help, withdraws, leaves the field.
   12. *Shows antagonism,* deflates other's status, defends or asserts self.

A Closure Activity

The final exercise suggested is a fitting one for the end of any group learning experience. It aids both the individual and the group in assessing the impact of the experience.

Goals: To provide individual and group feedback on the effectiveness and benefits of a group learning experience.

Time Needed: One hour

Setting: Concentric circles; groups of eight to twenty persons.

Procedure: Each individual is asked to take ten to fifteen minutes to prepare a written response to the following:

            1. Identify the overall expectations you had when you entered this particular group experience.

2. Identify, as best you can, your weaknesses as they have affected your ability to perform as well as you intended in this group.

3. Identify, as best you can, your strengths as they have affected your ability to perform as well as you intended.

4. Identify those aspects of the learning experience that you particularly value.

5. Identify those items or experiences that are of minimal value and/or things you would change if this experience was to be repeated.

After everyone has had a chance to respond, the facilitator should call time and ask the group to form two concentric circles (one within the other). People are to discuss what they have written with the individuals directly across from them. These sharings should be between two to three minutes in length. The facilitator will monitor the time and, at the end of each three minutes, ask the outside group members to move one seat to their right. The inner group members remain in their place. By doing this, each individual in the inner group will have an opportunity to talk with each individual in the outer group. Once the circle has fully rotated, the inner group will form one group and the outer circle will form a second. These two groups will then share their final statements with one another. Finally, the facilitator will ask the group for any additional remarks they would like to make concerning what they have discussed. This technique allows individuals to share their feelings, small groups to develop their own agenda of concerns, and the facilitator to get feedback about the experience. It can be a very beneficial sharing closure activity.

ENDNOTES

1. George Beal, Joe Bohlen, and Neil Raudabaugh, *Leadership and Dynamic Group Action* (Ames, Iowa: The Iowa State University Press, 1962), pp. 289–344.

2. Carol H. Weiss, *Evaluation Research* (Englewood Cliffs, N.J.: Prentice-Hall, 1972).

3. Edward A. Suchman, *Evaluative Research* (New York: Russell Sage Foundation, 1970).

SUGGESTED READINGS

Beal, George; Bohlen, Joe; and Raudabaugh, Neil. *Leadership and Dynamic Group Action.* Ames, Iowa: Iowa State University Press, 1962. (See especially Part III.)

Gibbard, Graham; Hartman, John; and Mann, Richard; eds. *Analysis of Groups.* San Francisco, Calif.: Jossey-Bass Publishers, 1974.

Pfeiffer, J. William, and Jones, John E., eds. 8 vols. to date. *A Handbook of Structured Experiences for Human Relations Training.* La Jolla, Calif.: University Associates, 1973–.

Stogdill, Ralph Melvin. *Handbook of Leadership: A Survey of Theory and Research.* New York: Free Press, 1974.

SELECTED RESEARCH JOURNALS

Many professional journals report the results of various studies and experiments on group dynamics, leadership, and communications. For those interested in small group research and the theoretical and research base from which the principles and techniques of group training have evolved, the following selected journals are recommended:

Administration Service Quarterly
Adult Education Journal
American Journal of Psychiatry
American Sociological Review
Educational Leadership
Harvard Business Review
Human Relations
International Journal of Social Psychiatry
Journal of Abnormal and Social Psychology
Journal of Applied Behavioral Science
Journal of Applied Psychology
Journal of Conflict Resolution
Journal of Contemporary Psycho-Therapy
Journal of Experimental Social Psychology
Journal of Organizational Behavior and Human Performance
Journal of Personality
Journal of Psychology
Journal of Social Issues
Journal of Social Psychology
Personnel Psychology
Sociometry

INDEX